I0799842

IMAGES
of America

WABASHA COUNTY

PLAT MAP of WABASHA VILLAGE
1854

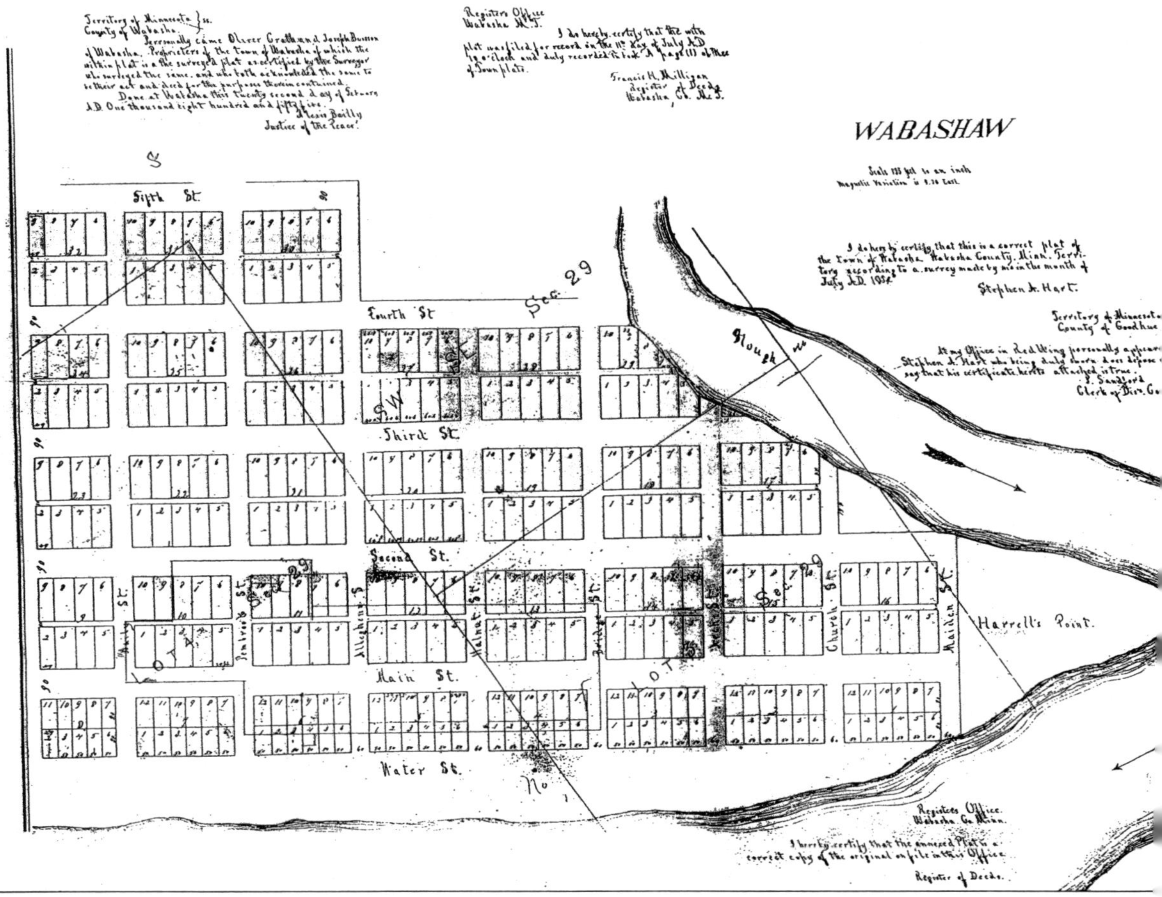

In 1854, Stephen A. Hart platted and laid out the town of Wabashaw (Wabasha). Bailey Street was named in honor of Justice of the Peace Alexis Bailey, and Pembrook Street was named for Pembrook S. Harrell, a riverboat pilot.

IMAGES
of America

WABASHA COUNTY

Judith Giem Elliott

ARCADIA
PUBLISHING

ISBN 978-0-7385-0054-6

Published by Arcadia Publishing
Charleston, South Carolina

Printed in the United States of America

Library of Congress Catalog Card Number: 98-83146

For all general information contact Arcadia Publishing at:
Telephone 843-853-2070
Fax 843-853-0044
E-mail sales@arcadiapublishing.com
For customer service and orders:
Toll-Free 1-888-313-2665

Visit us on the Internet at www.arcadiapublishing.com

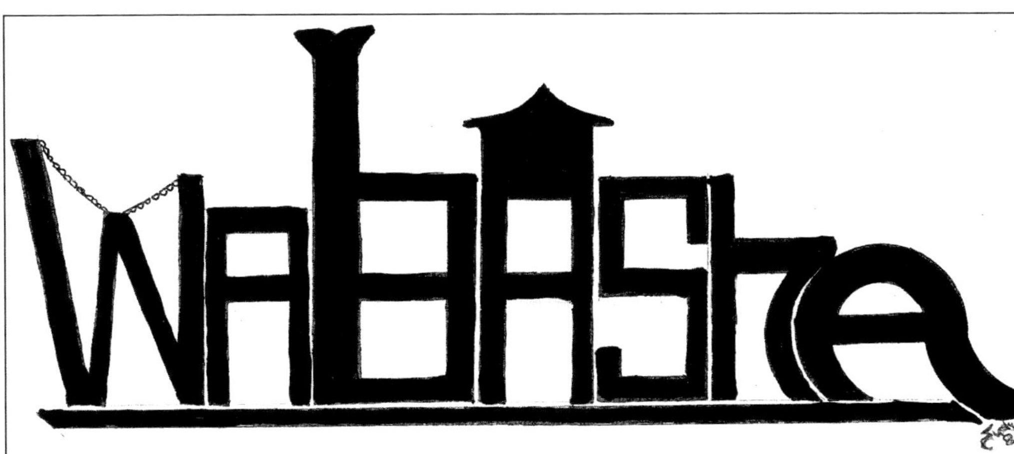

Contents

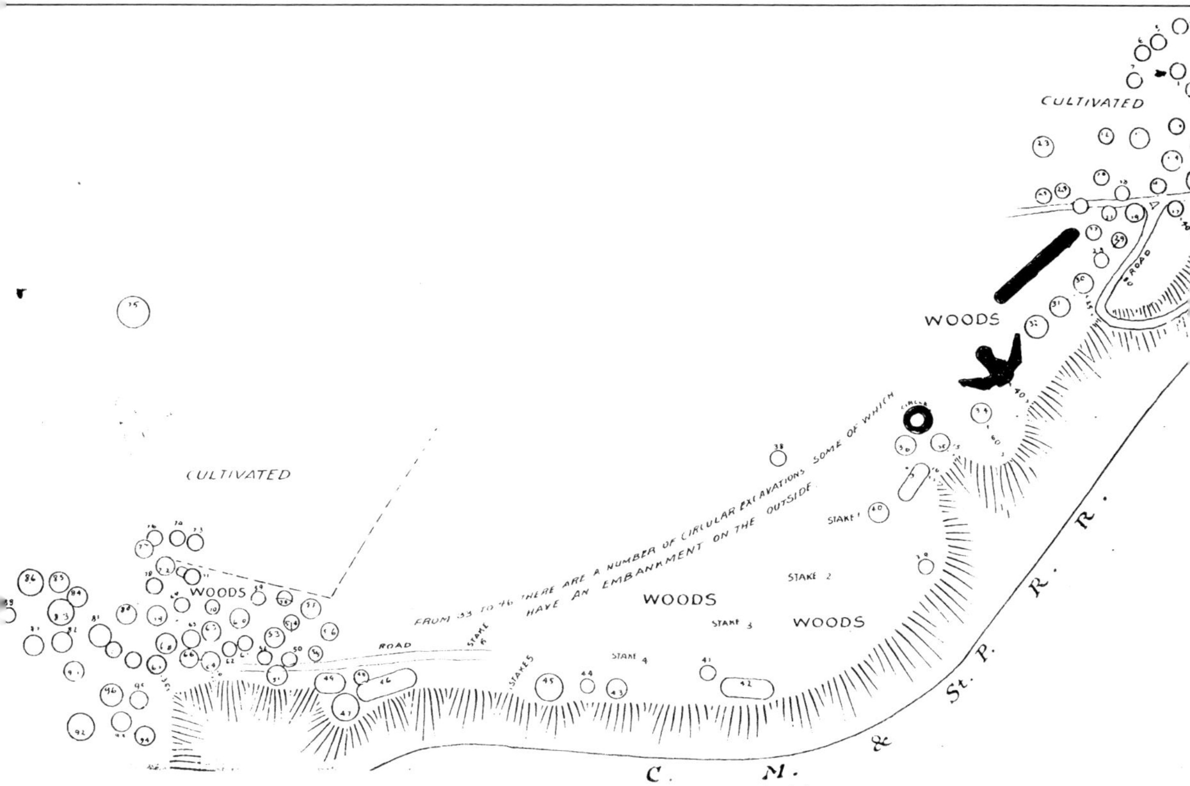

The "village" of Zumbro Valley Mounds in Glasgow Township is shown here on a map surveyed in 1885 by N.H. Winchell. The bird mound, which hardly had a head, was 63 feet long, 4.5 feet high in the center of the wing, one foot wide at the narrowest part of the body, and 2 feet wide at the end of the body.

Introduction

Wabasha County has been the home of people through countless generations. The earliest known people were called Mound Builders. Their homes were built of sand or earth in oval, round, square, triangular, and polygonal shapes. The largest mound in Wabasha County, located among the Zumbro Valley in Glasgow Township, was shaped like a bird. Many of these mounds have been obliterated by road construction, agriculture, and excavations by investigators. The chief territory of the Mound Builders was the Mississippi River Valley (including the Atlantic and Gulf, from North Carolina to Texas) and along the southern edge of the Great Lakes (from the St. Lawrence to the Fond Du Lac of Lake Superior). The mounds were built by the ancestors of the Mdewakantons.

The Mdewakanton band of Dahkotahs was one of the largest tribes in the U.S. in 1600. Their neighbors were the Shoshonees, Texano, Cheyennes, Iroquois, and Algonquin. In the 1800s the Dahkotahs, known as the Wa-pa-sha Band, were located at Wa-pa-shaw Prairie, the plain on which the city of Winona now stands. This is where Wabashaw II came into chieftainship. His band had about 70 bark lodges. Their traveling lodges, made of deer and elk skins, were carried on long poles; one end was fastened with breast straps to ponies, while the other was crossed with bars and left resting on the ground, a rod or so in the rear. Before they headed up the river, the women planted corn, potatoes, pumpkins, etc., on ground that was plowed for them by Mr. James Reed. Many early French explorers, and eventually men of Scottish, German, Swiss, and English descent, married into this band. Lieutenant Duncan Graham of Scotland came to Wabasha about 1834 and married Chief Wabashaw's sister Hazahotawin. In 1843, Mr. Graham named the village "Wabashaw" after the great chief Wabashaw II. Wabasha has been spelled various ways by white men as the Dahkotahs had no written language.

The earliest known pioneers were Augustine Rocque and his family. In 1826 they became the first white people, other than federal troops, to occupy a year-round residence in Minnesota. Augustine built a trading shanty on the west side of the slough in 1833. In 1834 Duncan Graham and his family built a shanty next to Mr. Rocque's. Oliver Cratte was sent by the government to be a blacksmith for Wabasha III's band. Joseph Buisson came a few weeks later, and Pierre Hortobese, a nephew of Wabashaw II, built a shanty on the other side of the slough. Francois LaBathe, a French trader, built a log house on the levee in 1840. In 1853, Pembrook Harrell erected a hotel on the levee named "Harrell's Exchange," but it burned in 1858. Nearly all the French traders here married into Wabashaw's family and today there are descendants all over the world that have their roots in Wabasha.

Before the arrival of steamboats, commerce and navigation had been conducted by means of keelboats and canoes. The keelboat was built much like an ordinary barge, but shallower, and had running boards on each side. The white men of the Northwest used a means of travel they had adopted from the American Natives—the birch-bark or dugout canoe. Small and light, such canoes were easily constructed, traveled with comparative rapidity (even against the current), and could be carried across the portages that were so often necessary if overland travel was to be avoided.

The first steamboat up the Mississippi was the *Virginia* in 1823, which ascended as far as Fort Snelling carrying troops. In 1853, the West Newton settlement in Greenfield Township, Wabasha County, took its name from the steamboat *Newton*, which had sank in the Mississippi River, leaving only its pilot house above water.

In 1856 one of the earliest buildings in Wabasha, the Anderson House, was built by pioneer Blois S. Hurd. The three-story building, originally known as the Hurd House, was constructed of solid bricks. Hurd's daughter Emma eventually married a carpenter, Mr. Ziba Goss, and in 1887 Goss nearly doubled the house's capacity by erecting the western wing. There were 45 rooms supplied with electric call bells, bathrooms, and incandescent electric lights. In 1909, William and Ida (Hoffman) Anderson purchased the hotel and renamed it the Anderson House.

The photographs in this book are from many private collections, including my own.

One

The Mdewakanton Band of Dahkotahs

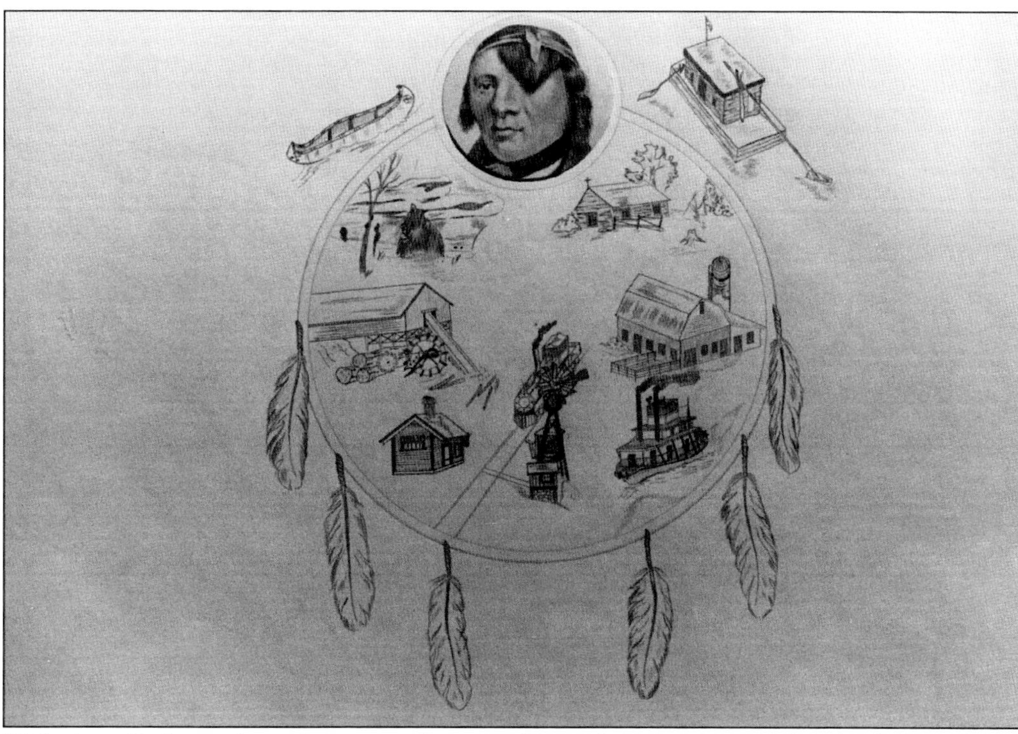

Wabashaw II, from whom the city and county derive their names, was the chief of the Keoxa band of the Dahkotahs. He lost his left eye during a game of LaCrosse, which was played by the Winnebago, Foxes, and Dahkotahs at Prairie du Chien, WI. He combed his hair down over the blind eye in a long cowlick. The Dahkotahs were divided into four main tribes in this area—the Warpekute, Sissiton, Warpetonwan, and Mdewakanton. Their way of life, before white men intervened, consisted of hunting, planting, socializing, and feasting. (Courtesy of Guyther Ray Spencer.)

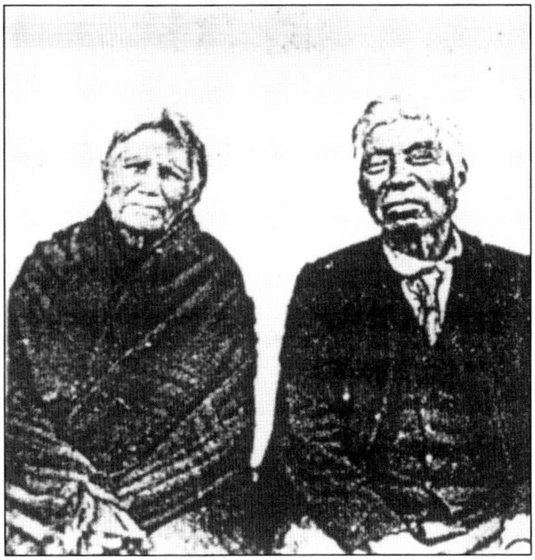

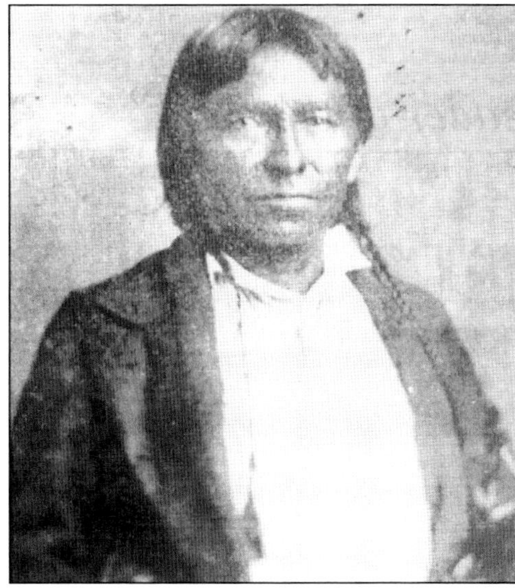

Left: Mah-pi-ya-a-ki-ci-ta, Soldier of the Clouds, is shown here with his wife, a daughter of Chief Wabasha II. He was the chief speaker of the virgin feasts at Ke-ox-ah (Winona). During the ceremonies he would step forward and address the virtues of chastity and warn "the denouncers" against the sin of bearing false witness. He also told the young braves that, if they knew of the lapse from virtue of any virgin applicant for vestal honors, they should denounce her. He died in 1899 at Hastings, MN. *Right:* Wabasha III, whose original name was Tahtapesaah (the Upsetting Wind), became chief to the tribe of 27 at the death of his father, Chief Wabasha II. Wabasha III signed the Treaties of 1836, 1837, 1851, and 1858. He was friendly with white men, but, from a sense of justice, sided with the Winnebago in their opposition to their removal to the inhospitable Long Prairie country in central Minnesota. He led his warriors in the Sioux Uprising of 1862 but was opposed to it, and was the first to make proposals of peace, even while his nation was still in arms.

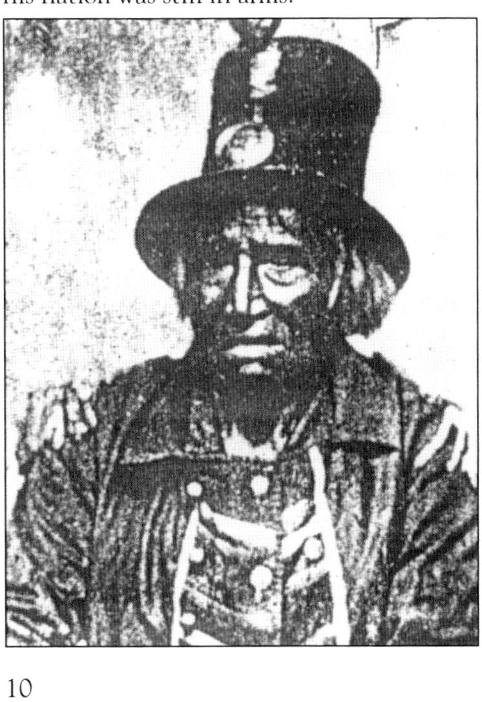

Ta-ma-ha, who was born at Prairie Aux Ailies (Winona), was a noted hunter in his youth. After the disruption of the Mdewakanton band, he joined Red Wing's subdivision, and then joined Wabasha's. He told a writer that, while following game into a dense Tamarach thicket during one of his hunts, a sharp, dry, twig entered one eye and destroyed its sight. (Courtesy of N.H. Winchell's book *Aborigines of Minnesota.*)

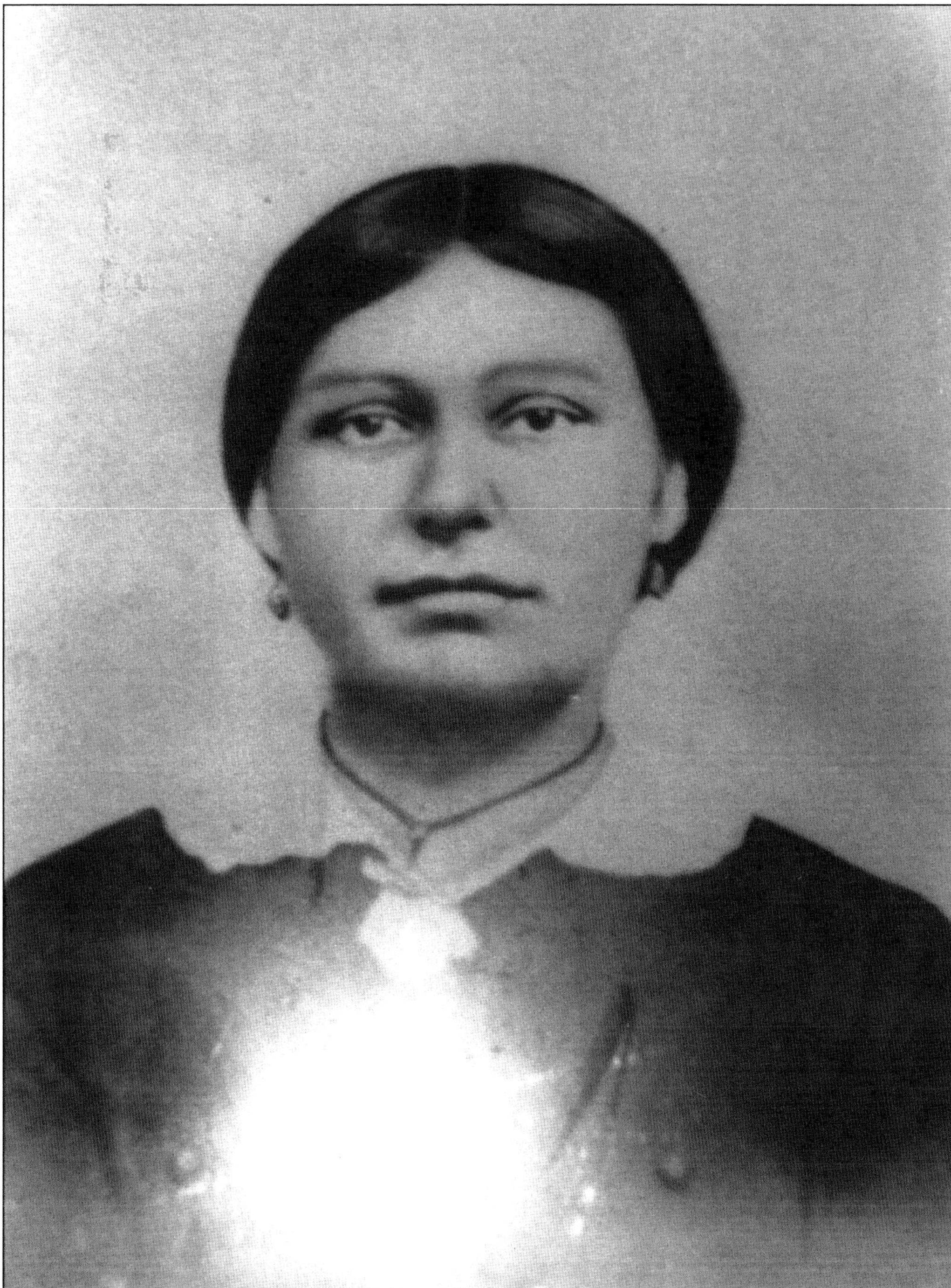

Matilda Rocque was born about 1842 in Minnesota to Joseph and Madeline (Robinson) Rocque. Joseph was born at Prairie du Chien, WI, and was listed in the 1850 census as being a farmer and hunter. Madeline was born in Minnesota to Dennis Robinson and a Mdewakanton-Dahkotah woman. Matilda's grandfather, Augustine Rocque, was the first to settle among the Mdewakanton band in 1826. (Courtesy of Merle Campbell.)

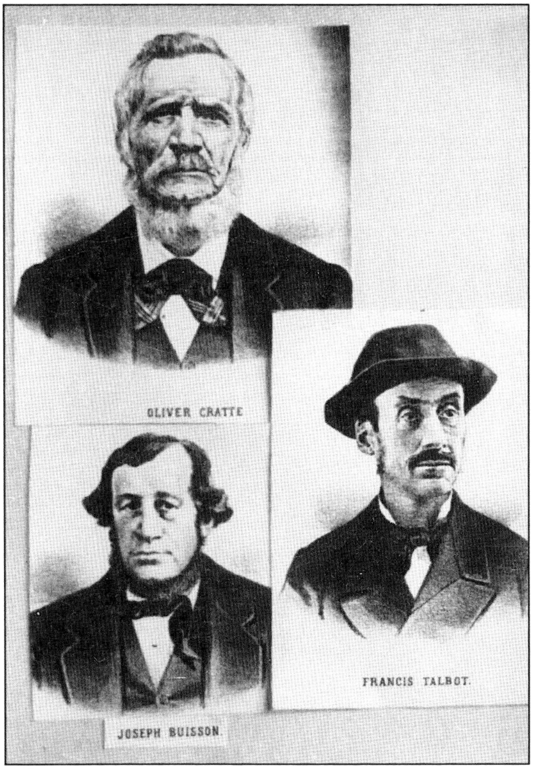

Oliver Cratte (top) arrived in Wabasha in 1838 and was appointed as a blacksmith for Wabasha III and his band at the Pepin Reservation. Francis Talbot (middle) first came to Wabasha in 1853. Joseph Buisson (bottom) married Nancy Graham, daughter of Captain Duncan Graham. Oliver Cratte and Joseph Buisson married into the Dahkotahs.

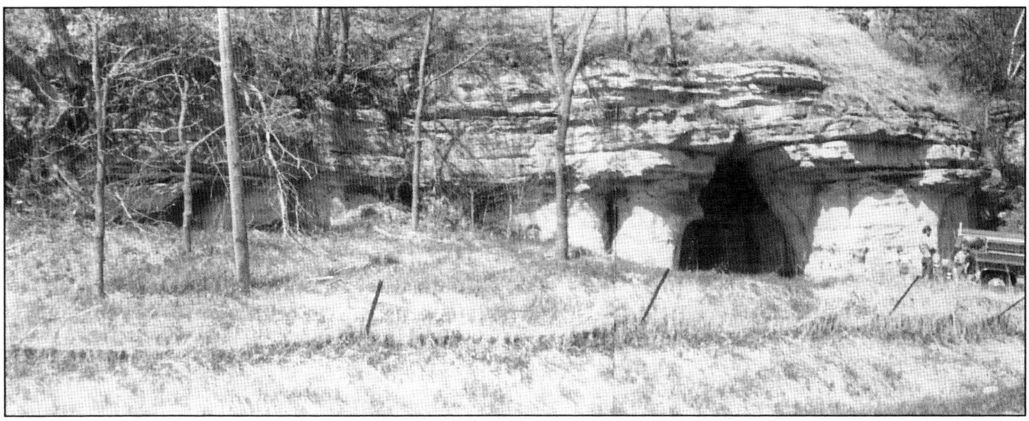

Mazeppa Cave, one of man's earliest homes, is located in the southeast corner of section 9, in Mazreppa Township, Wabasha County. The cave is about 70 feet deep and is made of solid limestone rock. It is 15 feet high and 12 feet wide at its entrance, but diminishes in size as you travel back. Hieroglyphics representing the birds, fish, and game animals of the region cover its walls, and a small passage at some distance above the floor runs back a ways. Early settlers used it as a shelter until they could build their homes. After being bought by a Mr. Frazier, it was eventually walled up; ever since it has served as an outdoor cellar.

Two

RIVERBOATS OF THE MISSISSIPPI

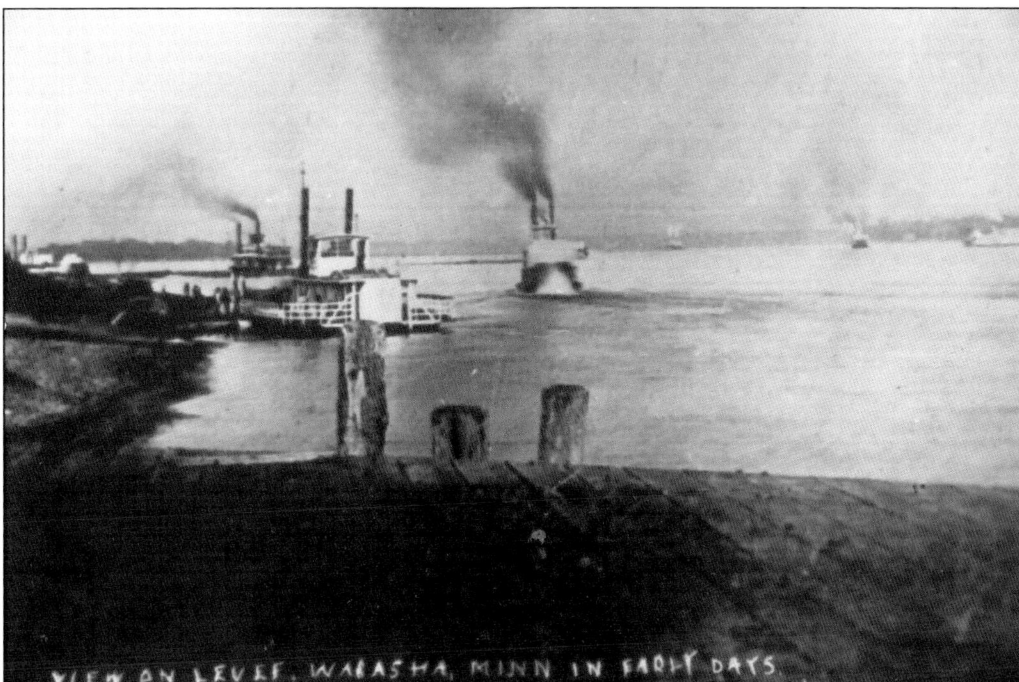

This is one of the earliest known photographs of steamboats on the Mississippi River at Wabasha. Steamboats and covered wagons were the primary modes of transportation in the area. Before the steamboats, there were keelboats and canoes, which the white men of the Northwest adopted from the American Natives. The boatmen themselves were more brawny and aggressive than gentle. Mark Twain, in *Life on the Mississippi*, mentions that "A common claim of the boatmen as that they were half horse, half alligator, and they had little respect for any authority not backed by superior physical strength. On the other hand, their labor was of the most exacting kind."

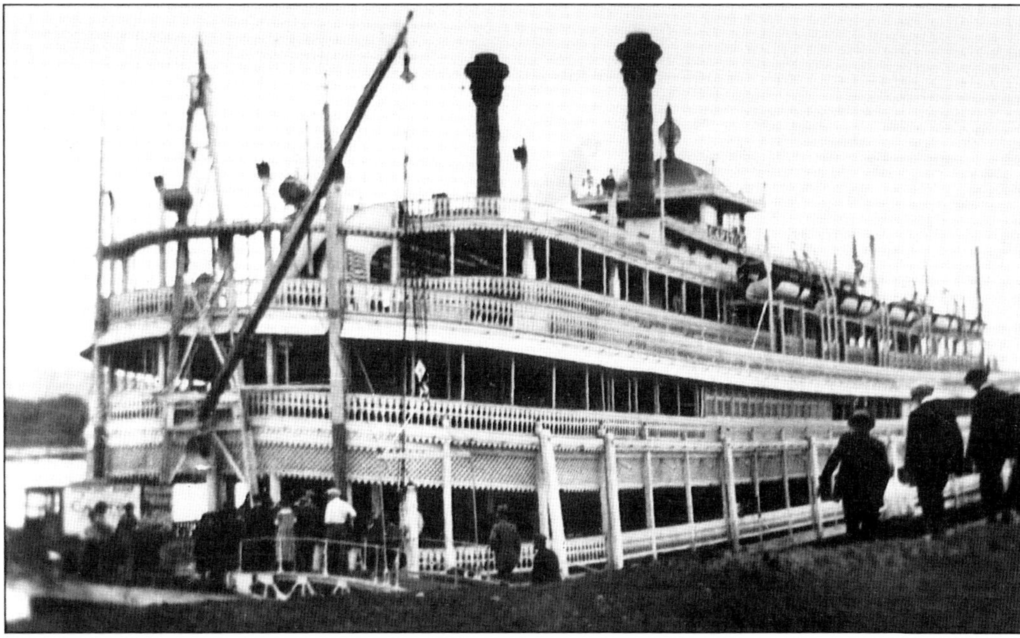

The picturesque old steamer *Capitol* is shown here at Wabasha in August 1923. One of the most famous excursion boats to ply the Mississippi River, she was dismantled in St. Louis by her owner, the Streckfus Line. For many years, the grand old steamer, one of the largest sternwheelers in the world, spent her summers near the headwaters of the Mississippi. Her last visit to Wabasha was in 1942.

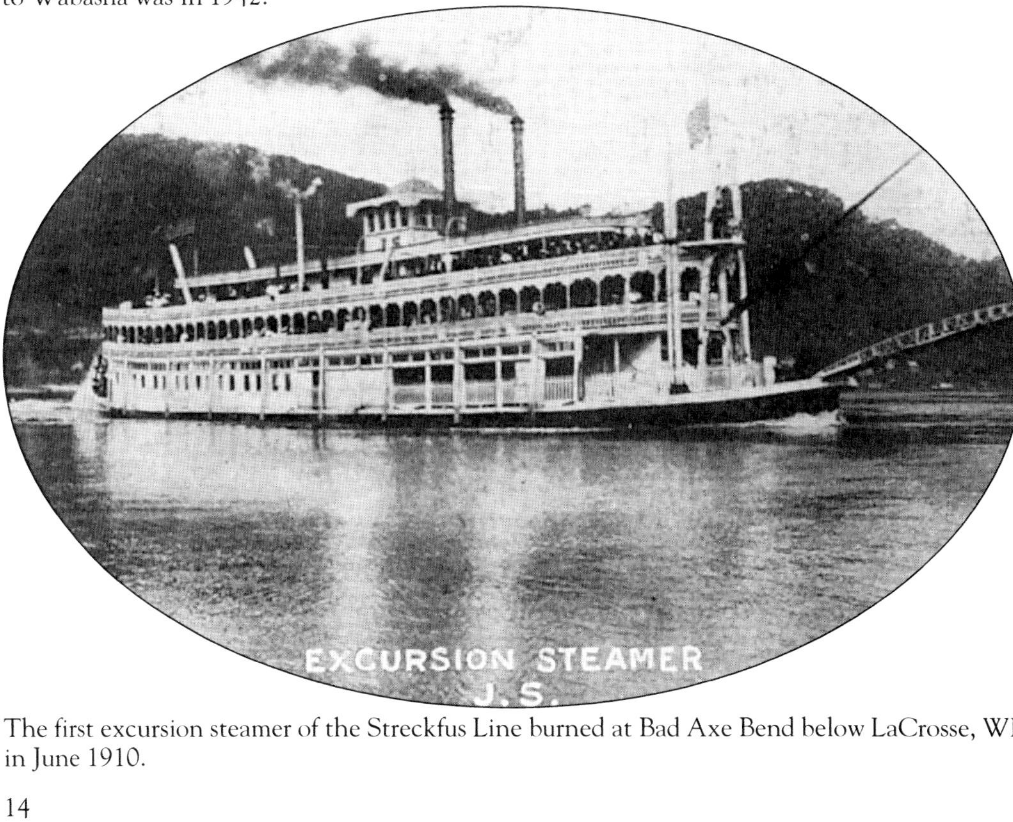

The first excursion steamer of the Streckfus Line burned at Bad Axe Bend below LaCrosse, WI, in June 1910.

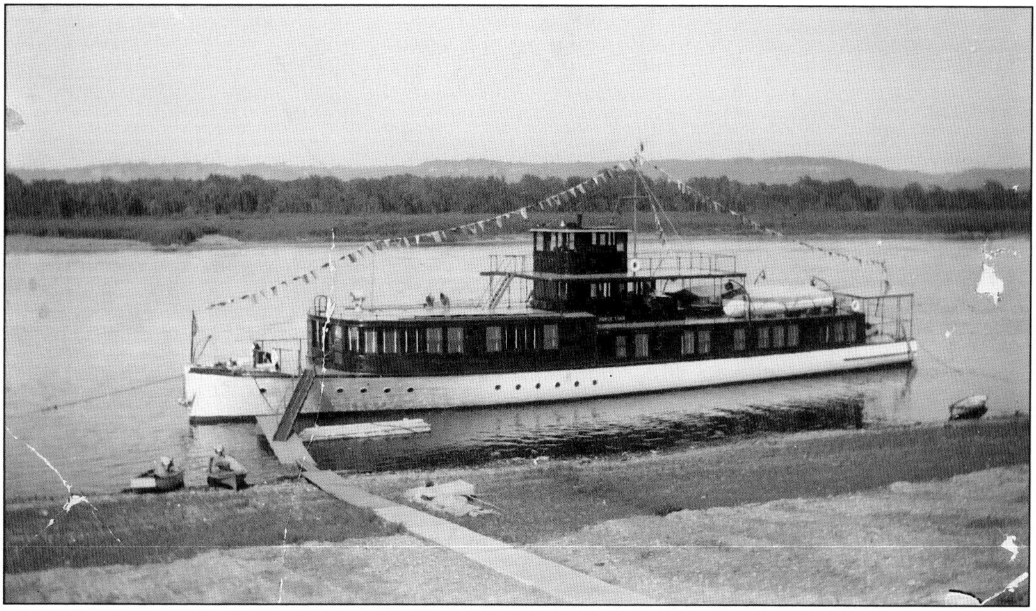

This photo was taken in 1934 at Wabasha by Rachel (Schurhammer) Giem. The owners of the *North Star* were Dr. Will and Dr. Charlie Mayo, the famous Mayo Clinic doctors. In their leisure time, they would cruise on the Mississippi River. After 25 years of boating, the Mayo's sold their boat to General T.Q. Ashburn, president of the Inland Waterways Corporation. The *North Star* was built in 1922. She had a length of 120 feet, a width of 24 feet, and was powered by a 200-hp marine engine capable of moving her along at 17 mph.

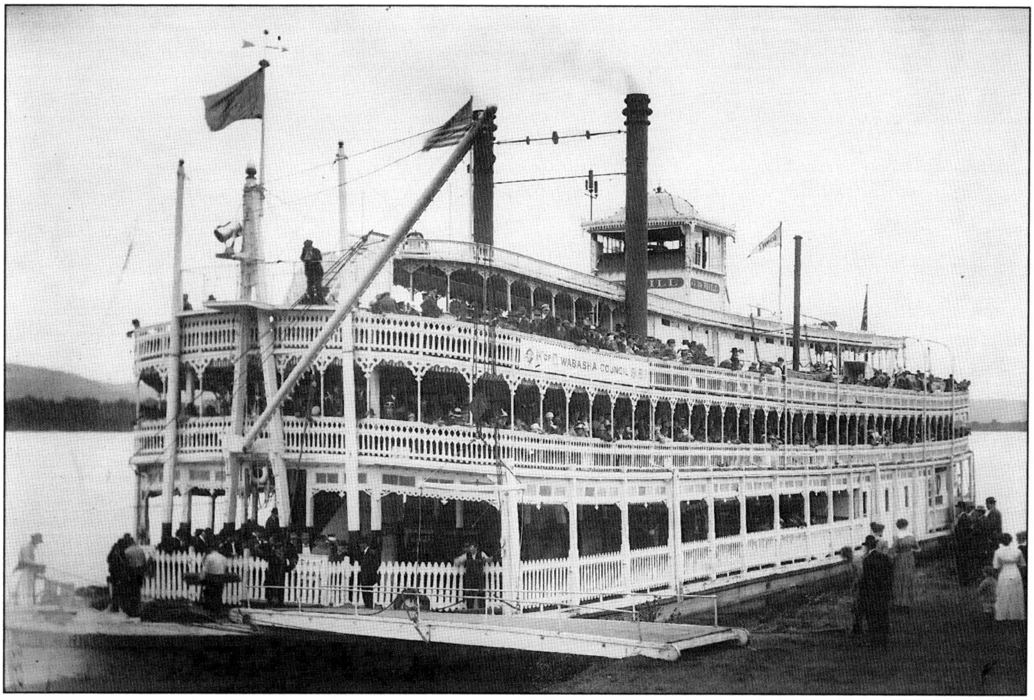

The steamer *G.W. Hill* is shown here on the levee at Wabasha, MN. She ran excursions between St. Paul and St. Louis for many years, and was operated by the Wisherd Line.

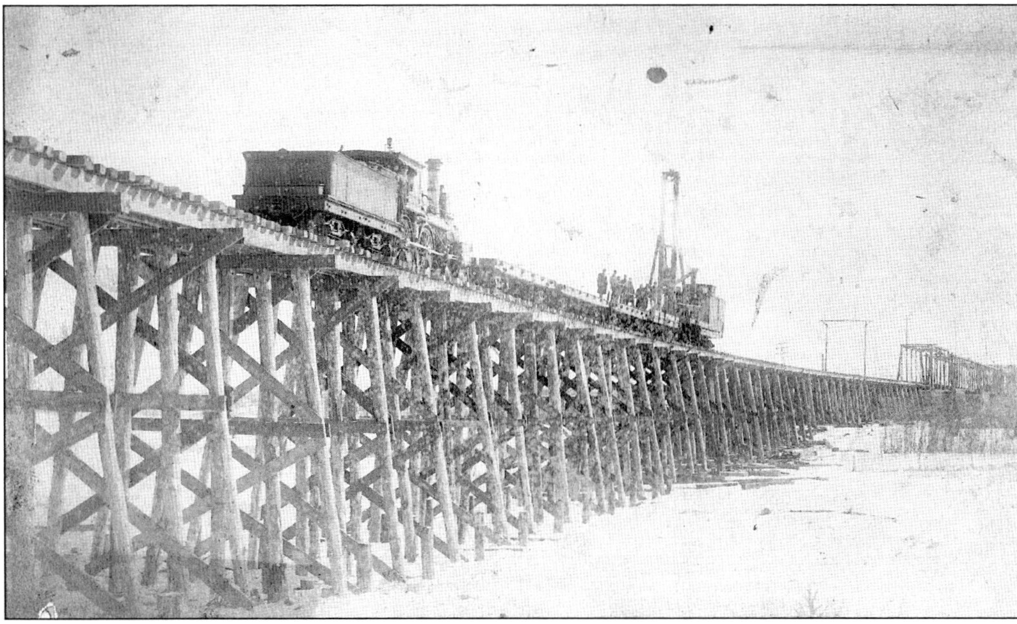

This 1882 photograph is of the pontoon bridge at about Read's Landing, MN. The pontoon, which is no longer in existence, was 400 feet long, 35 feet wide, 5 feet 11 inches deep, and drew 8.5 inches when launched. Its motive power consisted of two engines with 10-by-16-inch cylinders, and it cost $25,000.

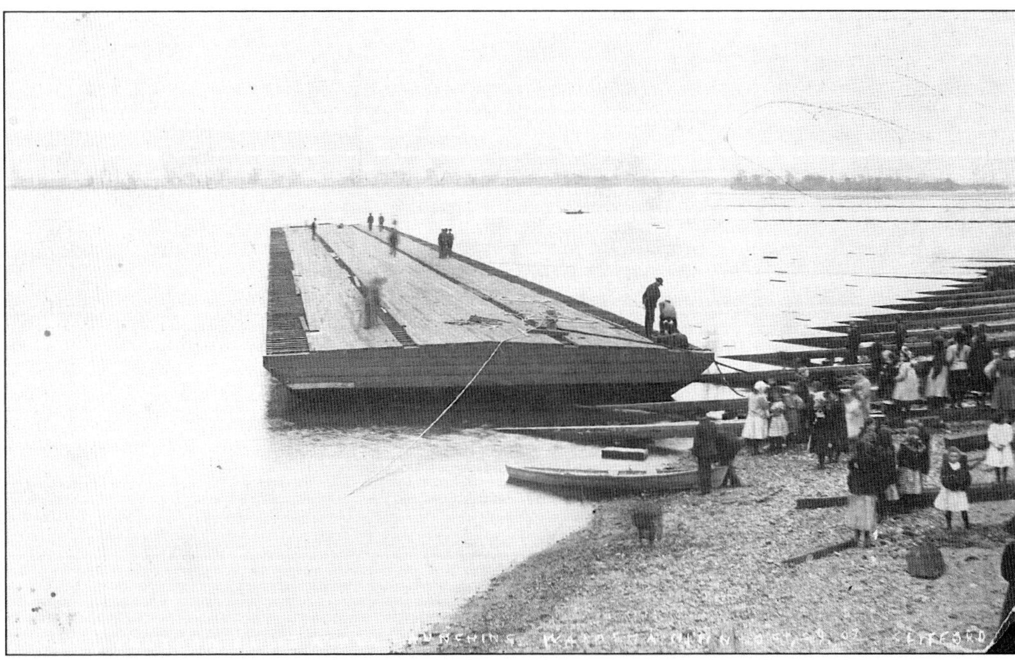

This pontoon was launched in 1907 at Wabasha. About 75 men were employed in getting her ready for the grand slide. Many schoolchildren witnessed the event. Hershel Cadwick was the foreman in the building and had full charge of the construction work.

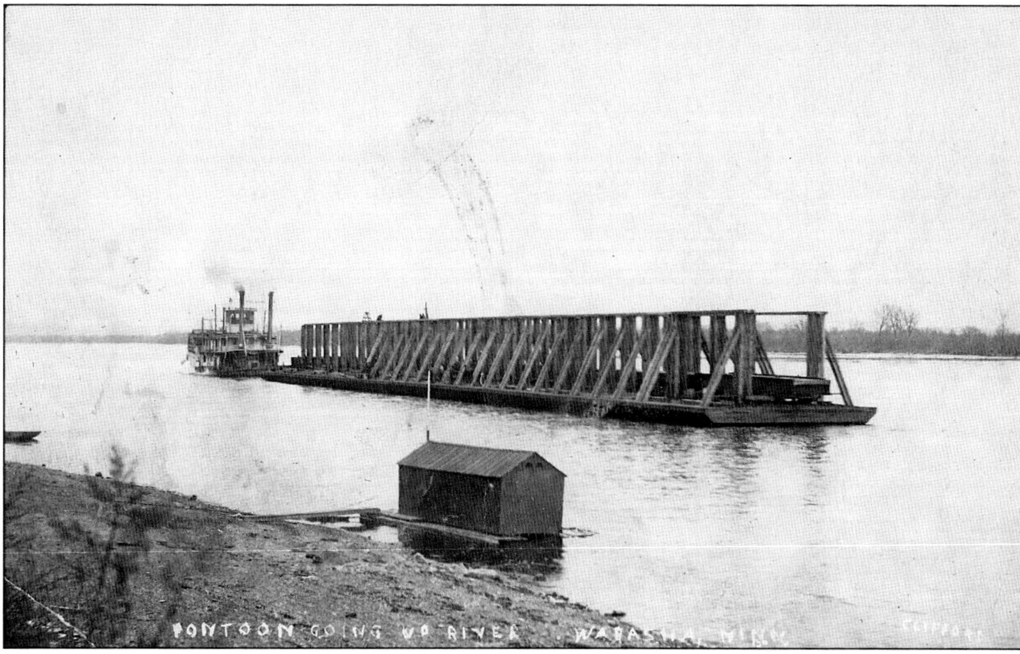

On October 27, 1907, the *L.W. Van San* towed the pontoon up the Mississippi River to Read's Landing to replace the pontoon built there. It was nearly 400 feet long and was used by the Milwaukee Road on the Chippewa Valley division.

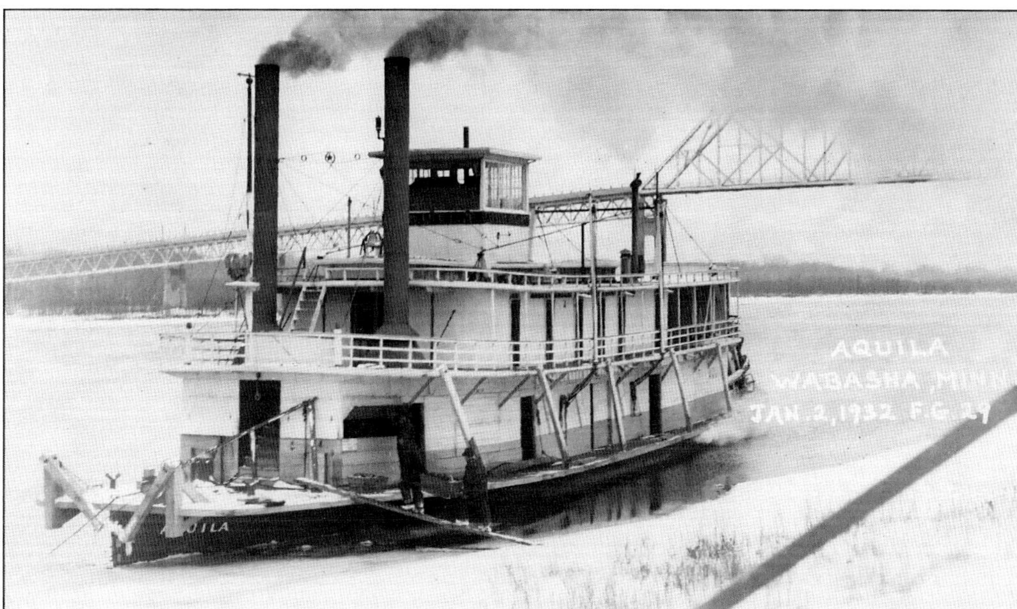

The *Aquila* at Wabasha was photographed on January 2, 1932, waiting to tow the world's largest single unit pontoon bridge. The *Aquila* was built at the Wabasha Boat Yard and was owned by Captain W.G. Peters of Wabasha. In the winter, Captain Peters harbored her at Fountain City, WI. (Courtesy of Gordon Schurhammer.)

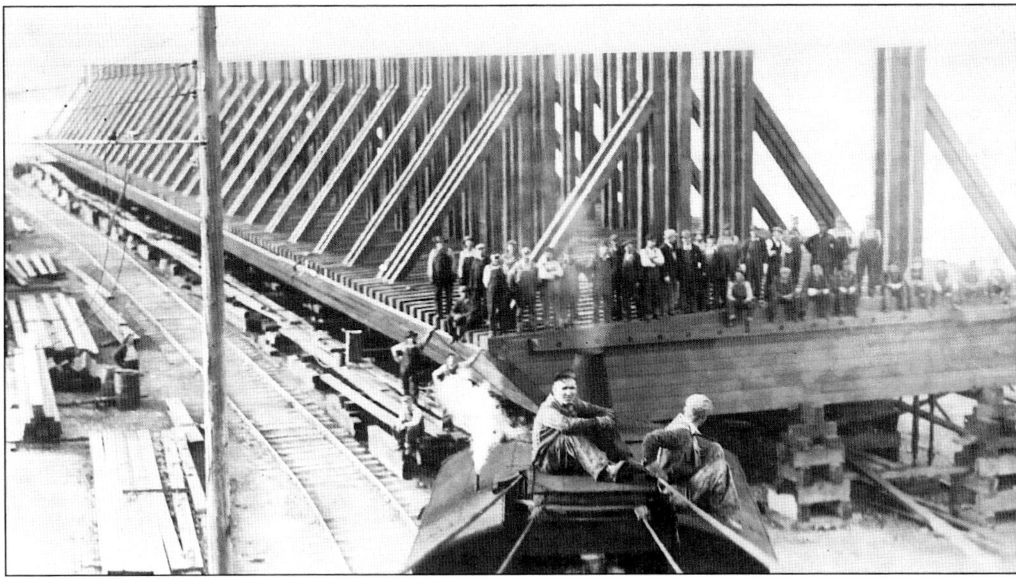

These men posed for a photograph shortly before the world's largest single unit pontoon was launched in 1932. The eight men who cut the ropes, which were spliced onto steel cables securely fastened to anchor pilings driven into the ground, were Walter Harms, Theodore Gosse, Clarence Stokes, Fred Boldt, James Fairchild, William Read, and Lawrence Davis, all of Wabasha and Read's Landing, and Steve Seleski of Hastings.

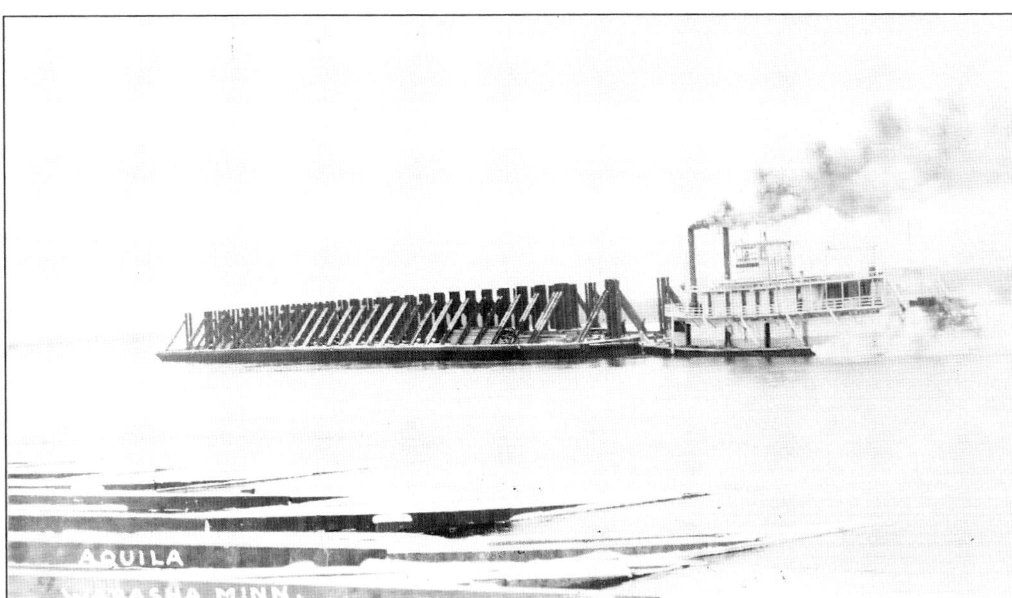

On January 2, 1932, this 1,900-ton pontoon was towed by the *Aquila* upriver to Read's Landing. The new pontoon cost the Milwaukee Road approximately $75,000 and was one of the biggest construction jobs undertaken. In 1962, it was taken to Lake City to serve as the breakwater at Lake City's municipal harbor. It was dismantled in 1984.

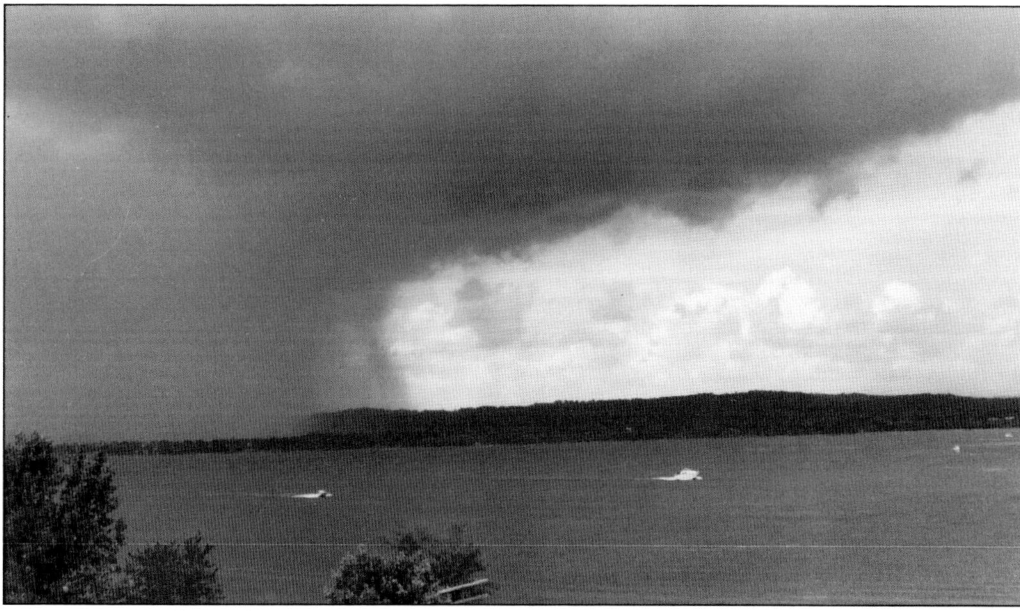

A rainstorm is shown here coming in over Lake Pepin in 1987. When you see this, you know it's time to get ashore! Over the years there have been several tragic losses of life on Lake Pepin. In June 1858, Julie and Rebecca Stout and their two sisters drowned during a squall when their small sailboat capsized. During the spring of the following year, the steamer *Aeolian* was crushed by ice, but perhaps the greatest tragedy occurred on July 13, 1890, when the *Sea Wing* capsized with 200 people on board; 125 of them drowned.

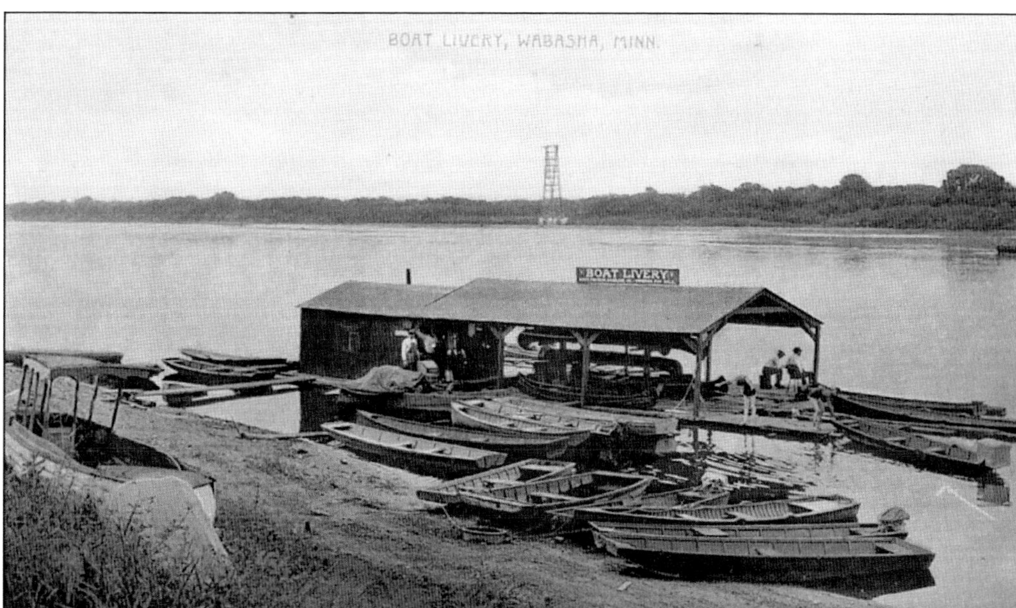

The Boat Livery in Wabasha along the Mississippi River was owned and operated by Ed O'Reilly for over 15 years. He kept a register in which all his patrons signed their name (one year over 1,000 people registered). Known as "Harmonica Andy," he has performed live on stage and during radio broadcasts.

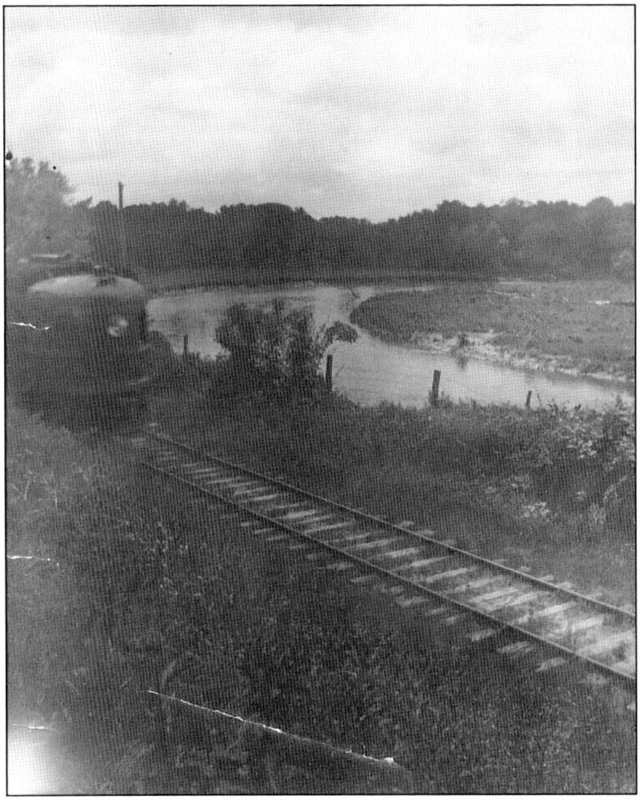

This c. 1940 photograph was taken in Greenfield Township near Kellogg. The Midland Narrow Gauge Railroad, completed on July 4, 1878, ran from Wabasha to Zumbrota along the Zumbro River. The Zumbro River originally bore the French name "Riviere des Embarras," meaning "a stream on which canoeing is hindered by driftwood."

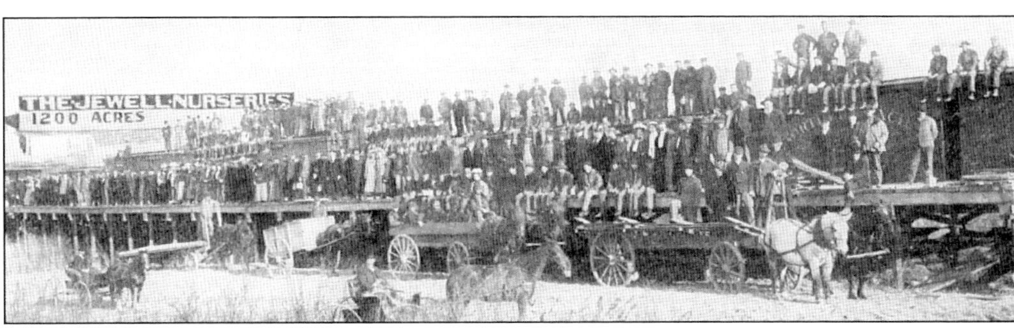

The Jewell Nursery in Lake City, MN, was started in 1868 by Dr. P.A. Jewell, with J.M. Underwood as foreman. At this platform during the packing seasons, 15 to 20 cars were loaded with Jewell trees and plants every day to be shipped to the northern United States and western Canadian provinces. The nursery is still in business today.

Three

Pioneers and Their Descendants

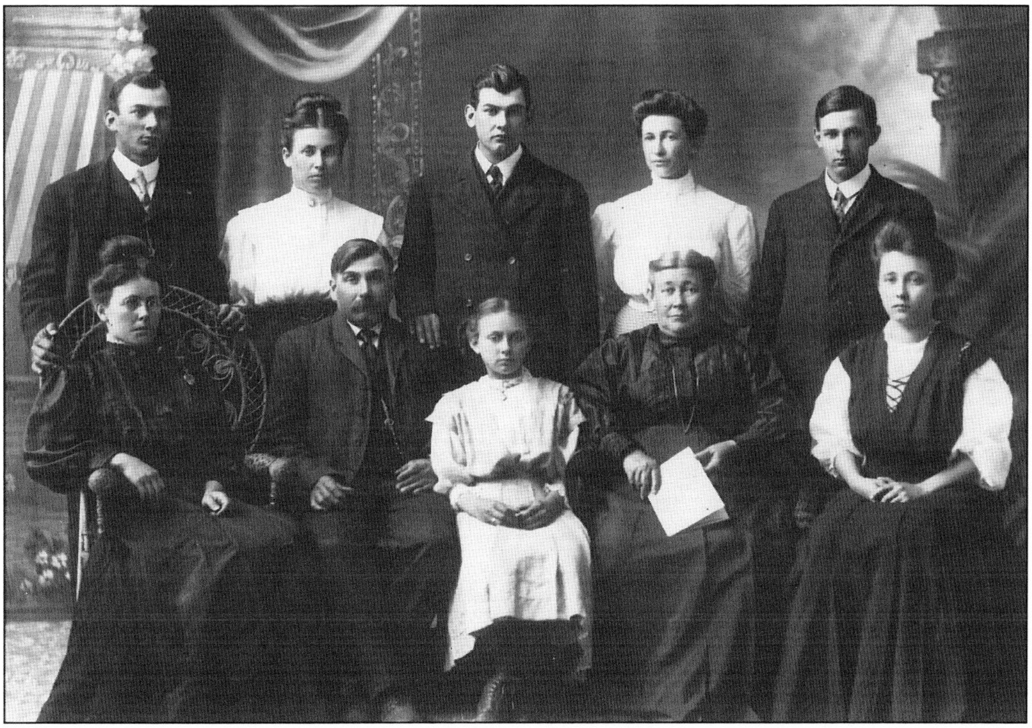

The members of the Valentine and Mellisa (Dull) Giem family shown here are, from left to right, as follows: (bottom row) Lydia, Valentine, Lotte, Mellisa, and Orpha; (top row) James, Esther, Jessie, Mary, and Elmer. The Giems settled in Elgin Township in 1856 when Valentine was only eight years old. His parents were Johann and Lucinda (Brundberg) Giem; Melissa's parents were Adam and Amelia (Campbell) Dull. (Courtesy of Don Nilles.)

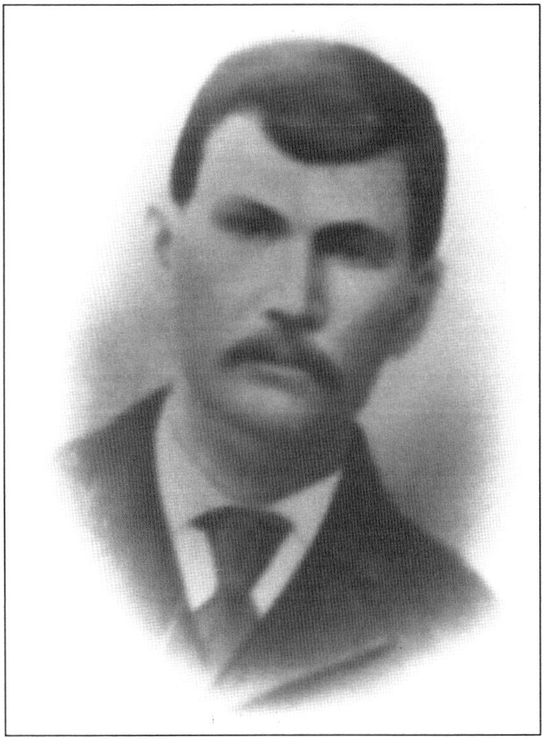

George Campbell, the son of George and Louise (DeChamps) Campbell, was born on March 1, 1846, in St. Paul, MN. He married Matilda Rocque in 1881 at Wabasha, and they had three children—Annie (John Valentine), George III, and Josephine. His second wife was Ida May Lampe, and they had six children—Ralph, Chester (Isabelie Adams), Margaret (John Hott), Ida (Lloyd Johnson), Gladys (John O'Connell), and Chaucey (Gladys Hartly). (Courtesy of Merle Campbell.)

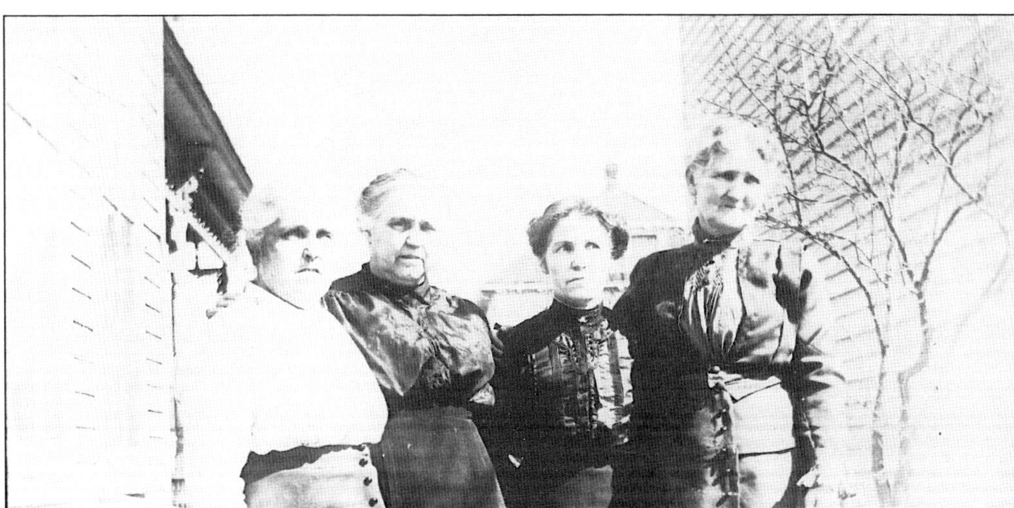

Lawrence and Mary (McDonough) Calhoun, early pioneers of Wabasha County, had three daughters. They are, from left to right, Anna (Mr. M. Cummings), Margaret (Martin O'Laughlin), and Maria (Patrick F. Ryan).

Leonard Pomeroy was born *c.* 1861 in Minnesota to Eliza Pomeroy of Tennessee. He married Phoebe Lee on August 19, 1883. They moved to Mazeppa and had eight children—Goldie, Frank, Archie, Jacob, Otis, Genevieve, Gladys, and a little boy.

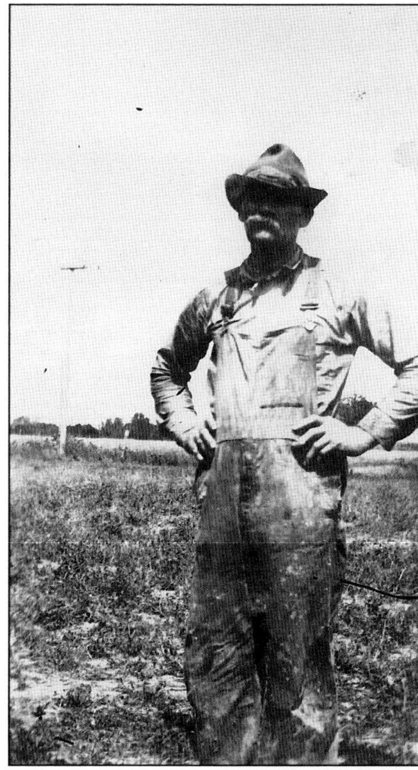

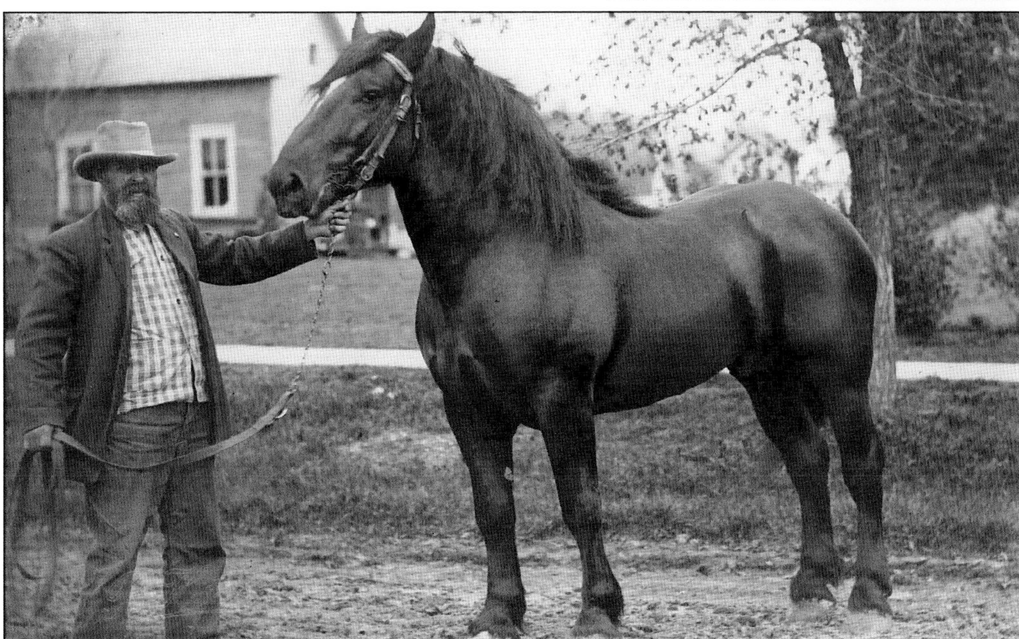

Philo A. Drew poses with his Percheron stallion "Juste" in a photograph recorded by the Percheron Society of America. Juste was foaled on March 1, 1909, and was bred by M. Poilpre, department of Sarthe. He was imported in March 1912 by J.W. and F.T. Peterson of Litchfield, MN. Philo lived in Plainview for many years and was married to Ella Curtis.

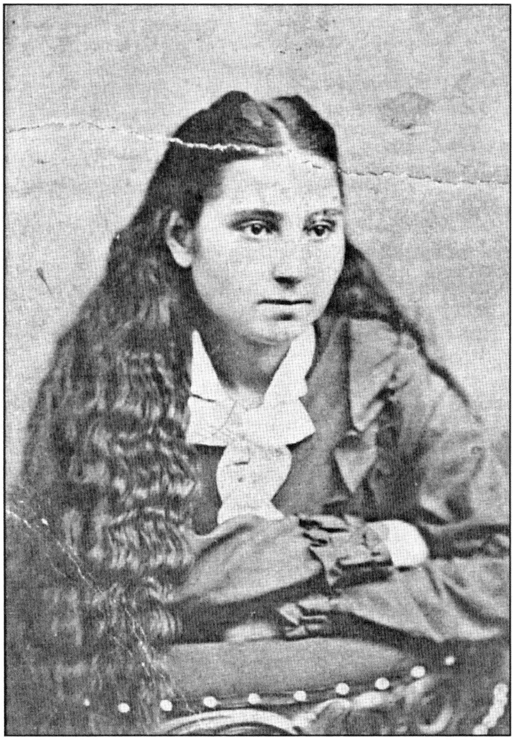

Eighteen-year-old Laura Ann Harrell, of French and Welch descent, was born in Wabasha on March 27, 1856. Her grandfather, John Harrell, arrived here in the early 1850s with his family. Laura's parents were George Harrell and Margaret McCollum. Her father was in the raft-towing business on the Mississippi River, being the captain on the steamers *Jim Watson* and *Ruby*. In 1853, the first hotel was erected on the levee in Wabasha by Pembrook and George Harrell. Known as "Harrell's Exchange," it burned in 1858, the same year Minnesota became a state.

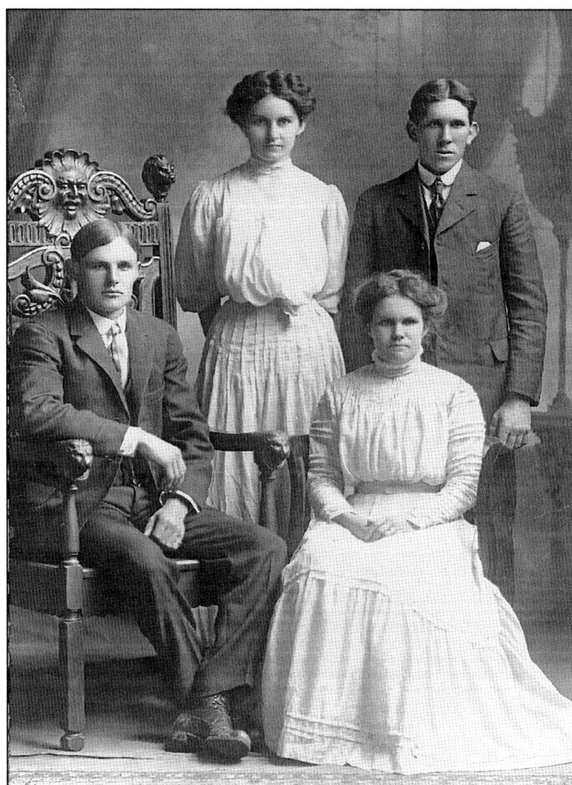

Paul and Mary (Schurhammer) Schmoker (both seated) are shown here shortly after being married. Their attendants, Clara and Joseph Schurhammer III, stand behind them. Paul is the son of William and Helen (Martin) Schmoker. Helen came to Wabasha County at the age of three. At the age of 21 she headed west with some friends, and she arrived in California in time to witness the "driving of the golden spike."

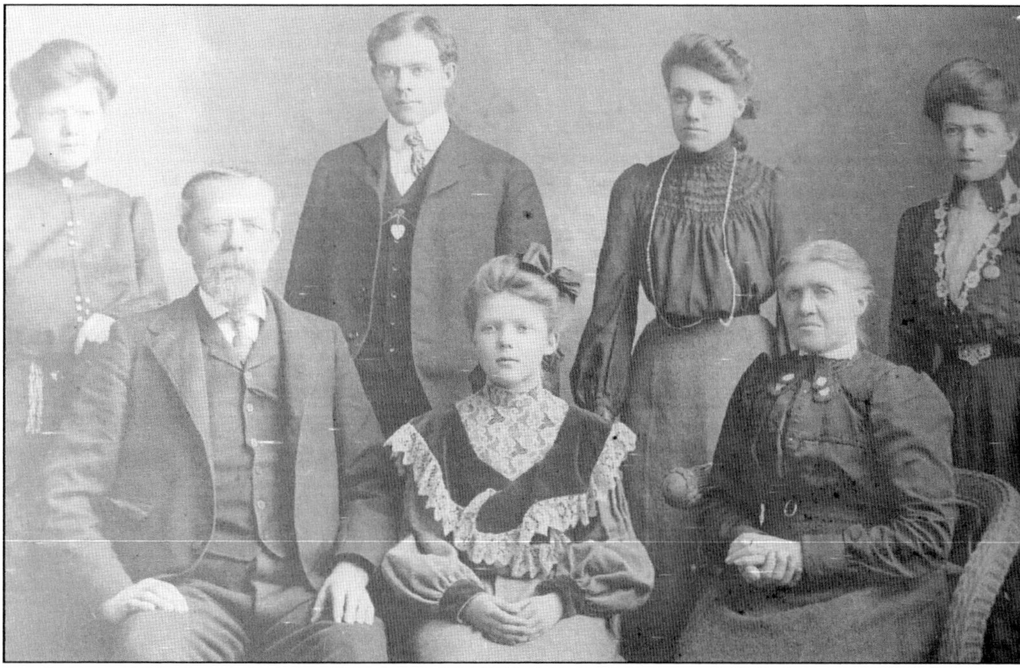

The family of Peter and Odelia (Baker) Howe poses for a photograph. Peter was born in Germany in 1851. In 1861, he came with his parents to Wabasha County, settling on a farm in Glasgow Township. His parents are John and Susanna (Leisen) Howe. Odila was born in Germany to John and Anna (Miller) Baker in 1849. Peter and Odila were married in 1875 at Wabasha. They had seven children—Katherine (Peter Schierts), John (Ruba Parson), Lizzie (Peter Stiever), Mary, Celia (Linn Pfeilsticker), William, and Susanna.

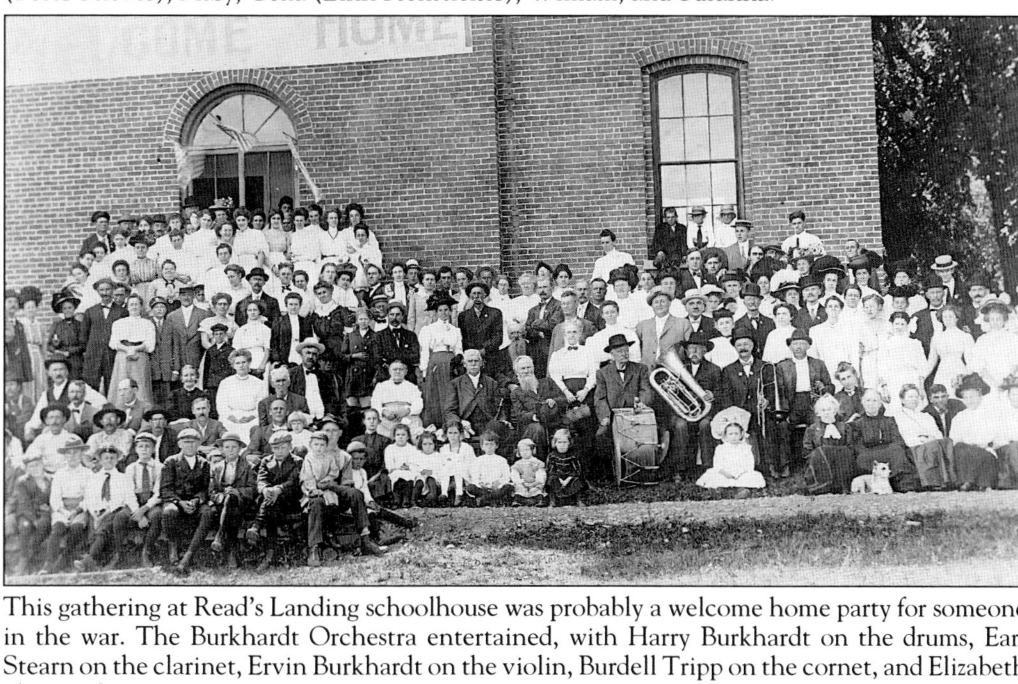

This gathering at Read's Landing schoolhouse was probably a welcome home party for someone in the war. The Burkhardt Orchestra entertained, with Harry Burkhardt on the drums, Earl Stearn on the clarinet, Ervin Burkhardt on the violin, Burdell Tripp on the cornet, and Elizabeth playing the piano.

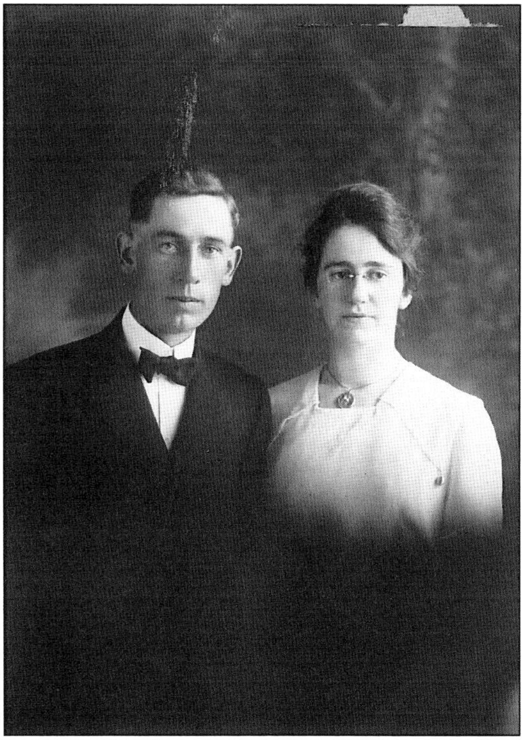

Archer and Grace (Geppert) Copp are shown here on their wedding day, November 29, 1917. The farm of the Copp family eventually came to be what is called a "100"-year farm, having been retained by the same family all those years. It was actually in the family about 110 years before it was sold by Verle Copp in the early 1900s. Archer had many interests, including raising all kinds of animals and birds. (Courtesy of Evlyn Dahling.)

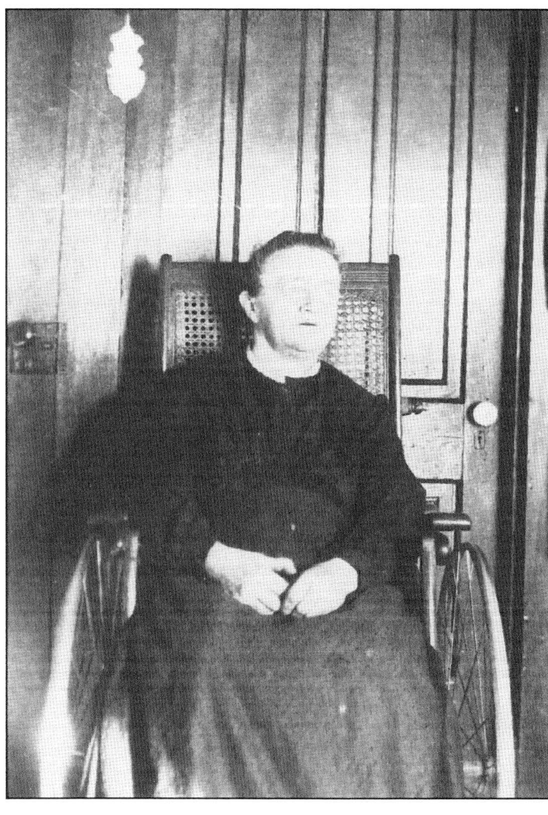

Helena (Bootz) Bahr-Huber was born in Germany to John and Marie Bootz. Helena and her husband, Frederick Bahr, came to the United States in 1881 and settled in Buffalo County, WI. Their children are Fred, Peter, Mrs. Fred Frommeit, Mrs. E. Jacobson, and William. In October 1881, Frederick passed away. Helena married John Huber in Wabasha in November of the following year. They had two children—Rose (Joseph Ryan) and John (Marie Burrichter).

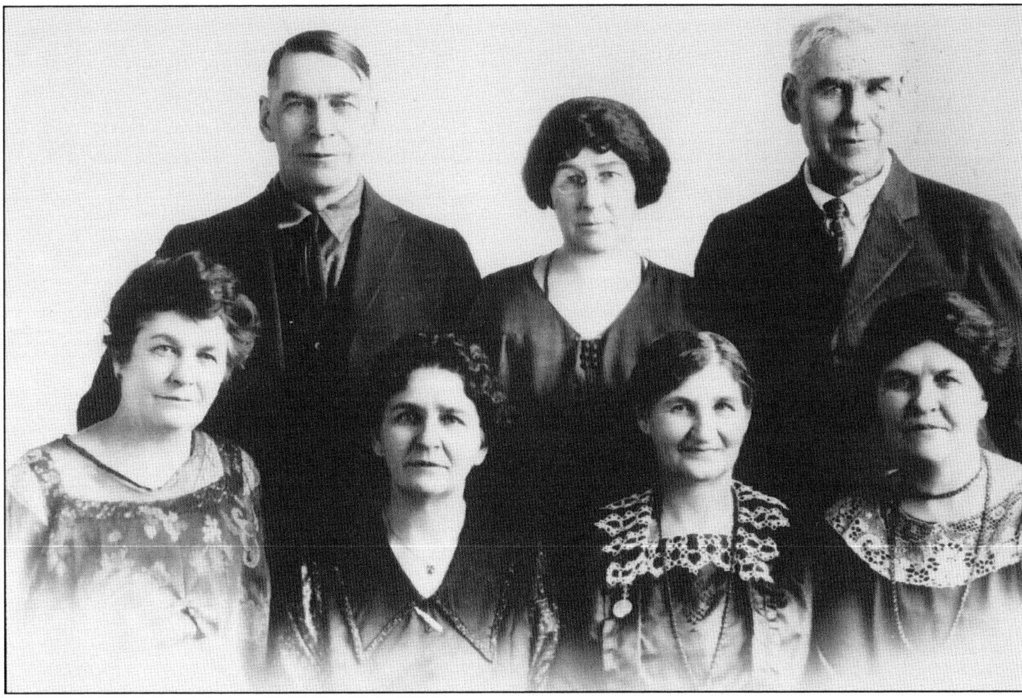

In this photo are 7 of the 11 Hellinger children. They are, from left to right, as follows: (front row) Anna, Clara, Mary, and Susan; (back row) Frank, Lucinda, and William. All these children were born in Glasgow Township to Thomas and Maria (Giem) Hellinger. The following was written by Ardis Dashiell: ". . . One day, while Thomas and Maria were outside working in the field near the house, a deranged neighbor set fire to their cabin in Glasgow. Charles died a month after the fire and Mary, who was the baby at that time, and sleeping in the same crib with Charles, was badly burned. She was crippled all of her life from the burns she received on her legs."

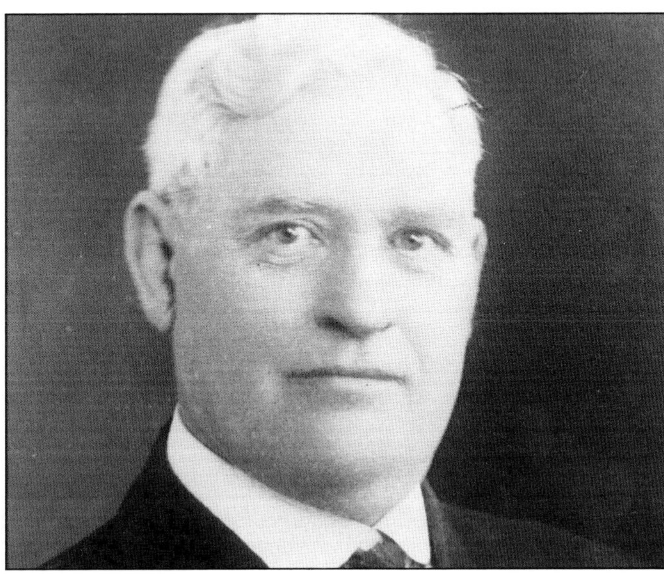

Mike Schouweiler was born on September 15, 1860, in Wabasha County. His parents were Michael and Catherine Schouweiler.

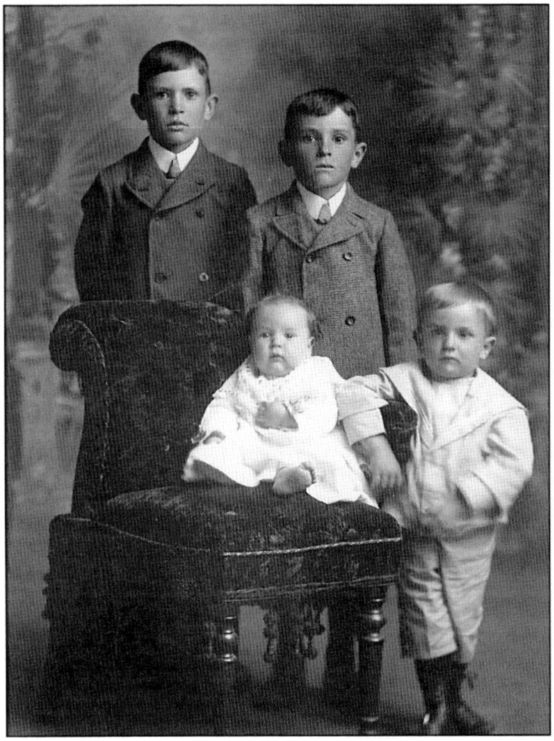

This photograph of the children of August and Anna (Jackson) Schurhammer was taken about 1907. They are, from left to right, as follows: (front row) Albert (Loretta Foley) and Andrew (Carnesea Petroff-Dorothy Grant); (back row) Arthur (Gladys Pomeroy) and Benjamin.

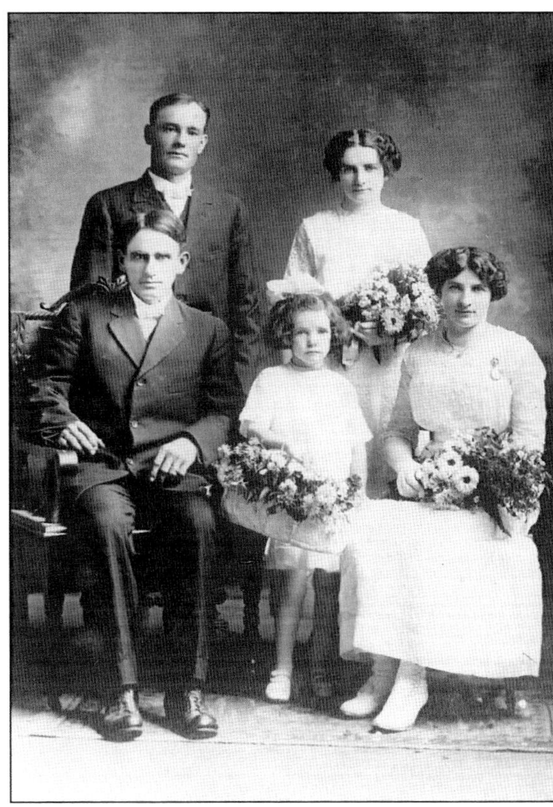

The wedding of Nick and Agnes (Norton) Klees took place on June 18, 1913, at Plainview. Nick was born in Highland Township in 1885. Agnes, who was born in 1889 to Mr. and Mrs. John Norton, had three brothers (Edward, James, and Dan) and two sisters (Mrs. Verne Wentworth and Mrs. Art Gosselia). Rick and Agnes were blessed with five sons and four daughters—Francis, Robert, James, Paul, Lester, Eleanor (Lloyd Gessner), Catherine (Ralph Wodele), Loretta (Leo Everman), and Rosella. (Courtesy of Dorothy Stoos.)

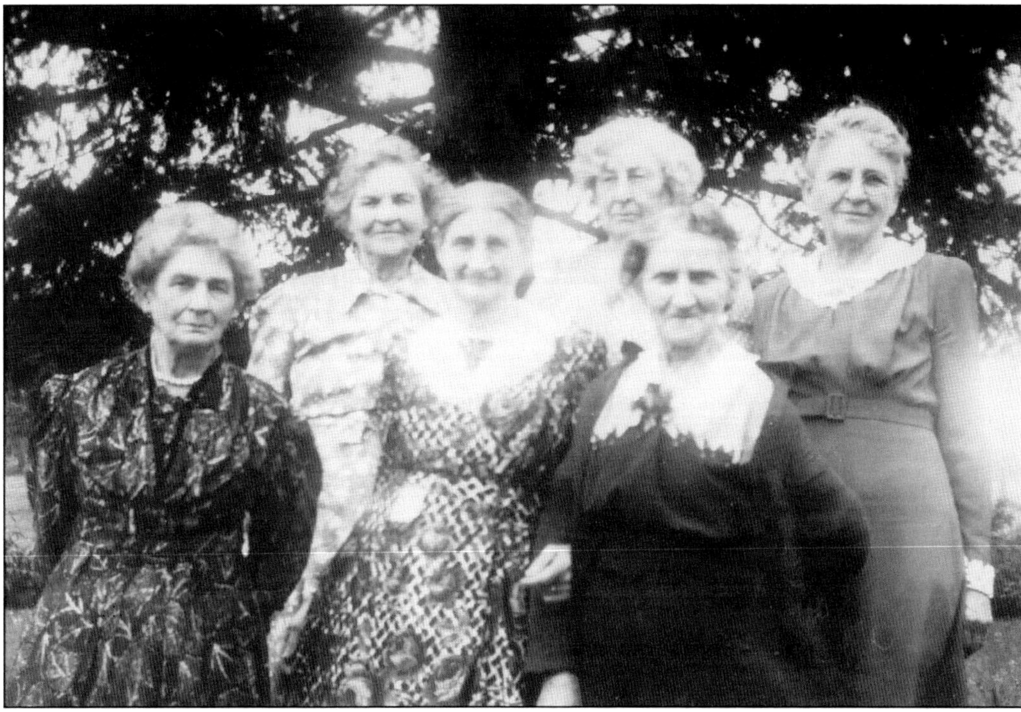

The Hellinger girls are, from left to right, Anna, Susie, Mary, Lucinda, Sara, and Clara. They were born in Glasgow Township to Thomas and Maria (Giem) Hellinger. On May 14, 1880, a tragedy fell upon the family—the loss of their beloved husband and father. Maria was left with her family of ten children and she needed John and Will to help support them. The boys wanted to go to Washington Territory to get homesteads, so Maria sold the farm and the family started west. (Courtesy of Ardis Dashiell.)

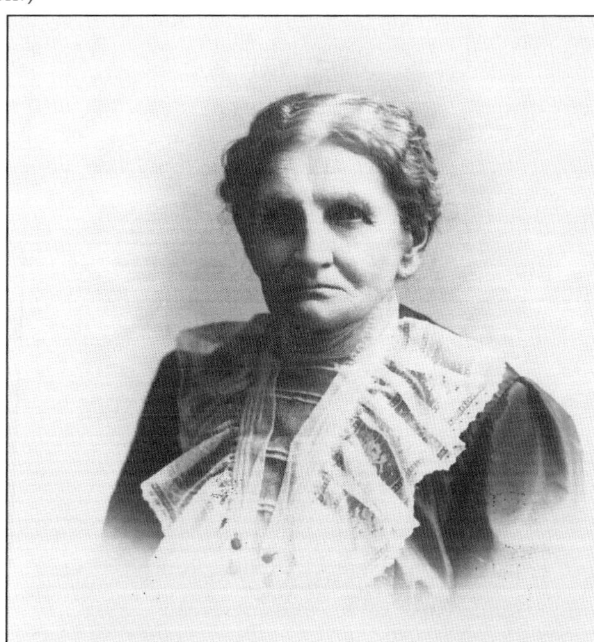

Maria (Giem) Hellinger was a pioneer in three states—Ohio (as a child of two in 1833), Minnesota (where she married and established her family in 1856), and Washington (as a widow with ten children ranging in age from 6 to 21 years in 1882). She was one of the people who established this country through a deep devotion to the responsibilities of rearing a family and a lifetime of hard work and perseverance. (Courtesy of Ardis Dashiell.)

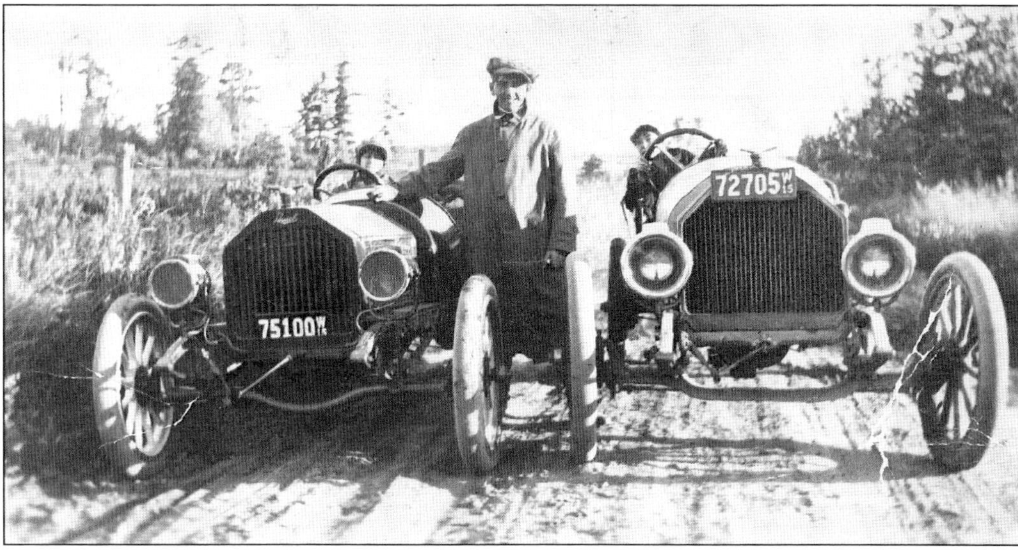

On the left is Julius Ausgaard in his homemade roadster #75100, and on the right is Arthur Chadwick in his homemade roadster #72705. Arthur was born in 1898 in Wabasha, and by the age of 14 he was working as a drayline driver for Jacob's Livery. When he was about 20 years old, he designed and built a garage with his sister Florence's husband, Julius Ausgaard. The garage, located behind the old Jacob's Livery, was doing quite well until the Klu Klux Klan burned it to the ground. It was never rebuilt. (Courtesy of Gladys Krusmark.)

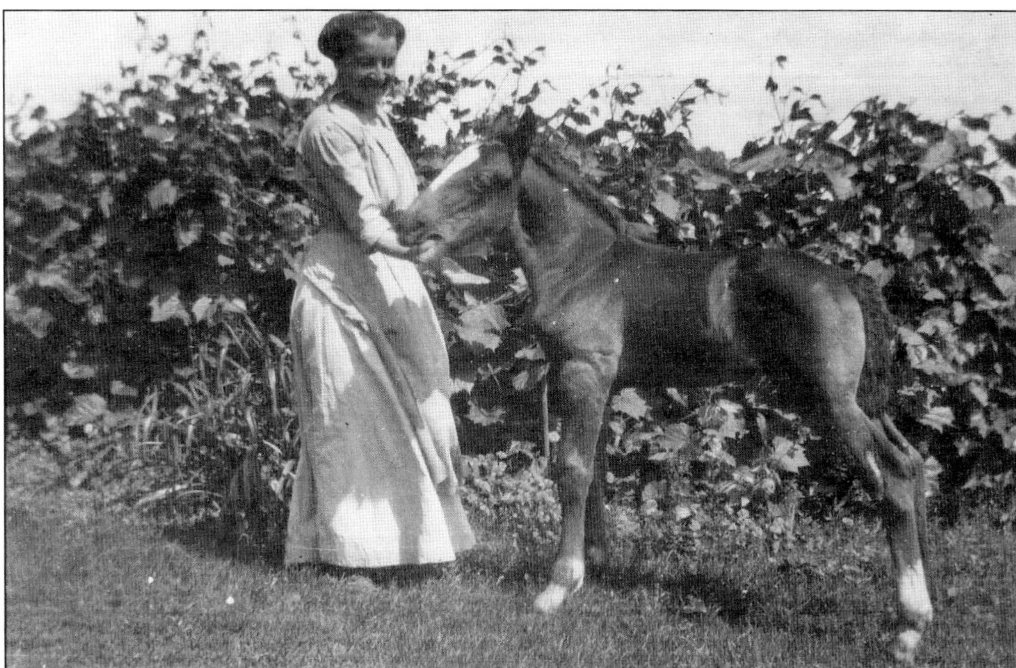

Rose Huber was born on May 3, 1884, in Greenfield Township to John and Helena (Bootz) Huber. John came to the United States with his first wife, Caroline Wacholtz. Caroline's parents, Thomas and Hannah, and their son John came with them and settled in Greenfield in the early 1850s. John and Helena married in Wabasha in 1882. Rose married Joseph Ryan.

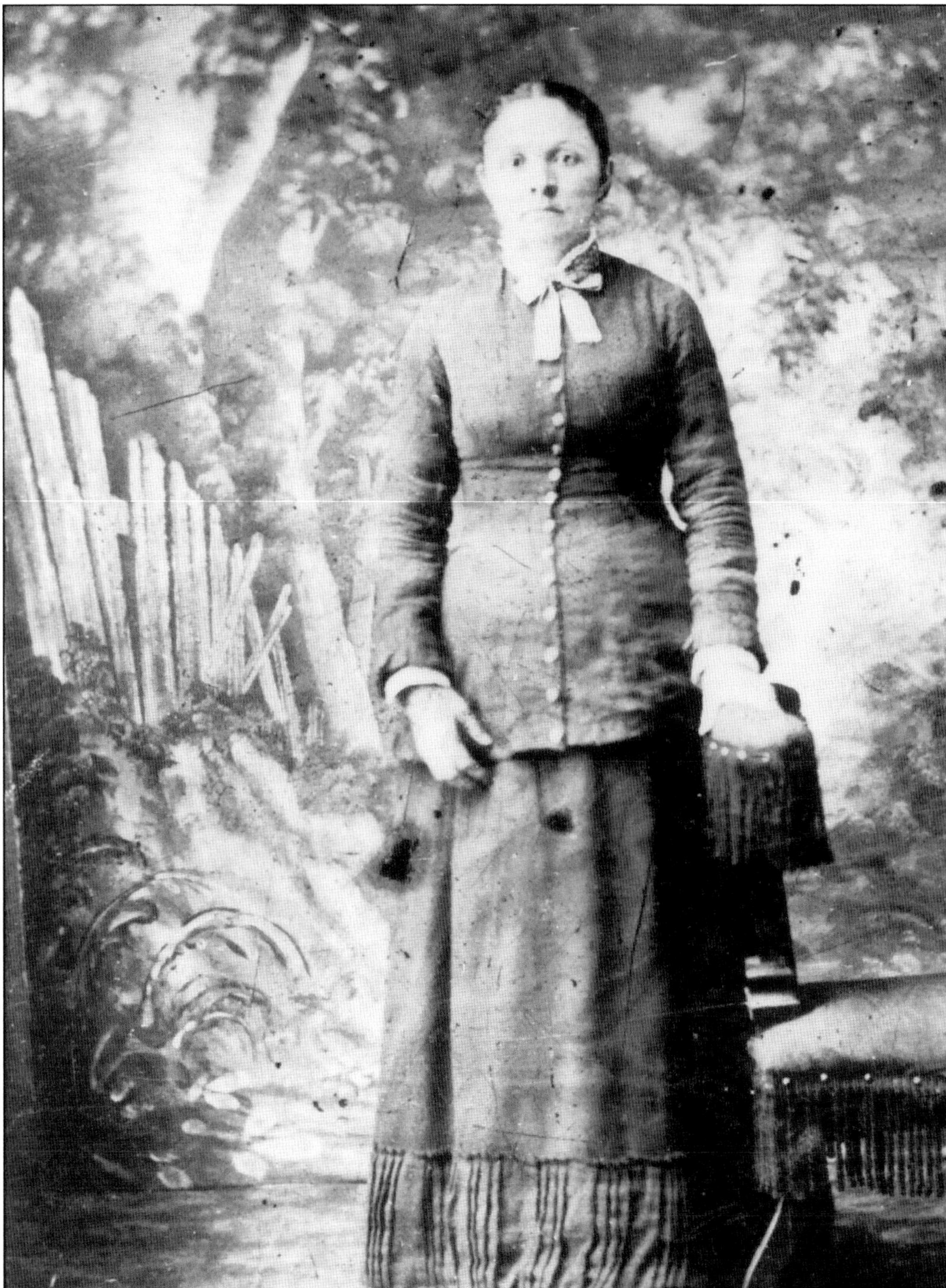

Margaret (Markadont) Giem was born about 1849 in Iowa. Her parents, Peter and Christena Markadont, came to Wabasha in the late 1850s and had four children—Margaret, John, Mary (Joseph Neigg), and Anna (Casper Schellenberger). Margaret married Jacob Giem and had six children—John, Ann, Emma, Peter, Jacob, and Henry.

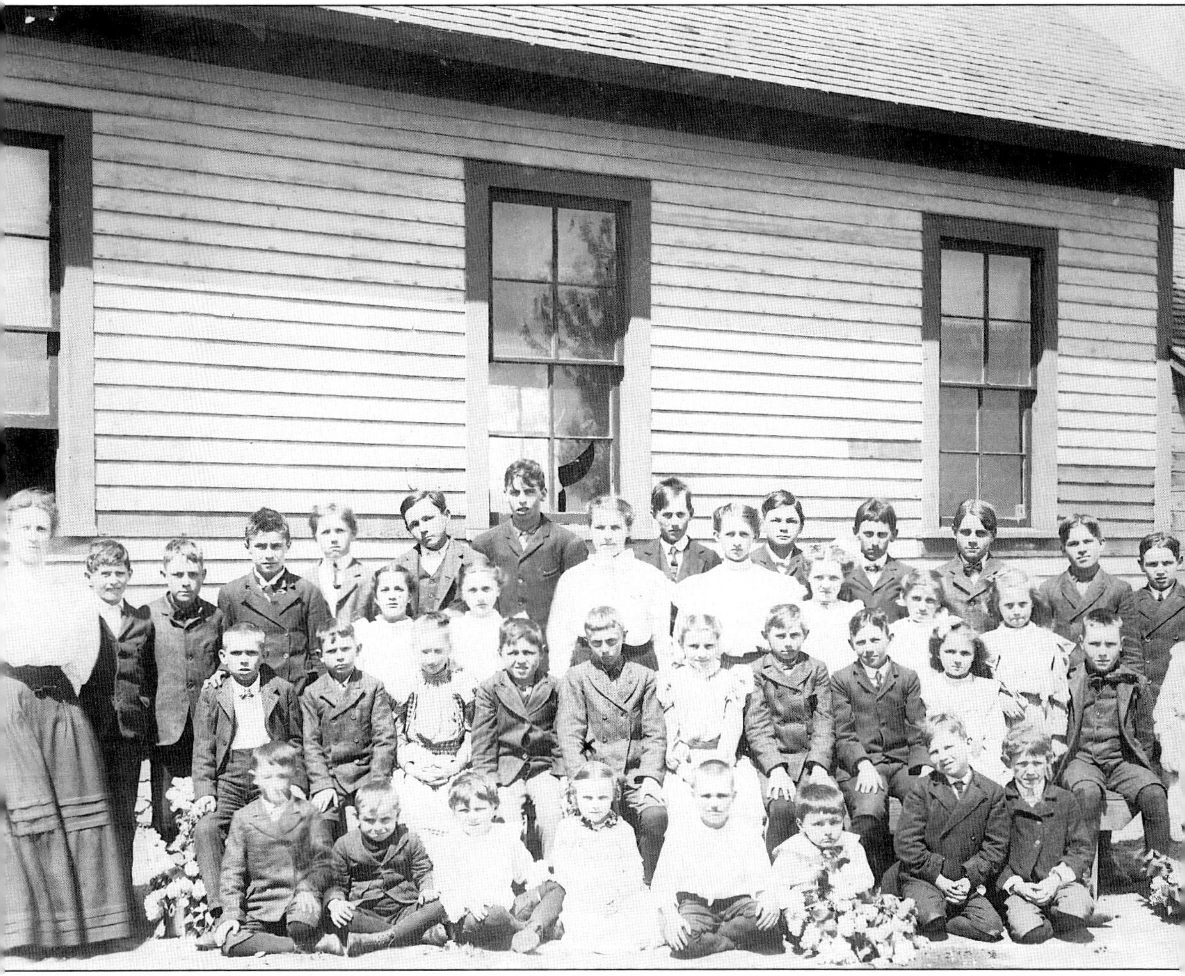

Teacher Kate Leonard is shown here with the class of 1906 at Kellogg. The students are, from left to right, as follows: (front row) Ben Schurhammer, Fred Senrick, and Neal McCaffery; (second row) Leonard Schurhammer, Arthur Schurhammer, May Geisler, Lawrence Buol, Frank Ryan, Sofie Shankey, Leo Freeze, Walter Dugan, Dorothy Buol, Walter Schurhammer, and Mary Peterson; (third row) Flora Freeze, Catherine Quigley, Margaret Drury, Josephine Geisler, Mary McCaffery, Marie Schurhammer, and Rachel Geisler; (back row) Joe Geisler, Lloyd Schurhammer, Mike Senrick, Harry Quigley, Chris Buol, Woodie St. Jacque, Theo Geisler, John Buol, Henry St. Jacque, Tom Barton, Ben St. Jacque, and Mike Drury.

Elizabeth (left) and her sister, Katherine Leisen, the daughters of Mathias and Catherine (Zeimetz) Leisen, have lived their entire lives in Wabasha County. Elizabeth married Peter Giem, and Katherine married William Deming. Their brothers are George, John (Mary Eischen), Albert (Margaret Eischen), Nicholas (Viola Dondlinger), and Joseph (Julia Stroot). Their sister Anna lived about six months.

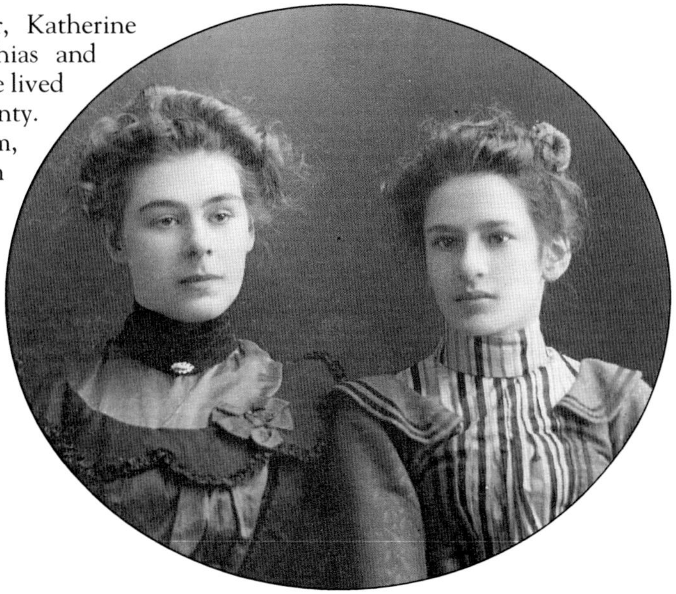

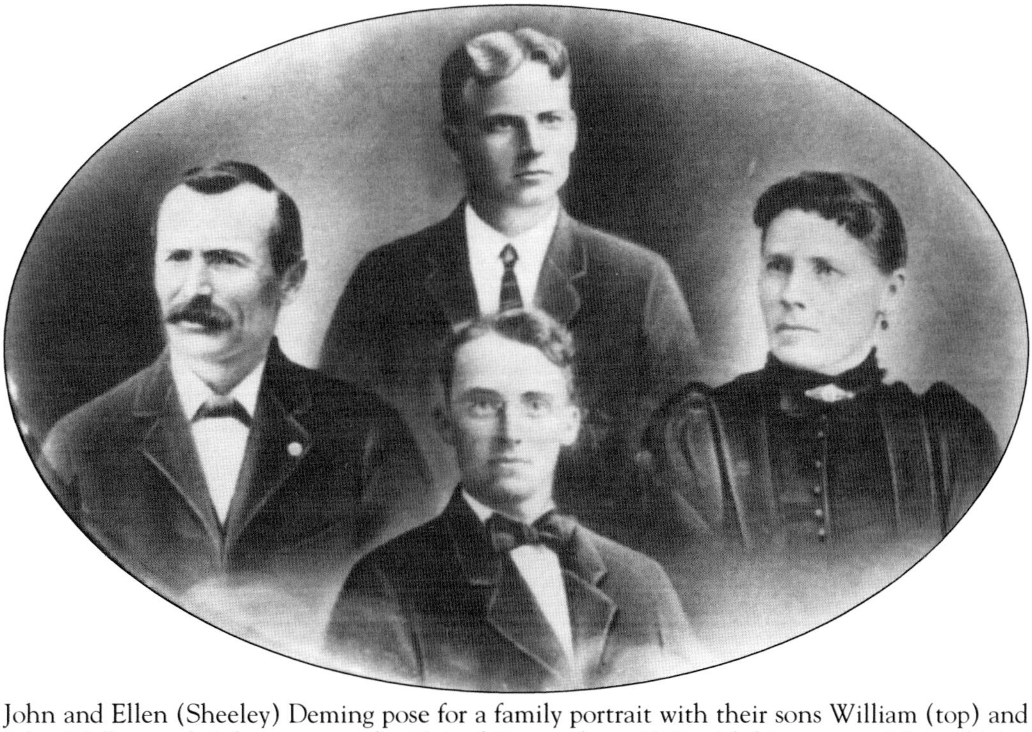

John and Ellen (Sheeley) Deming pose for a family portrait with their sons William (top) and John III (bottom). John came to the United States about 1853 with his parents, Mr. and Mrs. John Deming Sr., and settled in Wabasha County. He met and married Ellen in Wabasha in November of 1883.

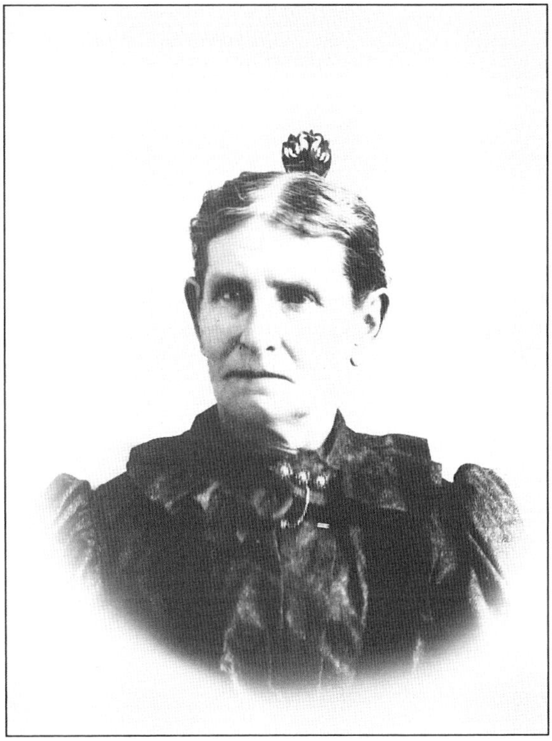

Maria Dorthea Fredericka (Giem) Hellinger, an early Glasgow Township pioneer, was born in Germany on December 14, 1834, to John C. and Dorthea (Meinhardt) Giem. Dorthea died when Maria was about 12 years old. In 1858 Maria married Thomas Hellinger and they had 11 children—John (Molly Mosley), Anna (John Drew), William (Mary Steffen), Charles, Maria (Frederick Timm), Frank (Martha Brooks), Sarah (Alfred Smith), Suzhannah (William Ivester), Clara (John Maurer), Elizabeth (Peter Selde), and Lucinda (George Brown). (Courtesy of Ardis Dashiell.)

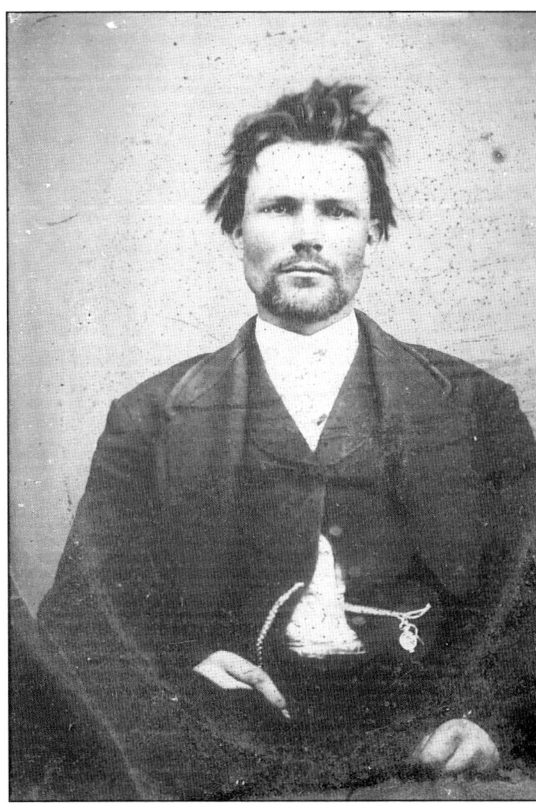

George Schurhammer was born in Baden, Germany, on April 21, 1852. At the age of three, he came to Wabasha County with his parents, Joseph and Magdelena (Tritschler) Schurhammer. George married Anna Braun at Alma, WI, on February 12, 1876. George and Anna's children are Josephine (Robert Sutter), Gustav (Olga Hammer), Simon (Mary Paul), Bodo (Lucy Gammons), Roy (Charlotte Cruzer), Phillip (Frances Bastian), and Reuben (Margaret Carroll).

This photo of Ira and Lucina (Norton) Buck was taken at Wabasha, MN. Ira (born *c.* 1816 in Monroe County, New York) and Lucina (born *c.* 1820 in New York) were married on February 6, 1838, at Parkman Township, Geauga County, OH. Ira was living in Palatine, Cook County, IL, when he enlisted in the Civil War. The Ira D. Buck family arrived in the 1870s at Wabasha, Wabasha County, MN. It was here that they lived out their lives. Their children are A.M., James (Emma Wetmore), Medora (Richard Lampe), Sarah (Alphens Allguer), Emma (John Confair), and Frances (David Hunt). (Courtesy of Merle Campbell.)

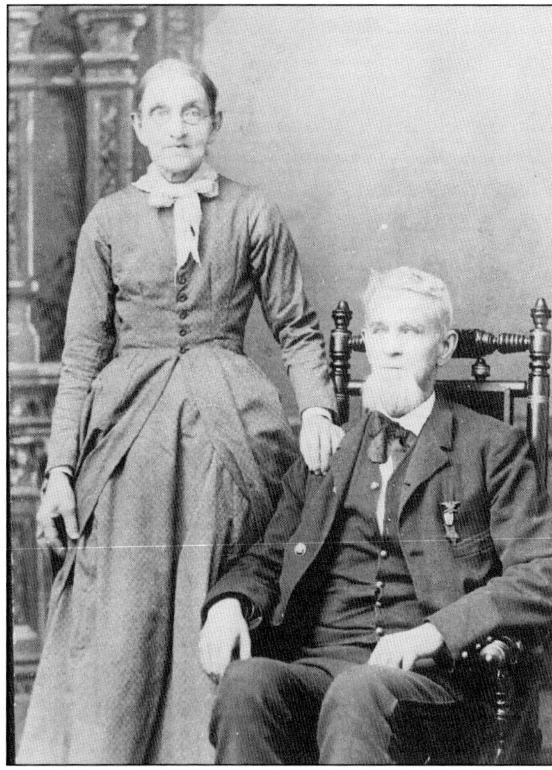

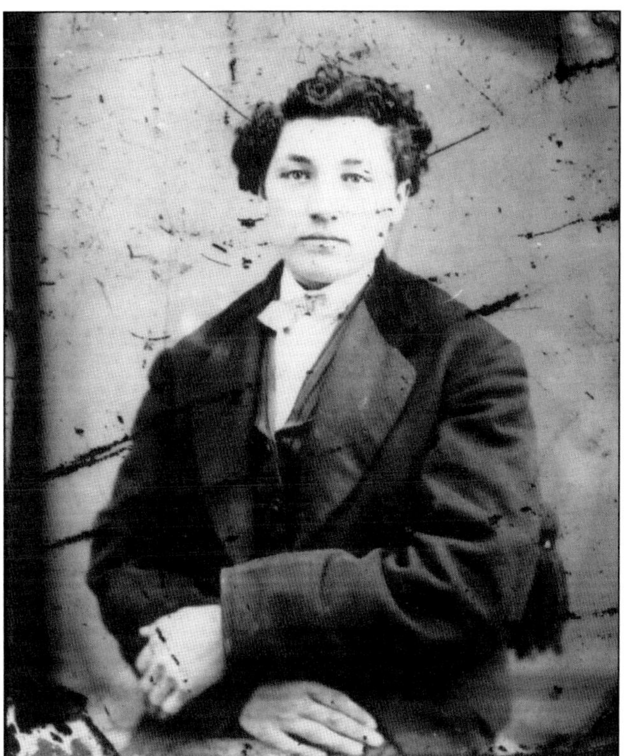

Jacob Schouweiler was born on November 18, 1854, in Wabasha County to Michael and Catharine Schouweiler. He died in Superior, WI, in 1895.

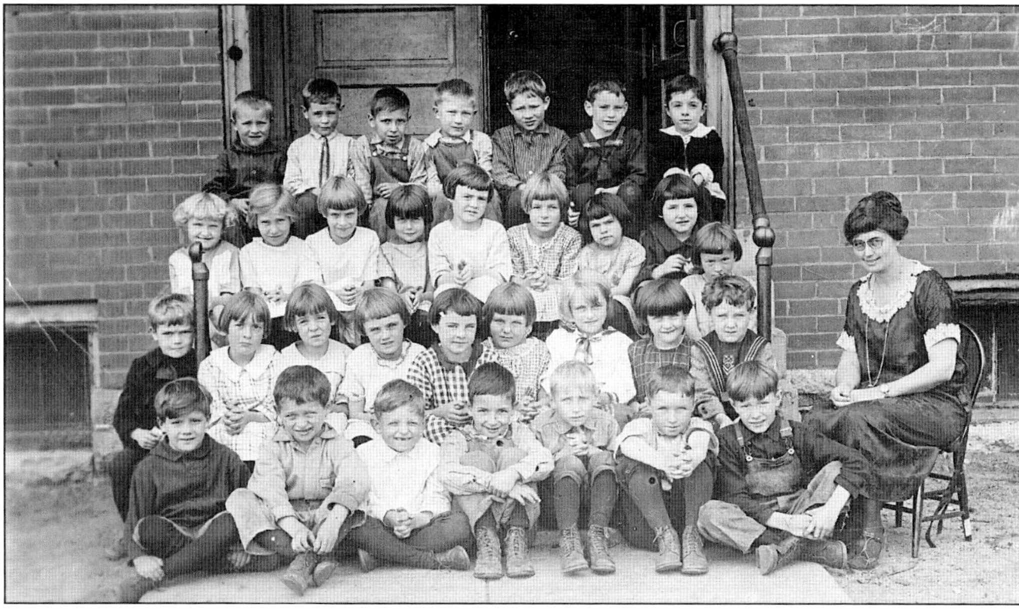

Teacher Mrs. Varvel is shown here with her first grade class at Kellogg. Among those shown here are Ervin Wehinger, Eugene Peterson, Donald Shones, Charles Hager, Kenneth Schurhammer, Eugene Deming, Jackie Reister, Margaret Canfield, Ethel Griggs, Josephine Giem, Wilma Schmoker, Marion Schurhammer, Jean McDonough, Helen Grant, John Blee, Louise Schurhammer, Sidney Schurhammer, Kathleen Blee, Mary McCormick, Alan Schmoker, Viola Graner, Burly Peterson, Tom Hager, Ignatius Straus, Ervin Barton, Bill Wehrenberg, ? Schones, Edward Quinn, and Immanuel Grant.

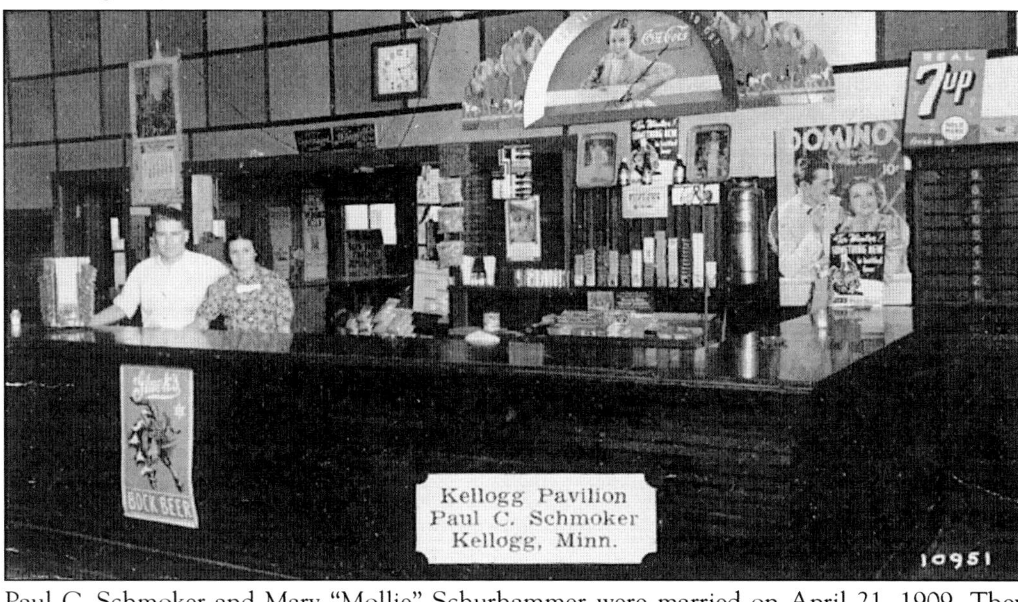

Paul C. Schmoker and Mary "Mollie" Schurhammer were married on April 21, 1909. They farmed on Sand Prairie near Kellogg, MN, until 1927, when they moved to Kellogg and built a dance pavilion. After operating the pavilion for 16 years, they started an Implement building at the same location. They retired in 1946, and were the parents of two children—Mrs. Helen Groetsch and Mrs. Mary Bricher.

Catherine Schouweiler, the daughter of Michael and Catherine (Klein) Schouweiler, was born on January 12, 1851, in Tiffen, OH. She married George Howe, the son of John and Susanna (Leisen) Howe, on May 7, 1868, and the two had eight children—Michael, Catherine, John, George Jr., Fora, Edward, Charles, and Lucille. (Courtesy of Dorothy Collard.)

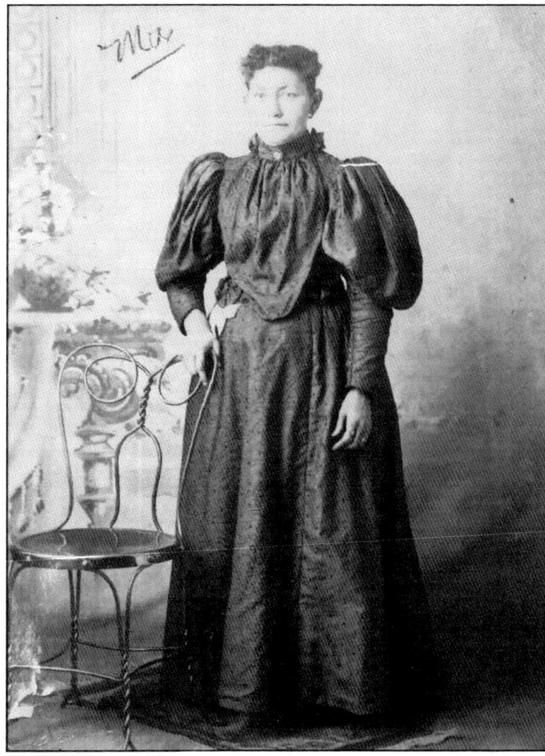

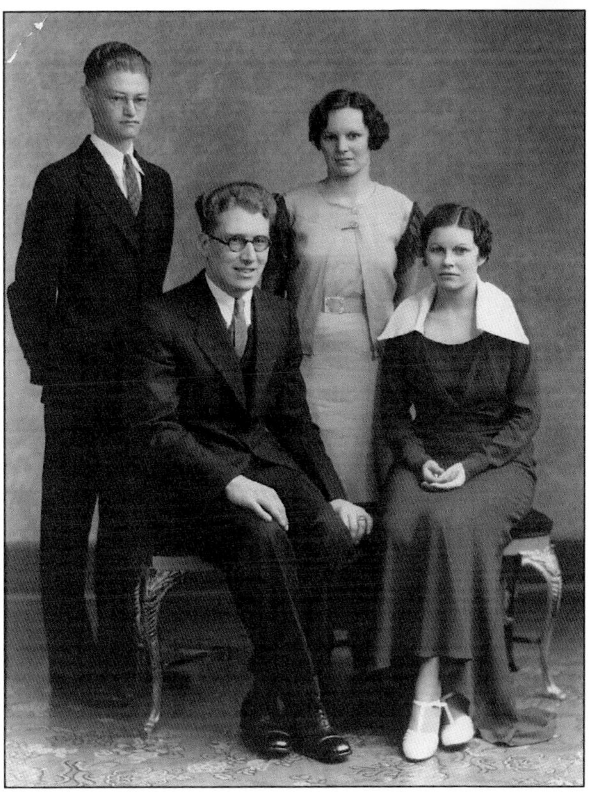

John and Mary (Schmoker) Bricher (both sitting) pose on their wedding day with best man Willard Bricher and bridesmaid Helen Schmoker. Mary and Helen are the daughters of Paul and Mary Mollie (Schurhammer) Schmoker. Their grandparents were among the early settlers of Wabasha County.

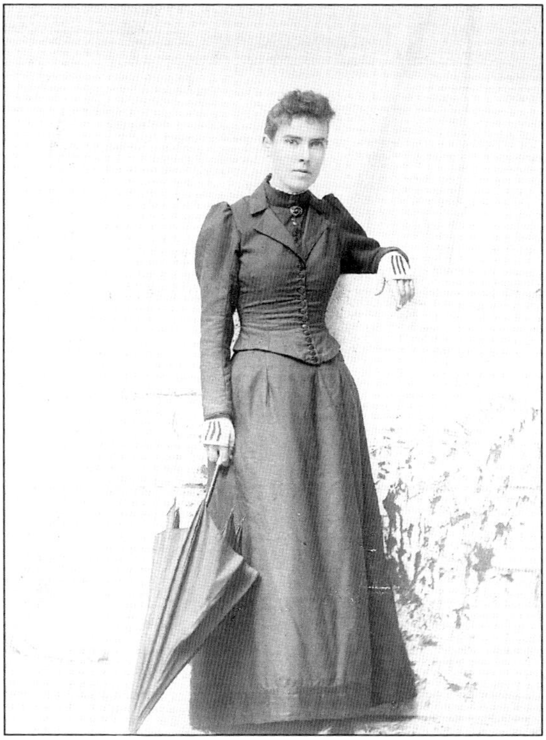

Alice Jackson, the daughter of John and Jane Jackson, was born July 17, 1877, in Greenfield Township. She married Christian Schurhammer in 1893, and the two spent their lives on their farm, working hard to clear the land. Alice and Christian's children are Lloyd, Walter, Woodruff, Rena, Orville, and Virgil Schurhammer.

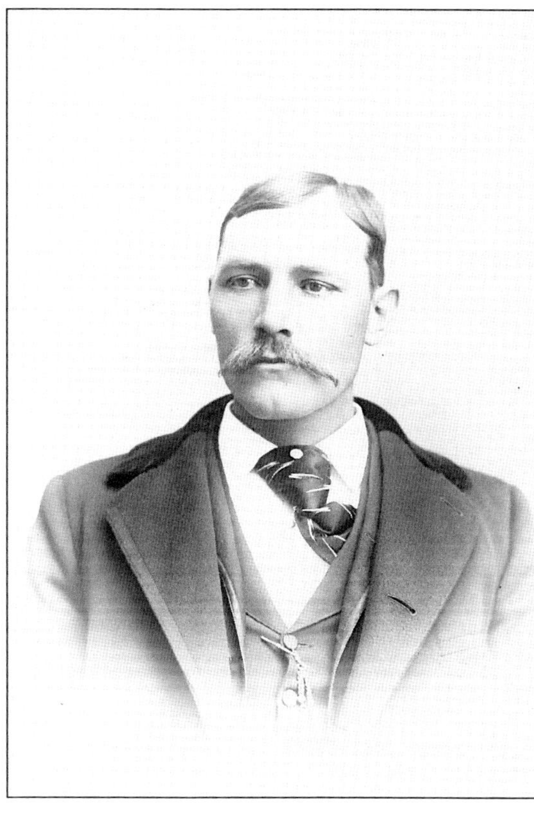

Christian Schurhammer was born to Joseph and Magdelena Schurhammer on January 19, 1864, on the family farm in Greenfield. He married Alice Jackson in 1893 at Alma, WI, and spent most of his life helping to carve Wabasha County's modern farm community out of the wilderness.

Joseph Schurhammer was one of Wabasha County's most respected early settlers. Born in Underglotteral, Amt Waldkirch, in a beautiful valley of Baden, Germany, he immigrated to America with his wife, Magdalena (Tritschler). After stopping in Iowa, they took a boat up the Mississippi River to Wabasha and settled in Greenfield Township in 1855. At the time the township was still a wilderness, Minnesota was not yet a state, and the nearest trading post was in Wabasha.

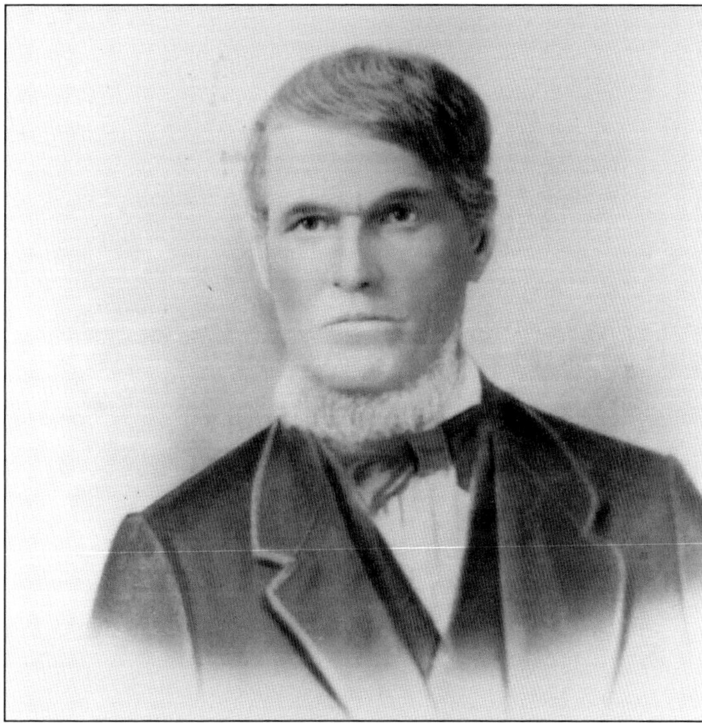

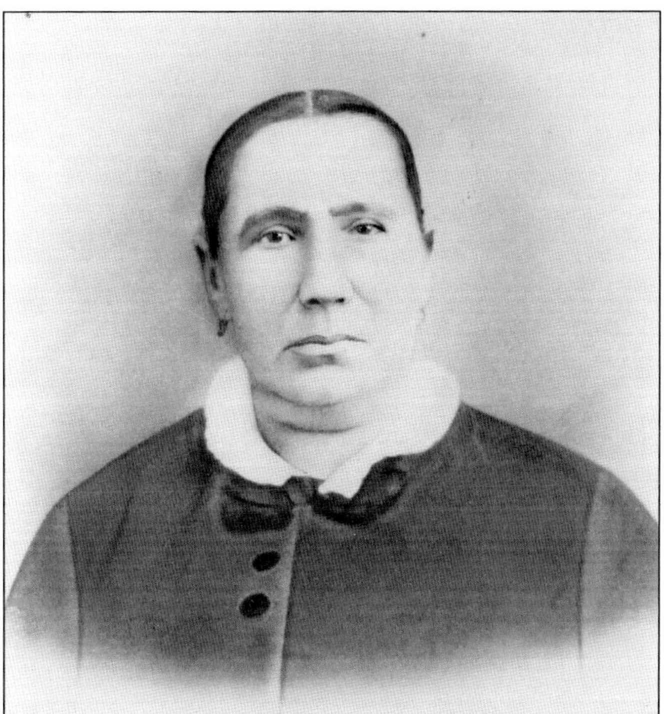

Magdalena (Tritschler) Schurhammer, the daughter of Michael and Barbara (Reichenbach) Tritschler, was born in Germany on July 7, 1831. She married Joseph Schurhammer in 1849, and together they immigrated to the United States. Mrs. Schurhammer met and coped with all the provocations, trials, and cares of the Minnesota frontier. Joseph and Magdelena had nine children—George (Anna Braun), Joseph (Sarah Huber), Andreas I, Wilhelmina (Thomas Hershberger), Christian (Alice Jackson), August (Anna Jackson), Andreas II, Albert, and Lawrence (Josephine Jorden).

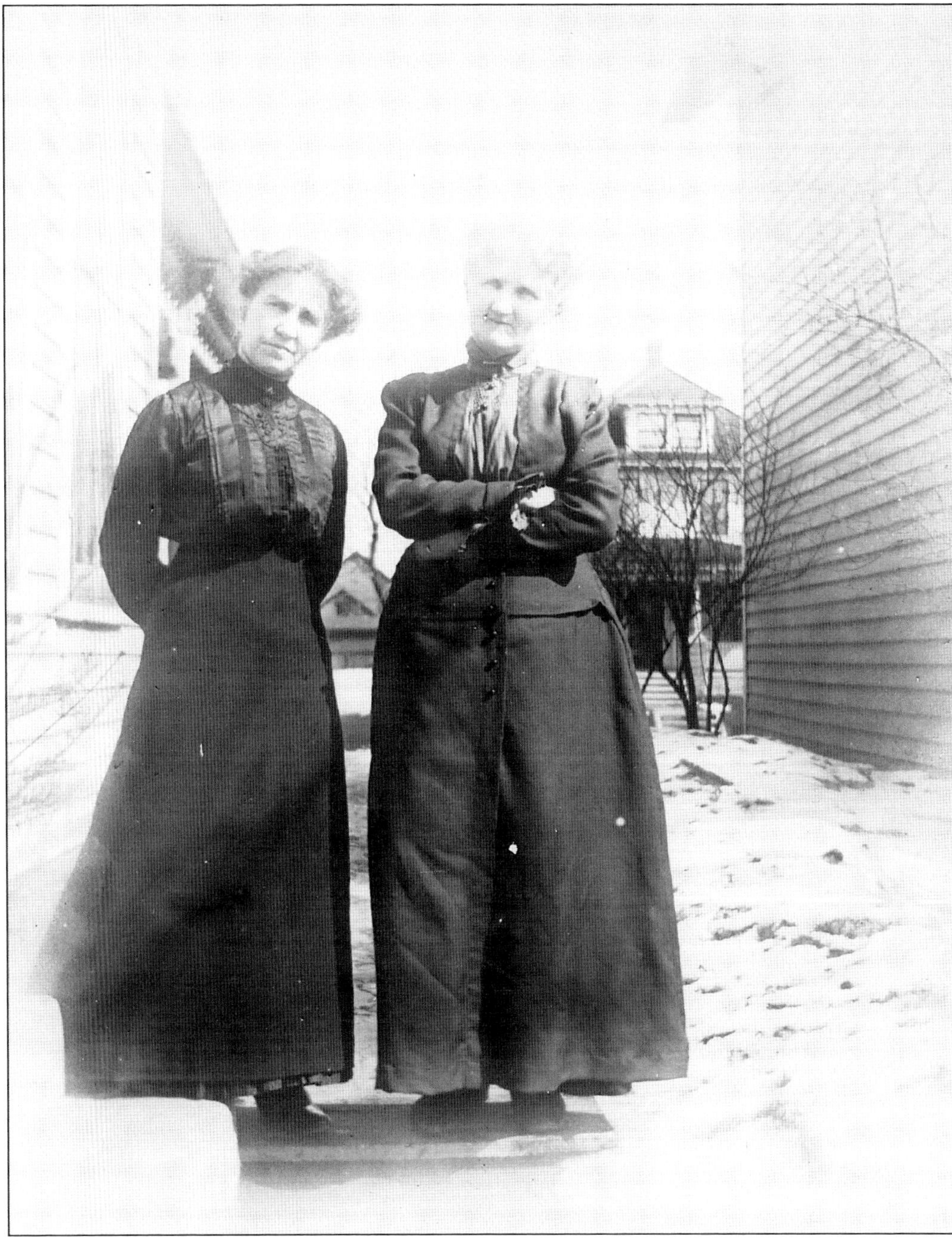

Margaret O'Laughlin (left) and Maria Ryan (right) pose for a photograph. Their father and mother settled in Wabasha County in 1854.

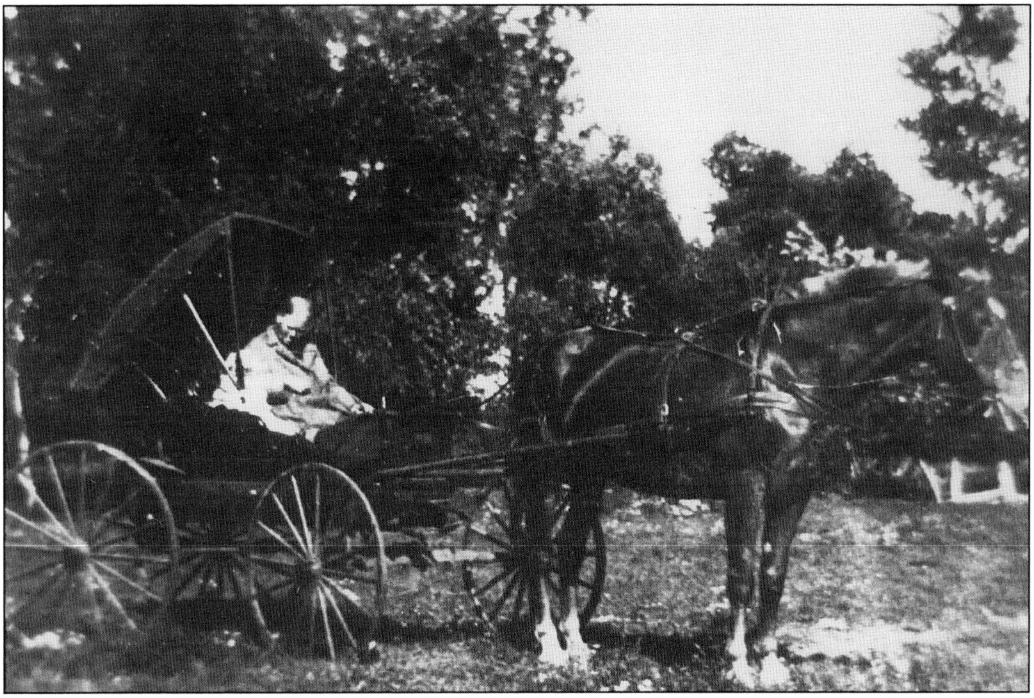

Sarah (Huber) Schurhammer is shown here in the carriage with Francis Spooner. She named the horse "Fanny." The photograph was taken in Greenfield Township about 1916. It shows how the pioneers traveled; they made their own wagons, clothes, furniture, and buttons, and produced food locally.

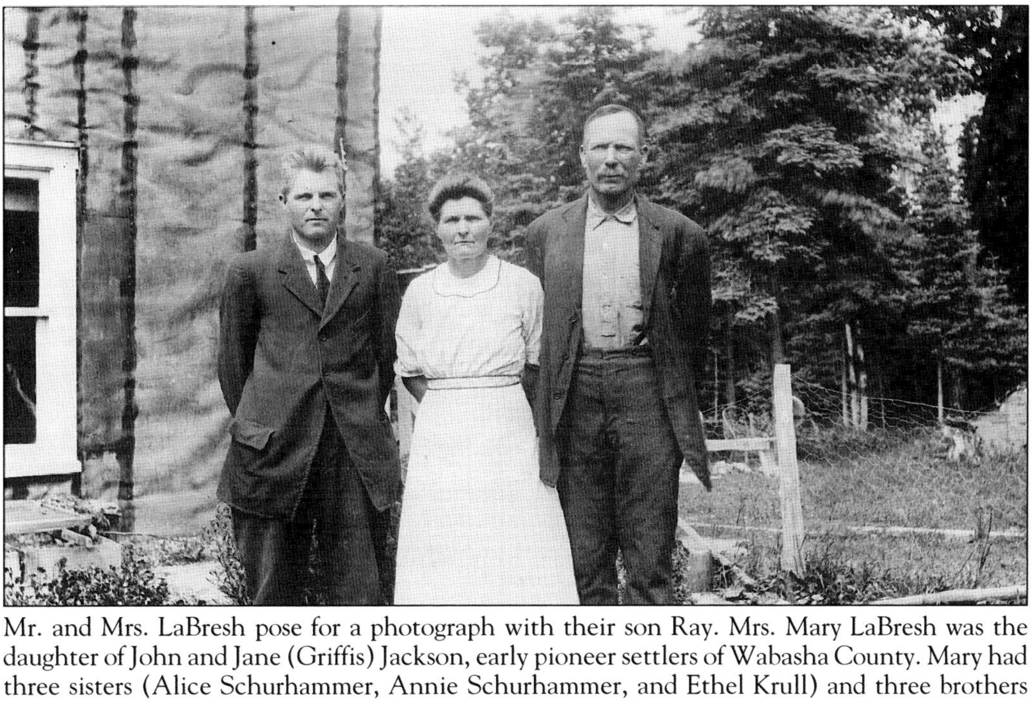

Mr. and Mrs. LaBresh pose for a photograph with their son Ray. Mrs. Mary LaBresh was the daughter of John and Jane (Griffis) Jackson, early pioneer settlers of Wabasha County. Mary had three sisters (Alice Schurhammer, Annie Schurhammer, and Ethel Krull) and three brothers (Samuel, John, and Bert, who died at age three).

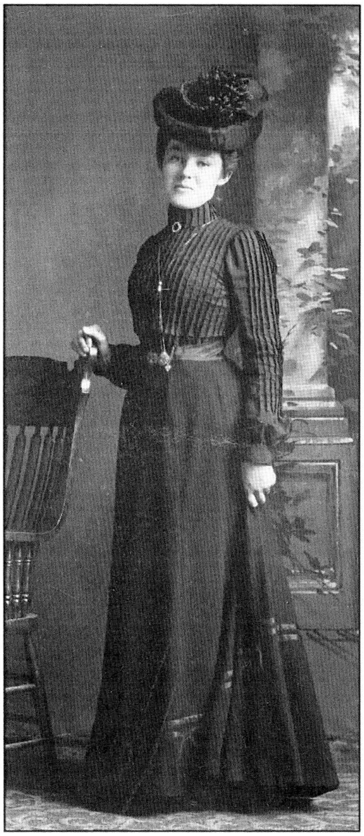

Elizabeth (Huber) Gustafson, the daughter of Albert and Bertha Huber, was born in 1880 at Wabasha. She married Charles Gustafson in 1902 and they had seven children—Elvin, Allard, Alfred, Louella, Alvira, Victoria, and Alvina. Mr. Gustafson worked in the lumber camps near Maine before moving to Chicago and working for the John Deere Company. He later moved to St. Paul, where he worked at the Street Car Company. He eventually relocated to Wabasha and was employed on the Milwaukee Road.

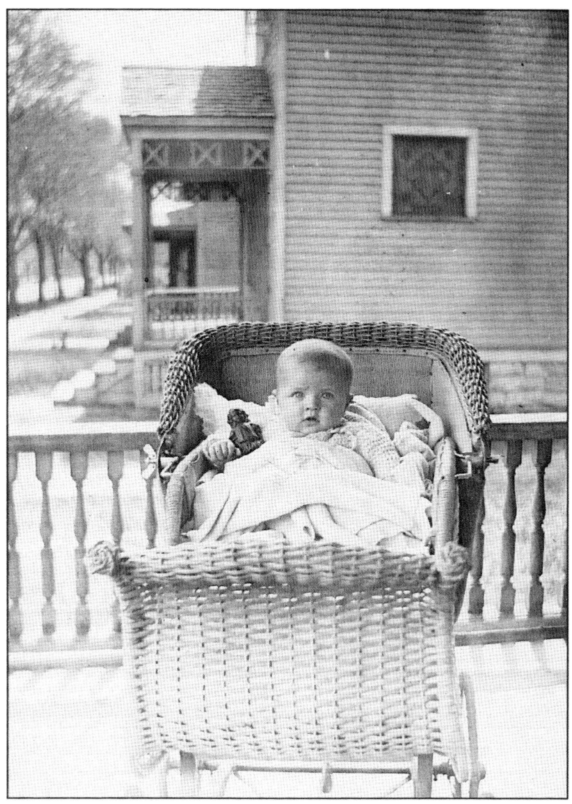

This five-month-old, posing quietly for a photograph in 1918, is the great-granddaughter of Lawrence and Mary (McDonough) Calhoun and the granddaughter of Anna (Calhoun) Cummings.

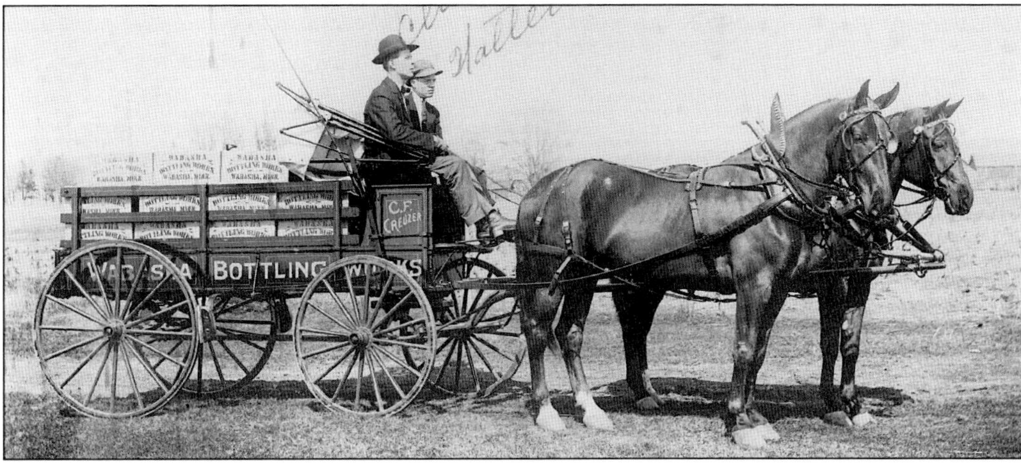

Charles F. Creuzer and his brother Walter deliver "pop" from their business, the Wabasha Bottling Works. On July 13, 1923, John and Joseph Meyer bought the business from Charles Creuzer. The business is no longer in existence. (Courtesy of Carla Schuth.)

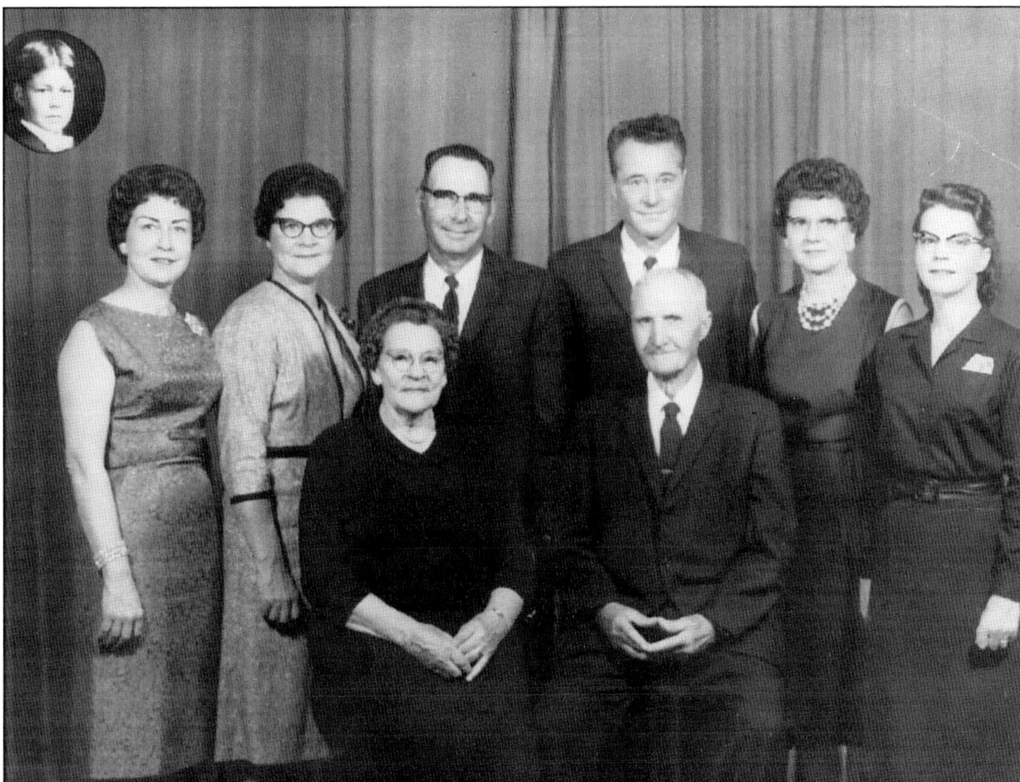

This portrait of the Giem family shows the following, from left to right: (sitting) Peter and Elizabeth (Leisen) Giem; (standing) Mary (Robert Passe), Margaret (Alphonse Kronebusch), Larry (Stella Eischen), Leo (Rachel Schurhammer), Josephine (Gerald Paine-Albin Konkel), and Beatrice (Mauritz Lindmark). The inset shows Peter and Elizabeth's son Joseph, who was born on April 17, 1902. On July 19, 1917, he was struck by lightning on the family farm in Minneiska Township and was killed instantly. (Courtesy of Rachel Giem.)

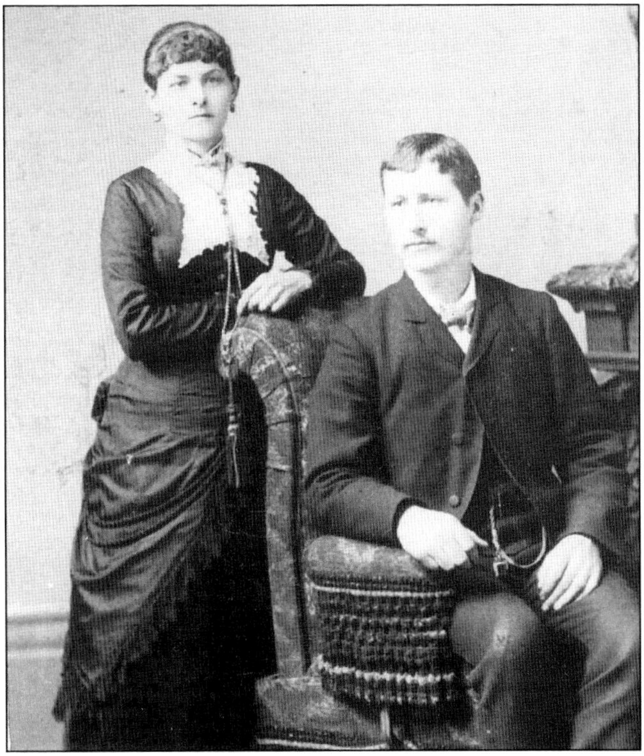

James E. Kennedy and Elizabeth Schouweiler are shown here in Wabasha on their wedding day—October 10, 1883. Elizabeth's parents are Michael and Catharine Schouweiler.

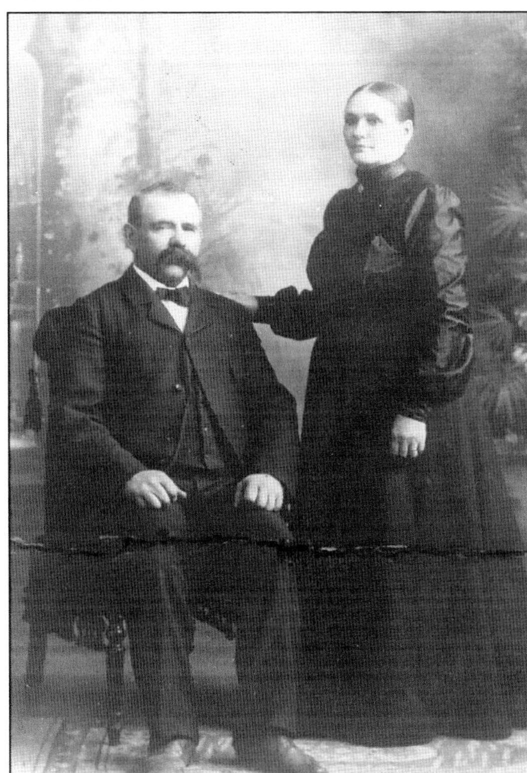

Mathias Leisen and Kathryn Zeimetz were married by Father James Trobee at the St. Felix Church in Wabasha. Mathias was born on March 17, 1848, in Germany, and he immigrated to the United States with his parents, George and Elizabeth Leisen, at the age of 12. Kathryn was born January 9, 1854, at Zeffern, Germany, to Mr. and Mrs. Martin Zeimetz. Mathias and Kathryn had eight children—Elizabeth (Peter Giem), George, John (Mary Eischen), Katherine (William Deming), Anna, Albert (Margaret Eischen), Nicholas (Viola Dondlinger), and Joseph (Julia Stroot).

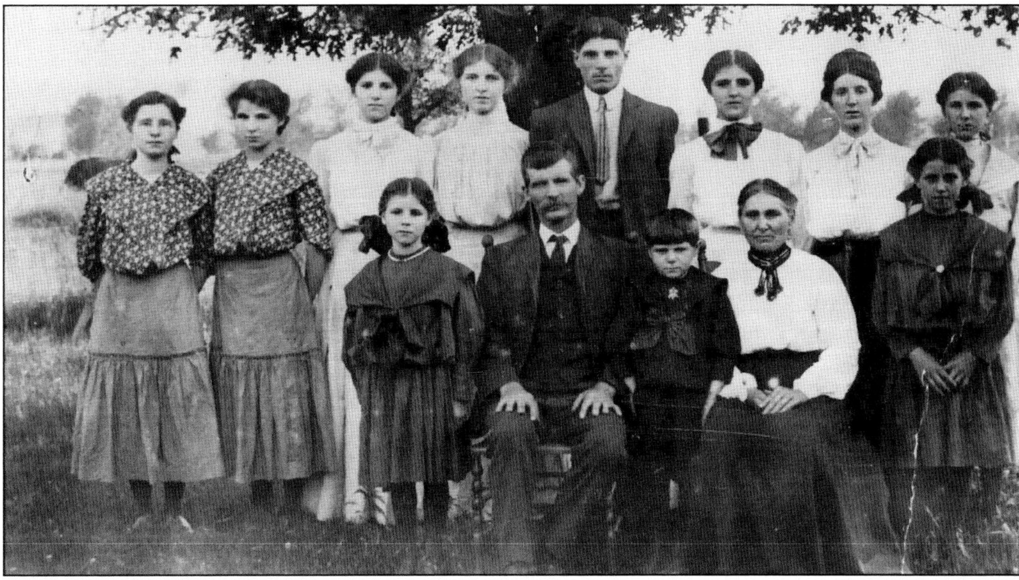

This *c.* 1906 portrait of the Lorenzo and Laura (Harrell) Curtis family shows the following, from left to right: (front row) Ruth (Joseph Woodward-Robert Schucard), Lorenzo, George (Letty Simmons), Laura Ann, and Vida; (back row) Jessie (John Allen), Jennie (Raymond Hendricks), Edna (Anthony Pryor), Margie (Albert Nelson-Claude Brownell), Roy (Mabel Krinke), Nine (Alvie Brown-Walter Belford), Maabel (Jim Shumway-John Hartwick), and Alta (Leonard Schurhammer).

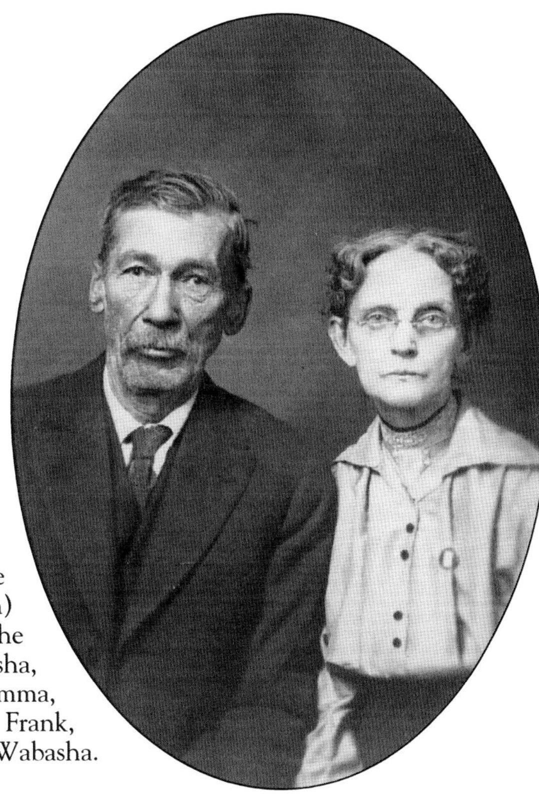

David Lillburn Hunt was born in Illinois on January 10, 1849, to James and Luann (Woodward) Hunt. Frances N. Buck, the daughter of Ira D. and Lucina A. (Norton) Buck, was born in Illinois about 1859. The two were married about 1870 in Wabasha, MN, and have nine children—Henry K., Emma, James, Elizabeth, Lucina, Jesse, David, Frank, and Willard—all of whom were born in Wabasha. (Courtesy of Merle Campbell.)

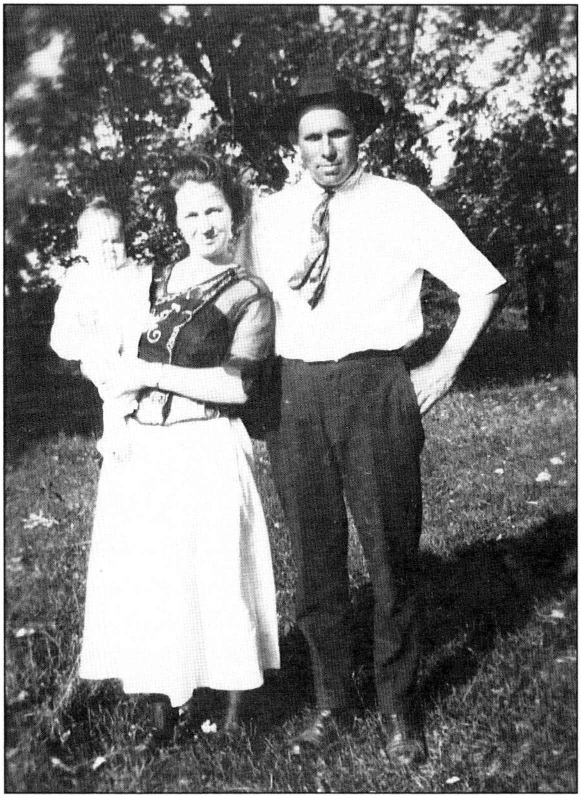

Valentine Schurhammer and Lorraine Braun were married on October 30, 1917, and are shown here with their daughter Mary. Valentine was the son of Joseph and Sarah (Huber) Schurhammer; Lorraine's parents were Robert and Mary (Theisen) Braun. Valentine and Lorraine had five children—Mary (Arnold Greden), Robert (Lucille Wolfe), Valentine Jr. (Gertrude Rademacher), and twins Dean (Bertha Rademacher) and Donald (Laura Lindmark).

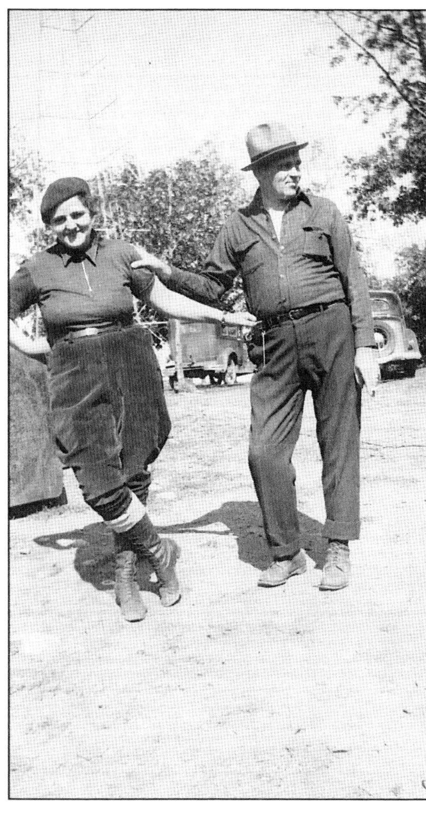

Walter Belford and Nina Curtis were married on September 28, 1930. Nina, who died in 1970, was born in 1888 in Plainview to Lorenzo and Laura (Harrell) Curtis. Her grandparents on her father's side were Orin and Rachel (Pepin) Curtis, early settlers of Wabasha County.

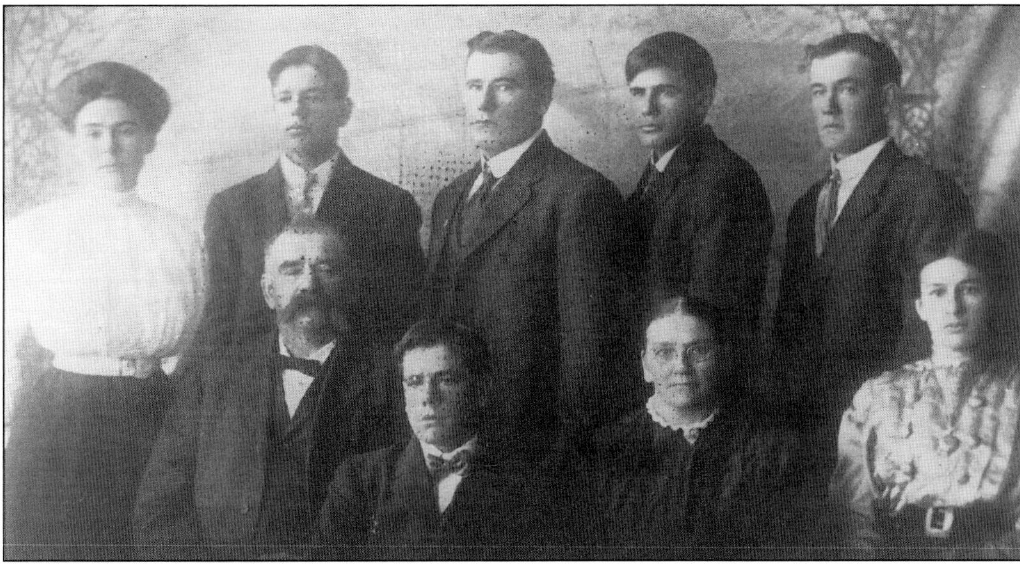

This portrait of the Mathias and Catharine (Zeimetz) Leisen family shows the following, from left to right: (front row) Mathias, Joseph, Catherine, and Katherine Leisen; (back row) Elizabeth, Nicholas, George, Albert, and John. Mathias's parents, George and Elizabeth (Baker) Leisen, settled on a farm in Glasgow in 1861.

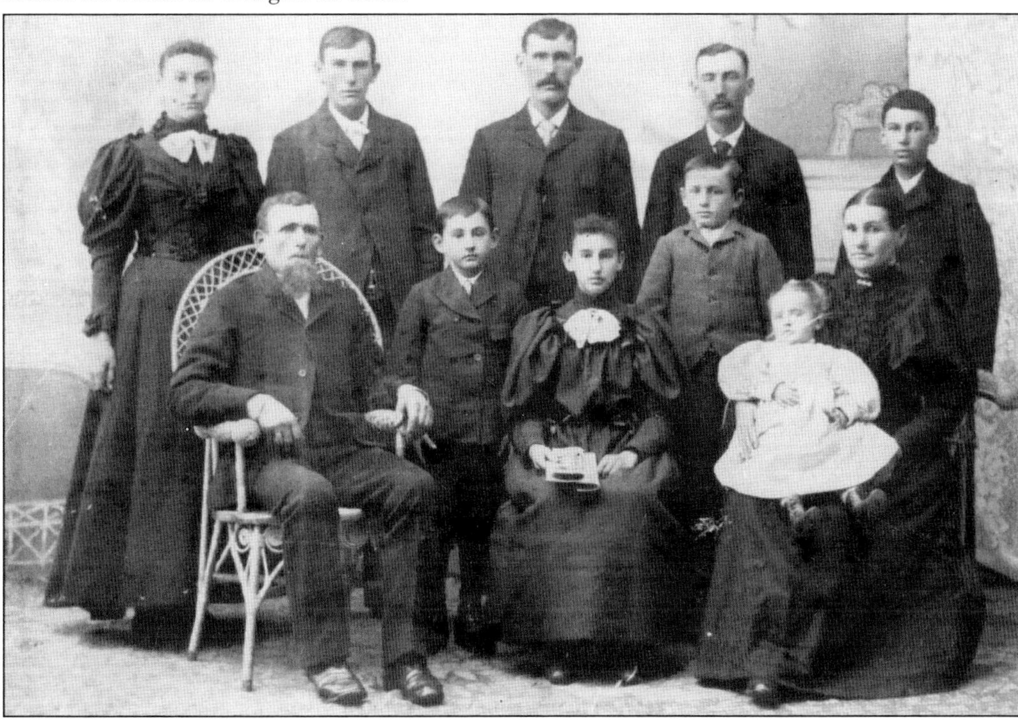

The Stephan and Magdalena (Zeimetz) Klees family is shown here *c.* 1898. From left to right, they are as follows: (front row) Stephan, Bill, Margaret, Nick, Marie, and Lena; (back row) Catherine, Michael, Martin, Leonard, and John. Stephan Klees left Germany when he was a young man, settling in Sparta and Port Washington, WI, before coming to Wabasha County. Magdelena's parents were Mr. and Mrs. Martin Zeimetz.

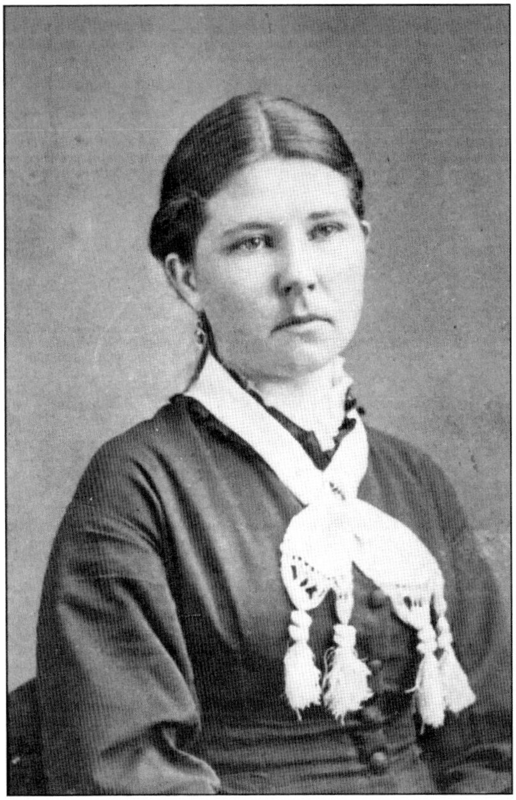

Sarah Huber was born to John and Caroline (Wacholtz) Huber on November 6, 1856, in Canada. In the early 1850s her parents left Germany with their daughter Mary, Caroline's parents (Thomas and Johnna Wacholtz), and Caroline's brother John. Tragically, Mary didn't survive the overseas voyage—she fell ill and died onboard the ship in the Atlantic Ocean, and was buried at sea. The family settled in Wabasha County in 1858.

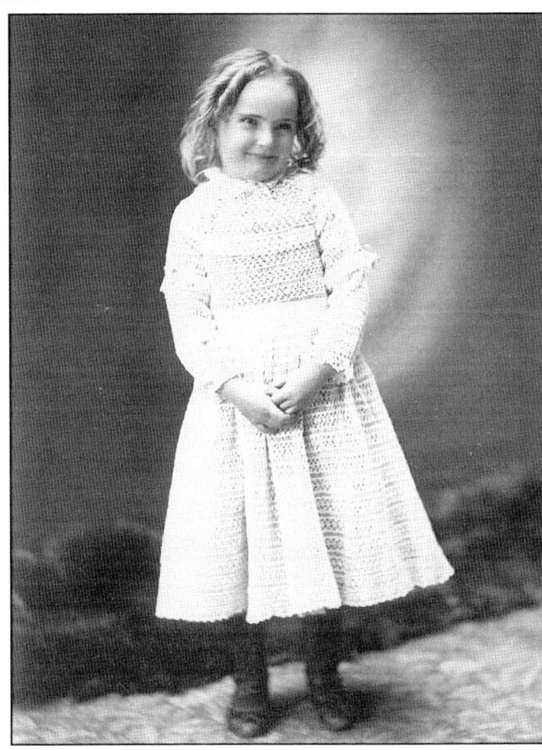

Ethel Jackson, who was born about 1881 to John and Jane (Griffis) Jackson, married Richard Krull. She had six brothers and sisters—Samuel, Mary LaBresh, Annie Schurhammer, John, Alice Schurhammer, and Bert (who died at the age of three).

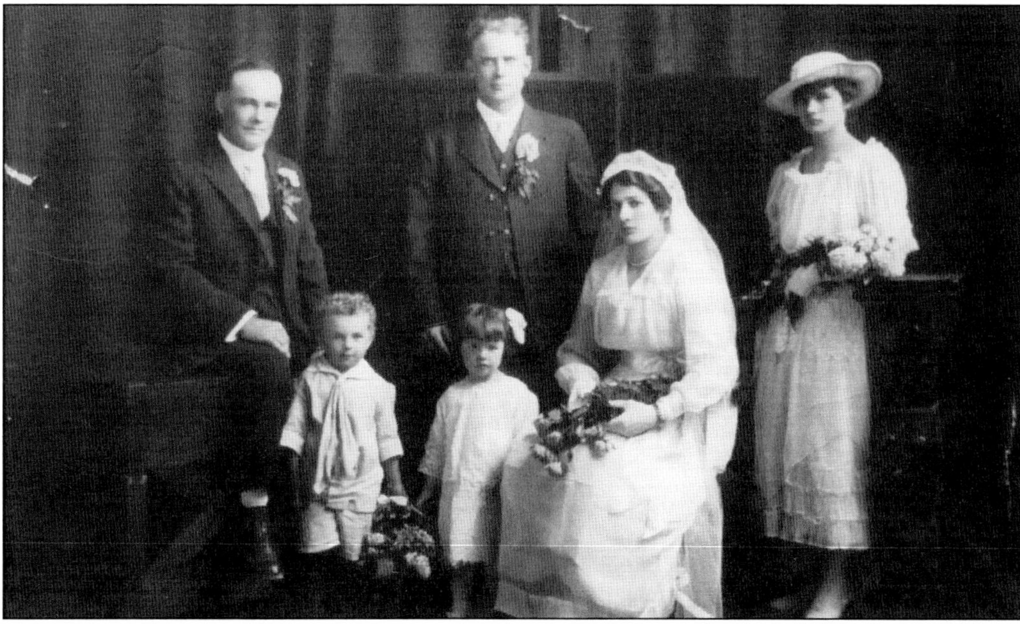

The wedding of William and Katherine (Leisen) Deming took place on June 6, 1917. Shown here with the newlyweds are bridesmaid Francis Deming, best man John Leisen, flower girl Beatrice Giem, and ring bearer Laverne Deming. In July 1914, William opened a machine shop in Kellogg, and in 1919 he erected a tile building, equipping it with the equipment necessary for acetylene welding and horse-shoeing. On January 15, 1920, he was killed in an explosion, leaving his wife to raise their two small children, Eugene and Katherine, on her own.

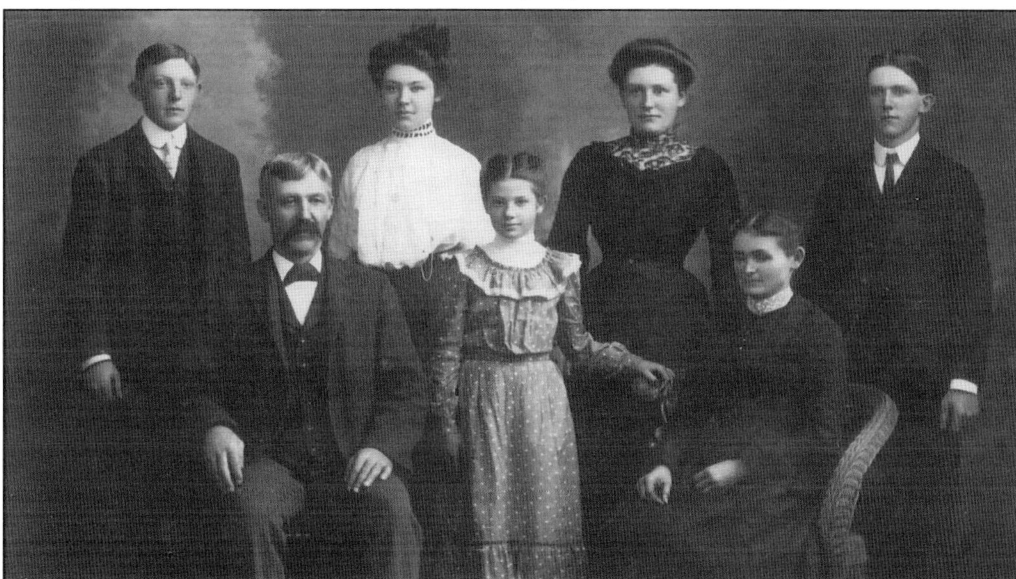

This portrait of the Albert and Bertha (Birkly) Huber family shows the following, from left to right: (front row) Albert, Louisa, and Bertha; (back row) William, Elizabeth, Caroline, and George. Albert and Bertha were married in 1879 and had nine children—Elizabeth (Charles Gustavson), John, Carolina (Hubert Marking), Albert Jr., George, William, Frank, Louie, and Louisa.

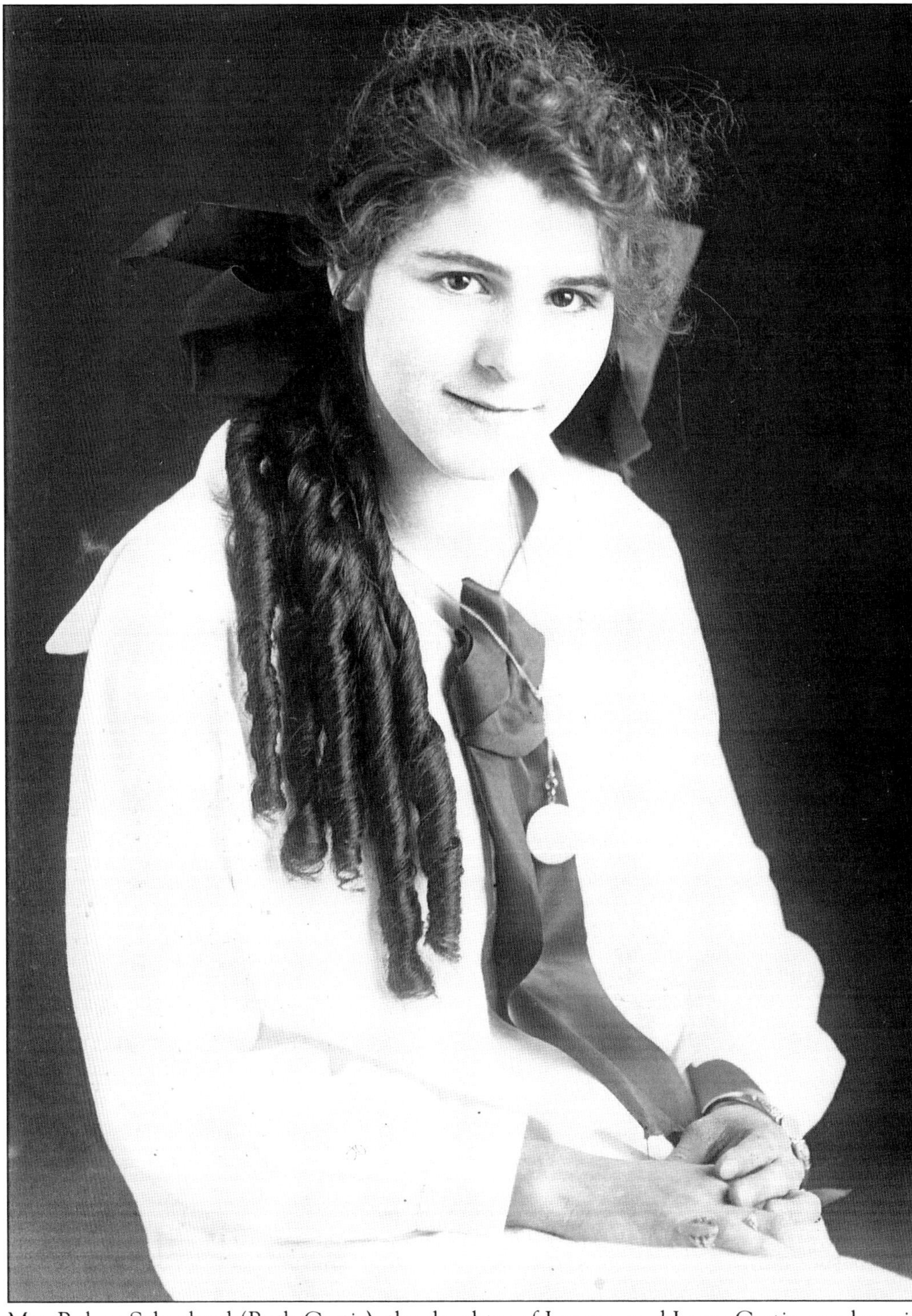

Mrs. Robert Schuchard (Ruth Curtis), the daughter of Lorenzo and Laura Curtis, was born in Kellogg, Greenfield Township. She lived in Plainview and Lake City before moving to Winona, where she was killed in a car accident on the Wisconsin dike road in 1935.

Lawrence Calhoun was born in Dublin, Ireland, on August 15, 1826, to Thomas and Mary (Hackett) Calhoun. When he was only a year old, his parents came to America, settling first at Shullsberg, WI, where the father engaged in mining. Lawrence's youth was spent in the city of Galena. In 1845 he came up the Mississippi to work as a lumberjack on the Chippewa River survey, and shortly thereafter he ran a keelboat on the Chippewa and the Mississippi Rivers. He married Mary McDonough Sullivan, and they had 12 children—Anna (Mr. Cummings), Marie (Patrick Ryan), Mary (John German), Sarah, Lydia, Minnie, Maggie, Katy, George, Aurelia, Clara, and Rosella.

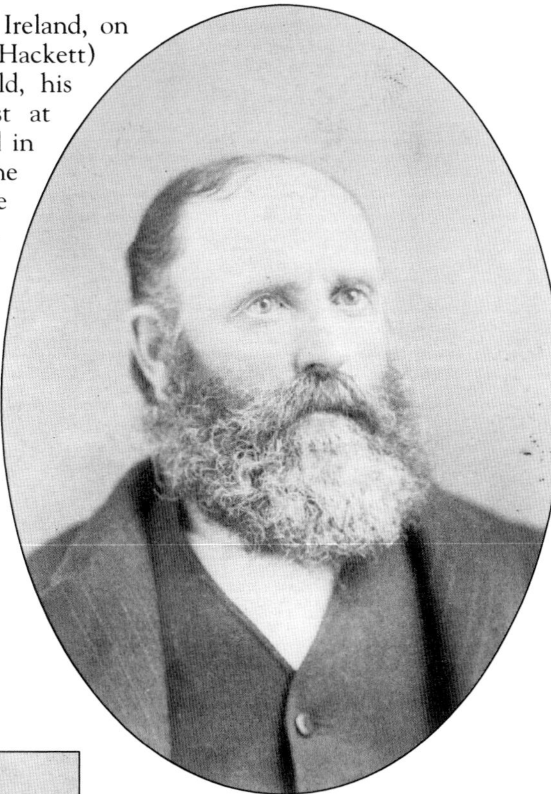

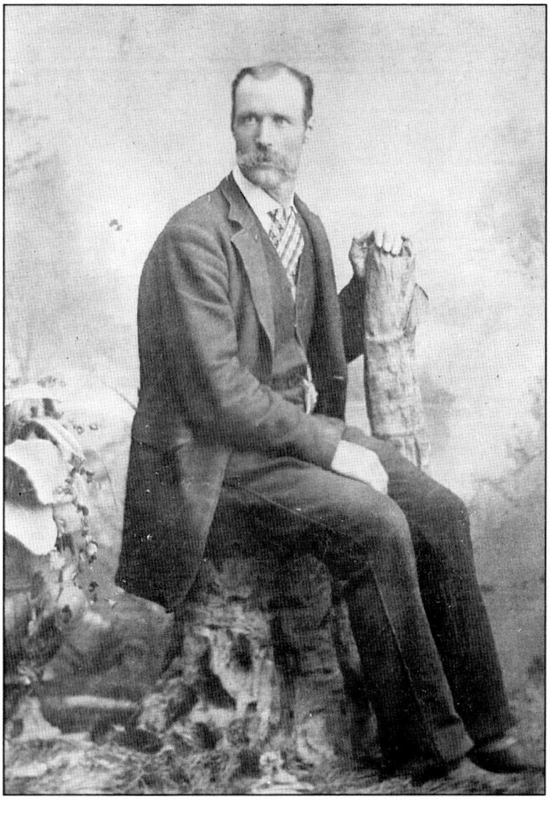

William Griffis was the son of Stephan and Elizabeth (Lampman) Griffis. He came to Wabasha County with his parents when he was a young boy, and was among the earliest settlers in Greenfield Township.

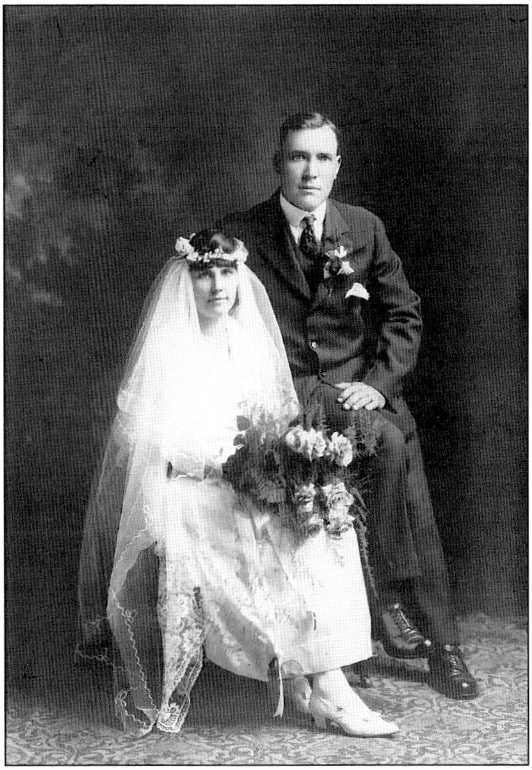

The wedding of Walter Schurhammer and Miss Maebell Ferch took place on September 14, 1921, at Ripon, WI. Walter was born about 1895 in Wabasha County to Christian and Alice Schurhammer. He received his education in the district school, and also worked for his father on the farm.

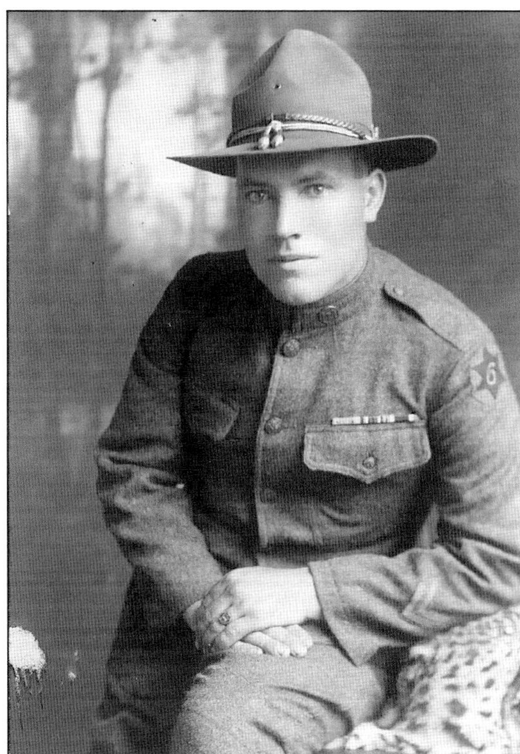

Walter A. Schurhammer enlisted in Wabasha as an engineer on February 5, 1918, and served one year overseas. He was a private in Company F, Regiment 318, in the Division of the 6th Sappers.

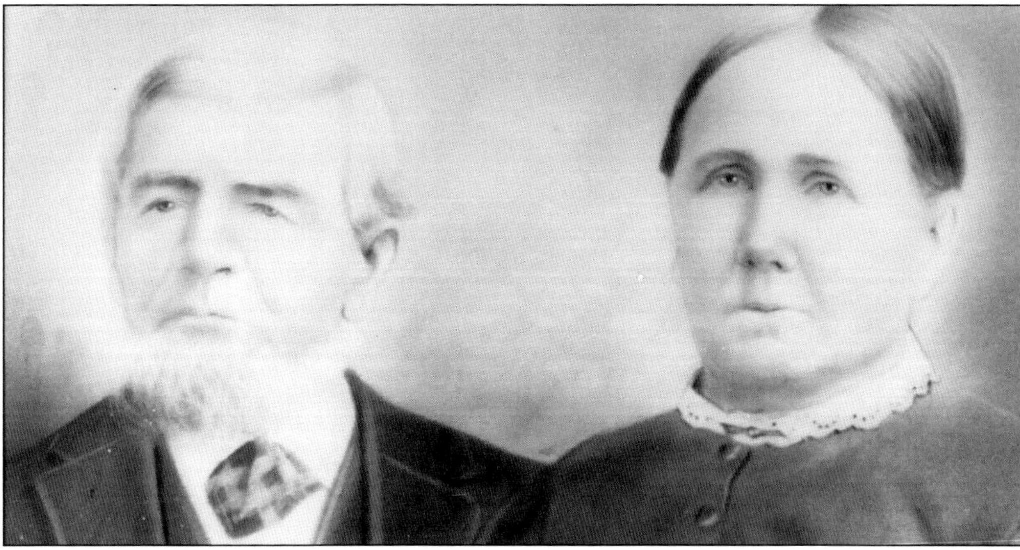

George Leisen, another pioneer of Wabasha County, was born on April 10, 1817, in Prussia. He married Miss Elizabeth Baker, a native of Seffern, near Treves Rhemish Province, Germany. Together they made their way to the United States, and in 1861 they settled on land in Glasgow Township, Wabasha County, where they spent the rest of their lives farming. George and Elizabeth were the parents of nine children—Mathias (Catherine Zeimetz), Anna (Nicholas Zell), John, Henry (Sarah Harncane-Mollie Stack), Maria (John Peters), Mary (John Nei), Elizabeth, Margaret (John Zeimetz), and Adelia (John Baker).

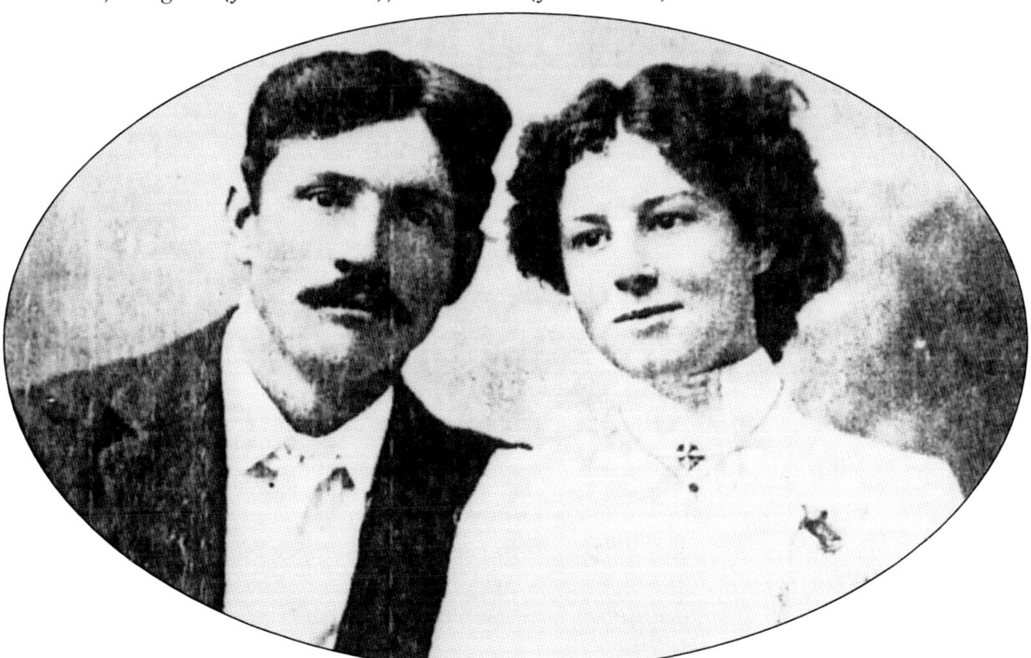

Jacob and Clara (Harriman) Giem Jr.'s wedding took place in 1902. Jacob, the son of Jacob and Margaret (Markadont) Giem, was born and educated in Wabasha. He played on a local baseball team while helping with his father's stonemason and carpenter business. Jacob left by train for Montana c. 1898, but eventually settled in Virginia, where he met Clara Harriman.

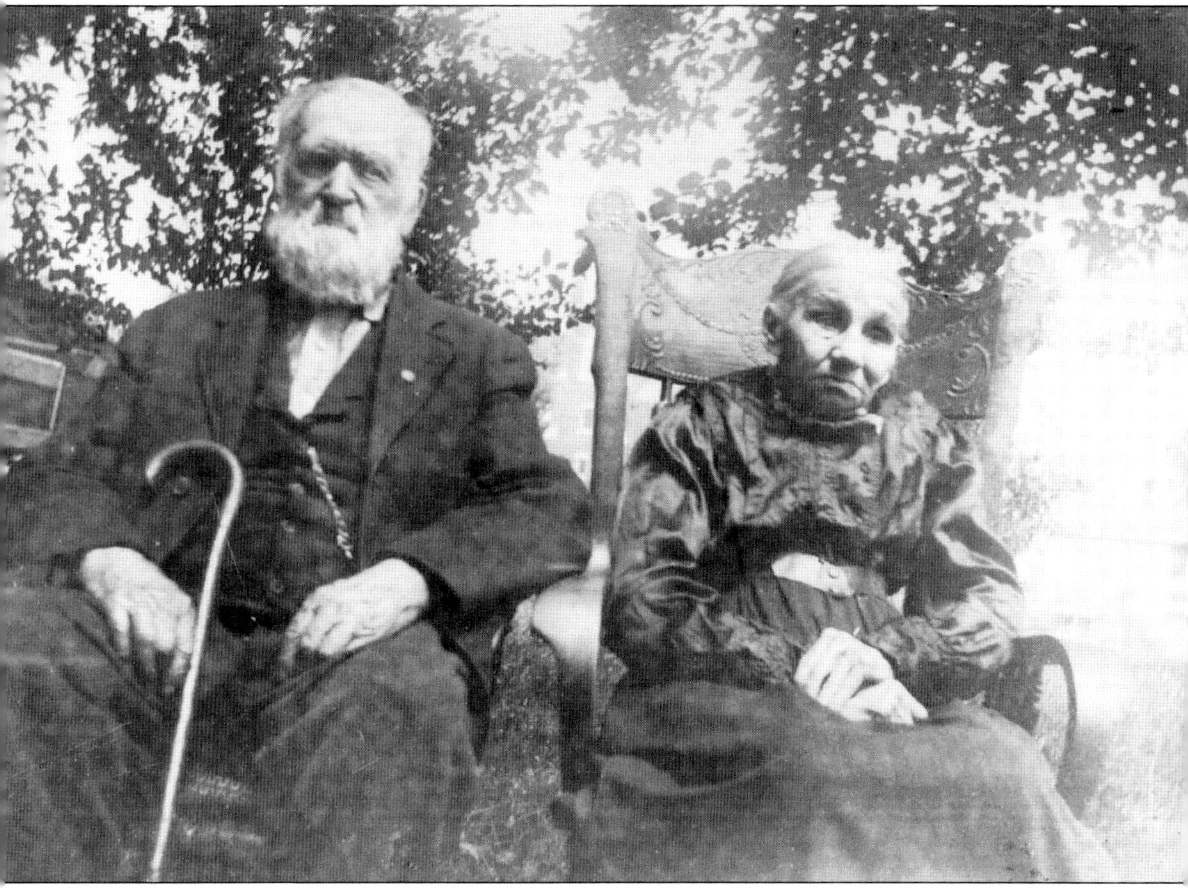

This photo, taken in 1916, is of Orin and Rachel (Pepin) Curtis, who settled in Plainview in 1877. Orin was born in New York to Benjamin and Roxie (Paine) Curtis, and Rachel was born in St. Thomas, Canada, to Charles and Hannah (Strawn) Pepin. In 1856, they lived in New Oregon, IA, where Orin was a doctor of veterinary medicine. When the Civil War began, Orin enlisted in Company I, 38th Regiment Iowa Volunteers. He was in the Battle of Gettysburg, the Battle of the Potomac, the Battle of Lookout Mountain, and many other important battles during the War between the States. Rachel's brothers, Charles, Abner, and Sylvenus Pepin, served in the same regiment. Orin and Rachel had seven children—Henry (Adelaide Morrison), Orin Jr., Lorenzo (Laura Harrell), Alice, Andrew (Jeanette Wright), Ella (Philo Drew), and Fred (Caroline Wright).

William Perkinson was born in Clithroe, Lancashire, England, in June 1833. He married Ellen Knight, the widow of John Easthan, on April 10, 1861. Ellen was born on October 26, 1831, and had a son, Richard Eastham, with John. William and Ellen came to the United States in 1864, settling first in Joliet, IL, where William worked as a guard at the state prison. They later moved to Wisconsin, where he was employed in a lumber business. In 1869, they came to Wabasha County. William and Ellen had four children—Joseph, Elizabeth (Wesley Lindsey-William Cox), James (Mary Barnes), and Margaret (Wallace Whipple). Richard Eastham married Helen Dale. (Courtesy of Kenneth Tiedemann.)

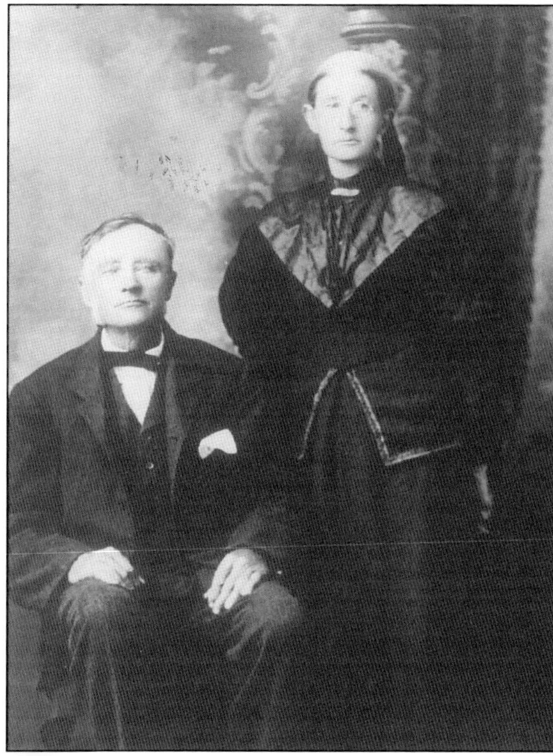

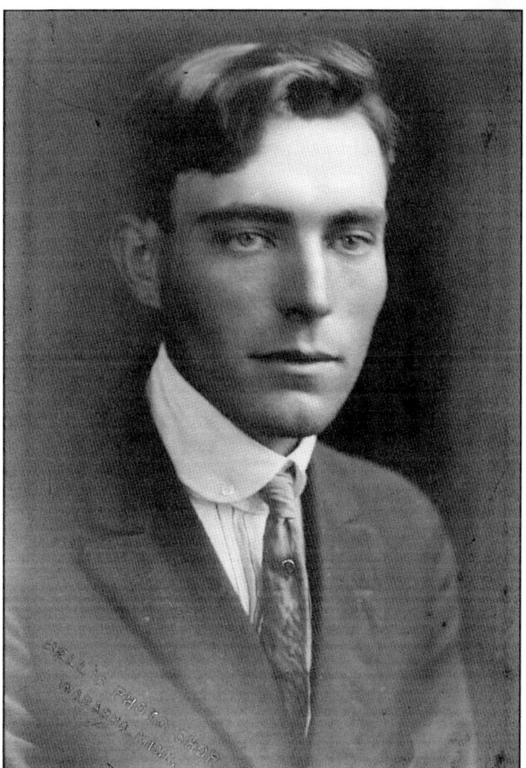

Woodie Schurhammer was born in 1898 in Greenfield Township to Christian and Alice (Jackson). The head of the family line, Wilhelm Schurhammer von Glotteral (1653–1684), was from a rich agricultural region in Germany known for its fine grape vineyards and farms, and as far as can be gathered from information compiled, the family was in the wine-making business.

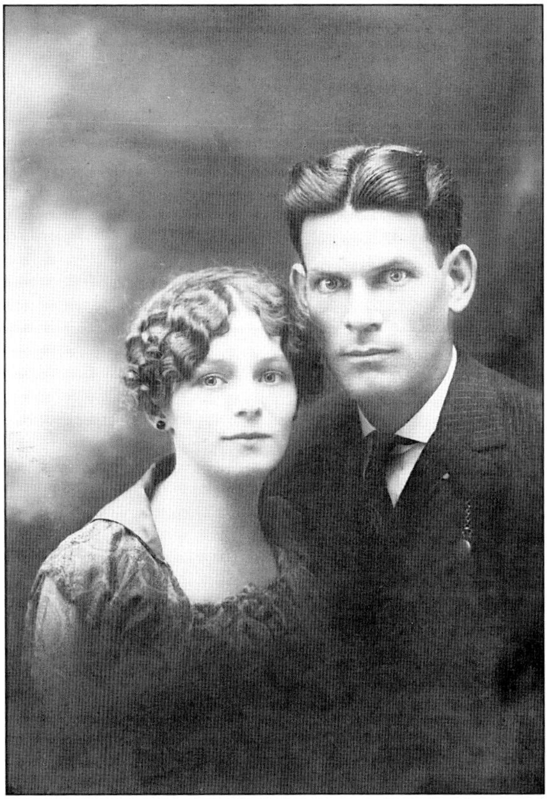

The wedding of Emil Schurhammer and Hazel Thompson took place in Chicago, IL. Emil was born April 10, 1855, in Wabasha County. On April 17, 1917, he fell off the Chicago Telephone Building. He struck his head and shoulders, fracturing his skull, and died at the Park Avenue Hospital.

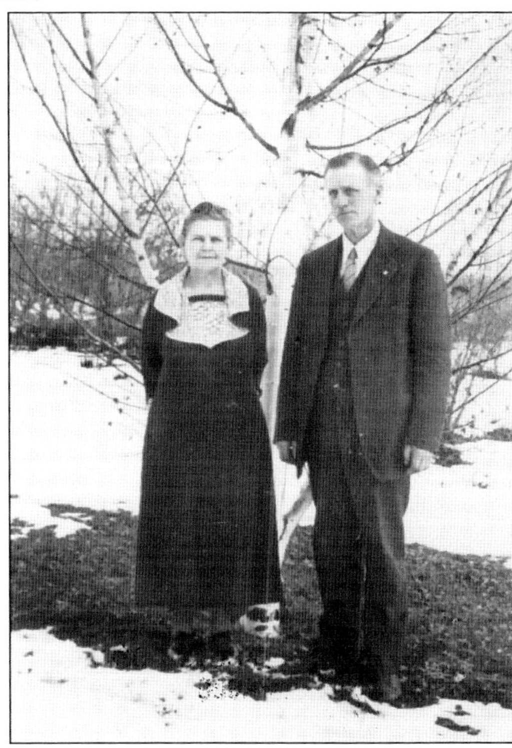

The seventh Hellinger daughter, Elizabeth, and her husband, Peter Selde Jr., celebrated their golden wedding anniversary in 1942. Elizabeth's parents, Thomas and Maria (Giem) Hellinger, were among the early pioneers of Wabasha County. Thomas was killed in 1880 in an accident on the Wabasha and Glasgow Road, when he apparently fell from his wagon and became entangled in the harness and double trees between the horses. (Courtesy of Ardis Dashiell.)

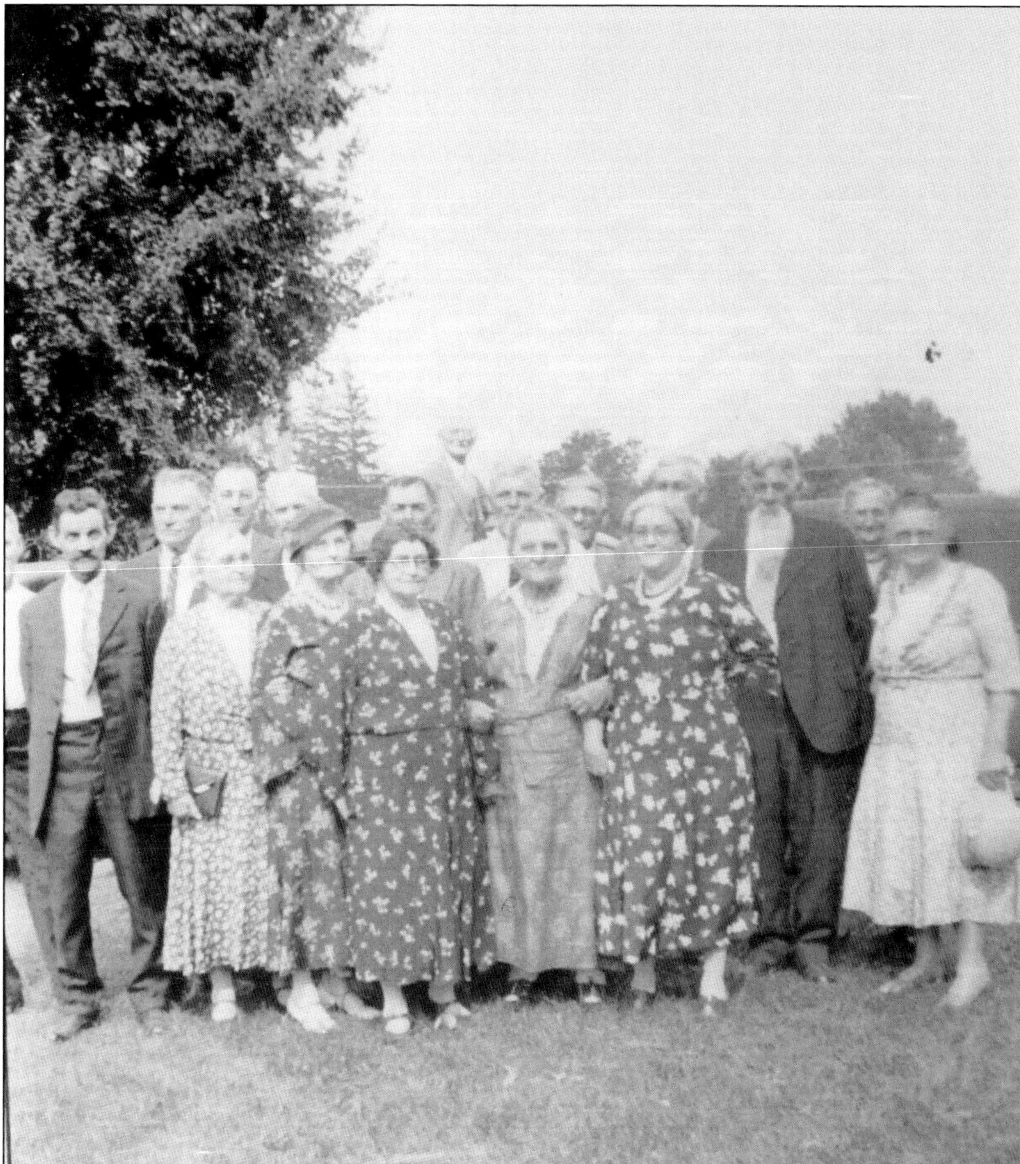

This 1932 Schouweiler family picnic took place in Wabasha. In the left front are the daughters of Michael and Catharine Schouweiler—Emma McDonough, Elizabeth Kennedy, and Catherine Howe.

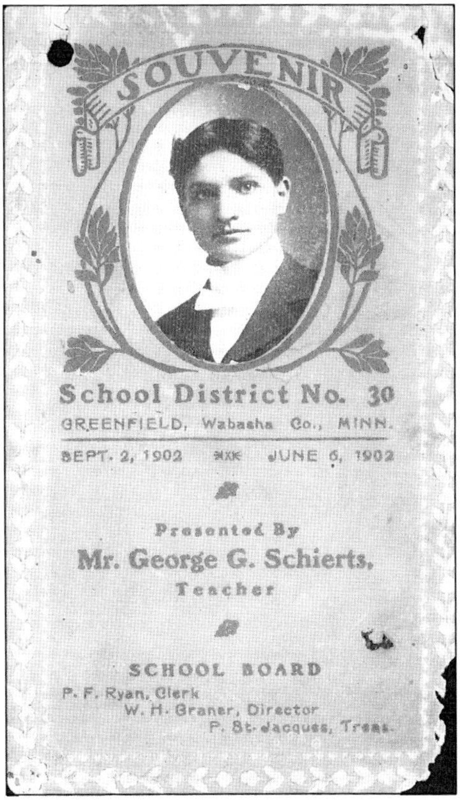

George Schierts was born on December 21, 1881, to Joseph and Elizabeth (Rohrer) Schierts in Conception, MN. He was the youngest of the Schierts's eight children—Frank, Mary, Anna, Katherine, John, Joseph, and Peter—and he attended rural and city schools in the Kellogg area. After graduating from Winona State Teachers College, he taught in the Kellogg area. He eventually married Genevieve Satory and they had three children—Florence (Clarence McKenzie), George Jr. (Vera Fredlemona), and Genevieve (Richard Stienley).

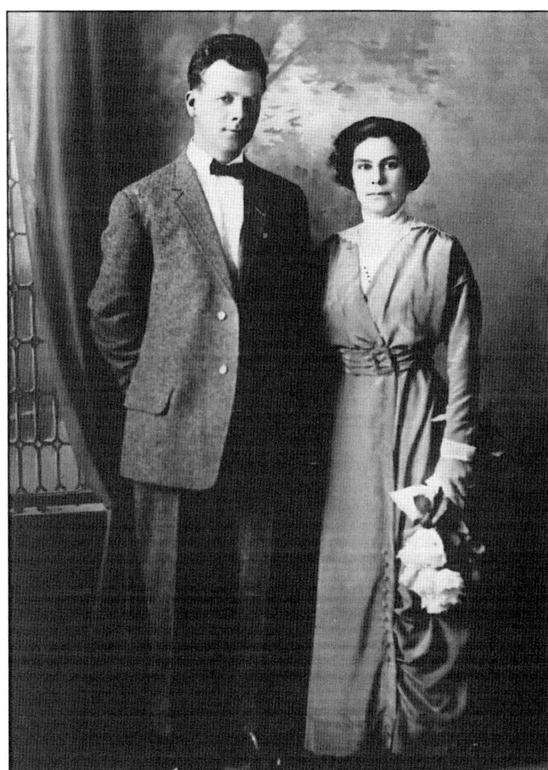

The wedding of Cornelius and Caroline (Schurhammer) Quigley took place on April 30, 1913. The couple had three children—Mary (Robert Borem), Margaret (John McAuliffe), and Richard. The Quigley family history begins with Cornelius's grandparents, Michael and Judith O'Donnoghue Quigley, who were born in the town of Nanagh, Tipperary County, Ireland, and came to Wabasha County in 1855.

On January 11, 1941, Leo Giem and Rachel Schurhammer were united in marriage. Leo is an avid hunter of deer, squirrels, and ducks. He killed his greatest prize, however, in 1974. While hunting southeast of Ely, MN, with his sons, Donald, Joseph, and Robert, and a friend, Chester Smith, Leo shot a 360-pound black bear with his shotgun! Rachel raised 11 children, was an avid cook, and canned tomatoes, dill pickles, carrots, beets, watermelon pickles, and pickled wax beans.

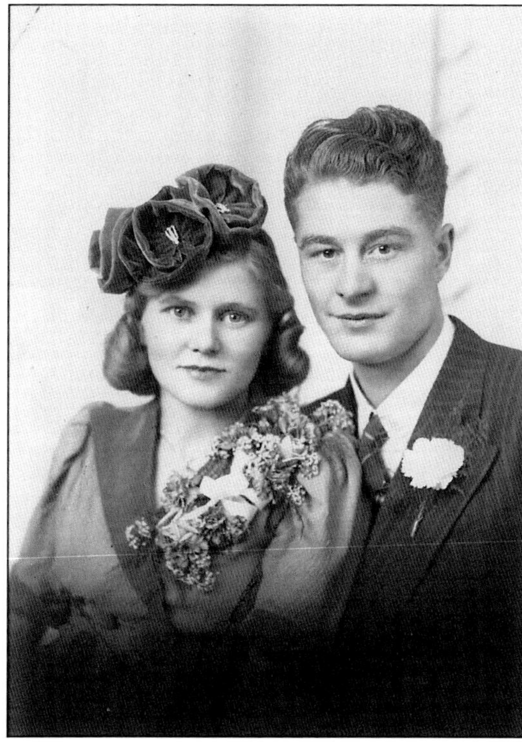

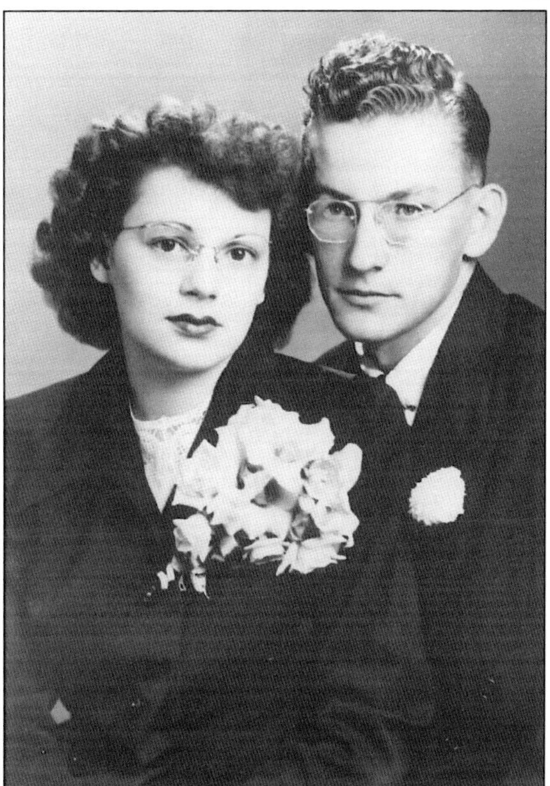

Dorothy Bernadine Leisen, the daughter of John and Nora Leisen, was born on August 24, 1929, in Kellogg, MN. She married Mryton Stoos on September 7, 1948, in Rollingstone, MN, and had a total of four children—Linda (Richard Kredermacher), David (Sandra Hardtke), Diane (Thomas Bronk), and Gary (Mary Rivers). Dorothy's history of Wabasha County, on the Leisen line, goes back to 1861 in Glasgow Township.

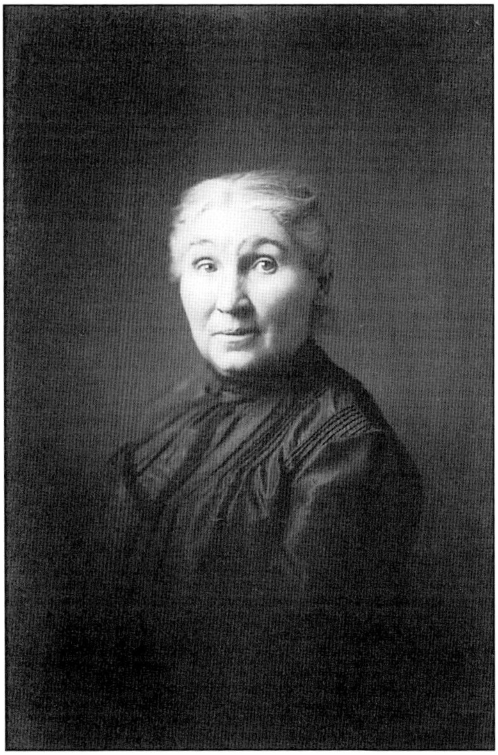

Mary Ann (McDonough) Drury was born on February 14, 1858, to Miles and Ann (Flaherty) McDonough. Miles was born in Ireland and came to America with his father, Patrick, and step-mother, Nappy Sullivan. He worked as a watchman for four years on Ohio and Mississippi River steamboats. Mary Ann, the second white child born in Wabasha County, had six sisters and three brothers—Nora, Patrick, Agnes, Edward, Maggie, Katie, Michael, Lydia, and Maud. She married Edward Drury at Wabasha, and was widowed in 1906.

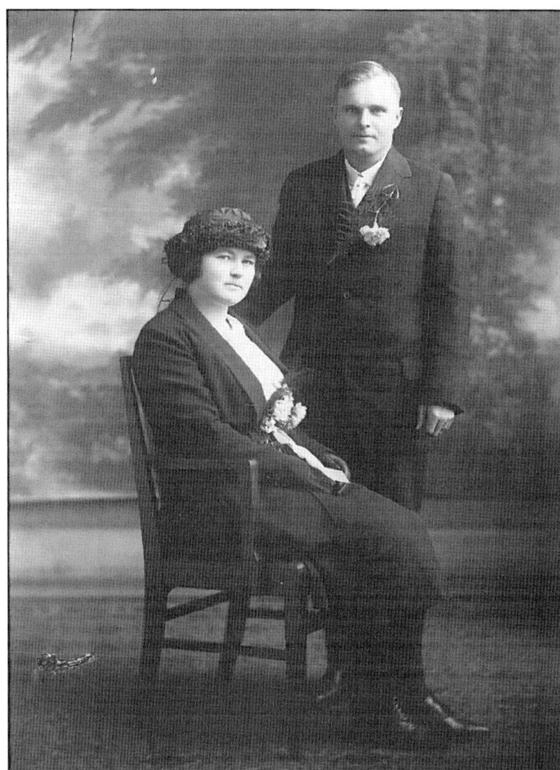

Raymond J. and Mary E. (Peterson) LaBresh were lifelong residents of the area. Mary (1897–1987) was born in Greenfield Township to Louis and Nellie (Mahoney) Peterson. She worked at the Anderson House, and with her husband at the former Pioneer Pearl Button Factory. The couple later worked together as the caretakers at the Villa Maria Academy at Frontenac.

In 1896 Maria Schurhammer was born to Joseph and Sarah (Huber) Schurhammer in a log house in Greenfield Township. She married Frank Spooner in 1913 in Wabasha. They farmed for five years near Kellogg and then for 20 years near Nelson, WI, before returning to rural Kellogg. During World War II, they worked in a shipyard in Seattle, WA. Marie is the oldest living Schurhammer, living in Wabasha County at the age of 101. Frank and Maria's children are Francis (Donald Karau), Margaret, Dorothy (Russell McDonough), and Frank Joy (Leona Tentis).

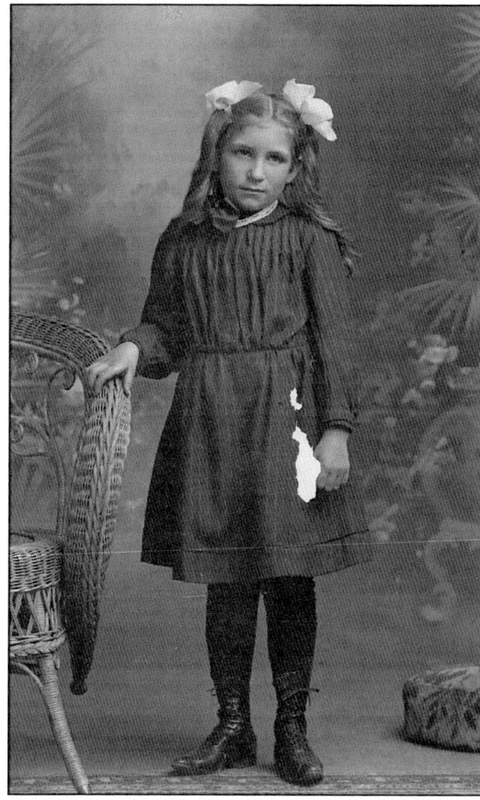

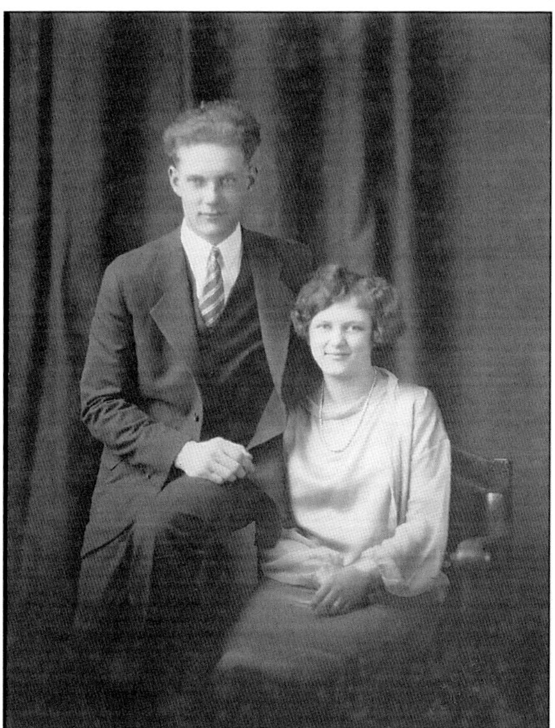

Jess Krusmark and Rose Klein got married on March 16, 1924, in Rochester, MN. They had three sons—Robert, Richard, and Jesse. In 1924, Jess moved his family to Lake City, MN, and went to work in Greenland to help build an airforce base. He also worked on the Alaskan Highway Project for a few months. In 1943, he worked for Hector Construction Company, and he contracted with the Plainview Creamery. His parents were Henry and Anna (Schwartz) Krusmark.

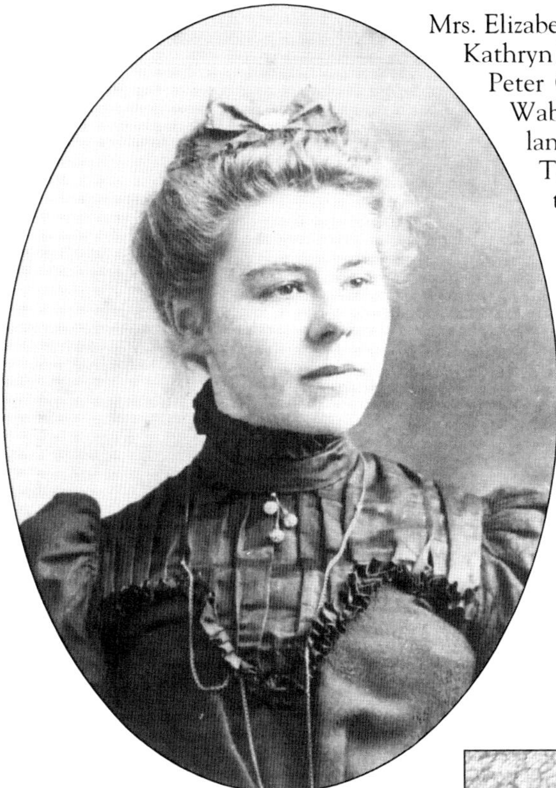

Mrs. Elizabeth (Leisen) Giem was born to Mathias and Kathryn Leisen on November 20, 1881. She married Peter Giem in 1901 at the St. Felix Church in Wabasha, and they farmed on her father's land in Section 31, Minneiska Township. Their first son, Joseph Henry, was born on the farm; he died there as well, after being struck by lightning. Their other children are Lawrence (Stella Eischen), Beatrice (Mauritz Lindmark), Margaret (Alphonse Kronebusch), Josephine (Gerald Paine-Albin Konkle), Leo (Rachel Schurhammer), and Mary (Robert Passe). Peter and Elizabeth lived to celebrate their 70th wedding anniversary—he died in 1971 and she died two years later.

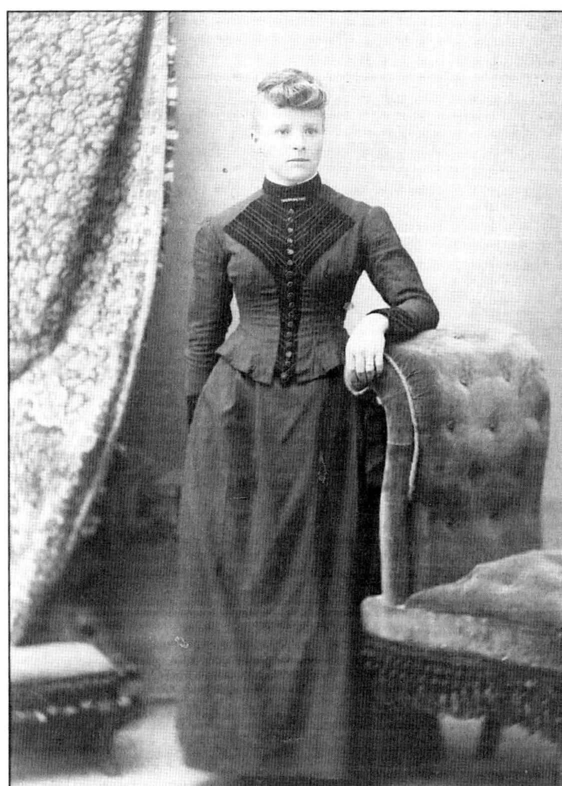

Annie Jackson, the daughter of John and Jane (Griffis) Jackson, was born in 1875, in Greenfield Township, Wabasha County. She married August Schurhammer in 1896, and had four sons—Arthur, Benjamin, Andrew, and Albert.

Another well-known resident of Wabasha is Peter Giem. Peter was born in 1874 to Jacob and Margaret (Markadont) Giem. His mother died when he was eight years old. Over the course of his life he worked on a farm in Theilman; in Wabasha on the St. Felix Church steeple; on the Mississippi River, putting logs on a raft and floating them downriver; and in the brick yards, mixing mortar. On April 9, 1901, he married Elizabeth Leisen, and they became members of the Old Settlers Association of Greenwood Prairie. One of the homes they lived in was mentioned in *Ripley's Believe It or Not* column: "Wabasha's famous house, that was remodeled at one time, leaving a corner-less, non-supported second-floor area." Peter always kept a vegetable garden, and had a pet carrier pigeon called "Henny Penny."

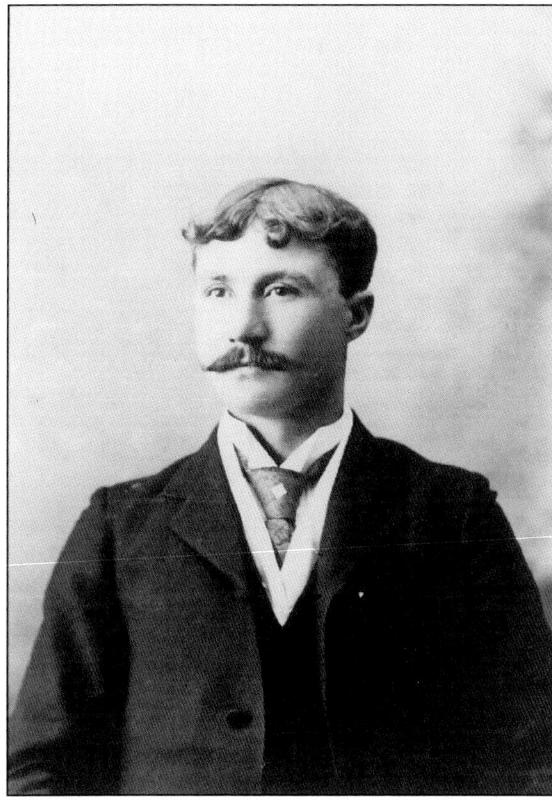

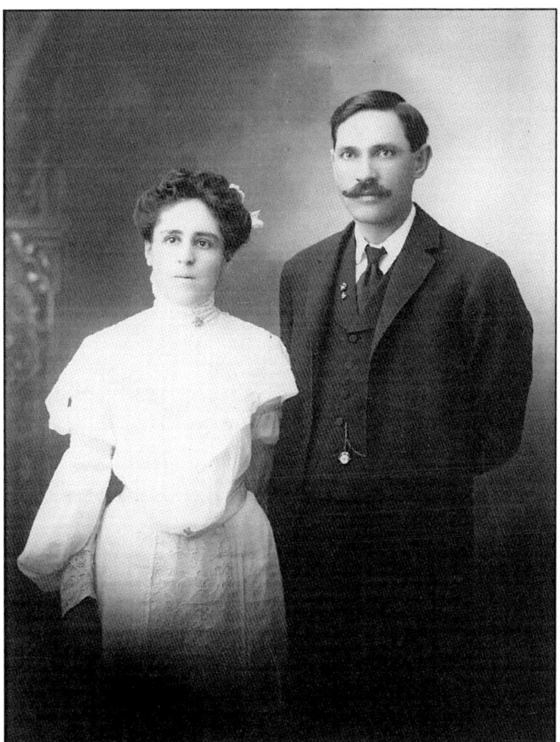

The wedding of Lawrence Schurhammer and Josephine Jordan took place in 1903. Lawrence, a talented musician, played in the Greenfield Orchestra before going on to lead the Wabasha Band. His son, Lawrence "Wacker" Jr., married Linda Roemer.

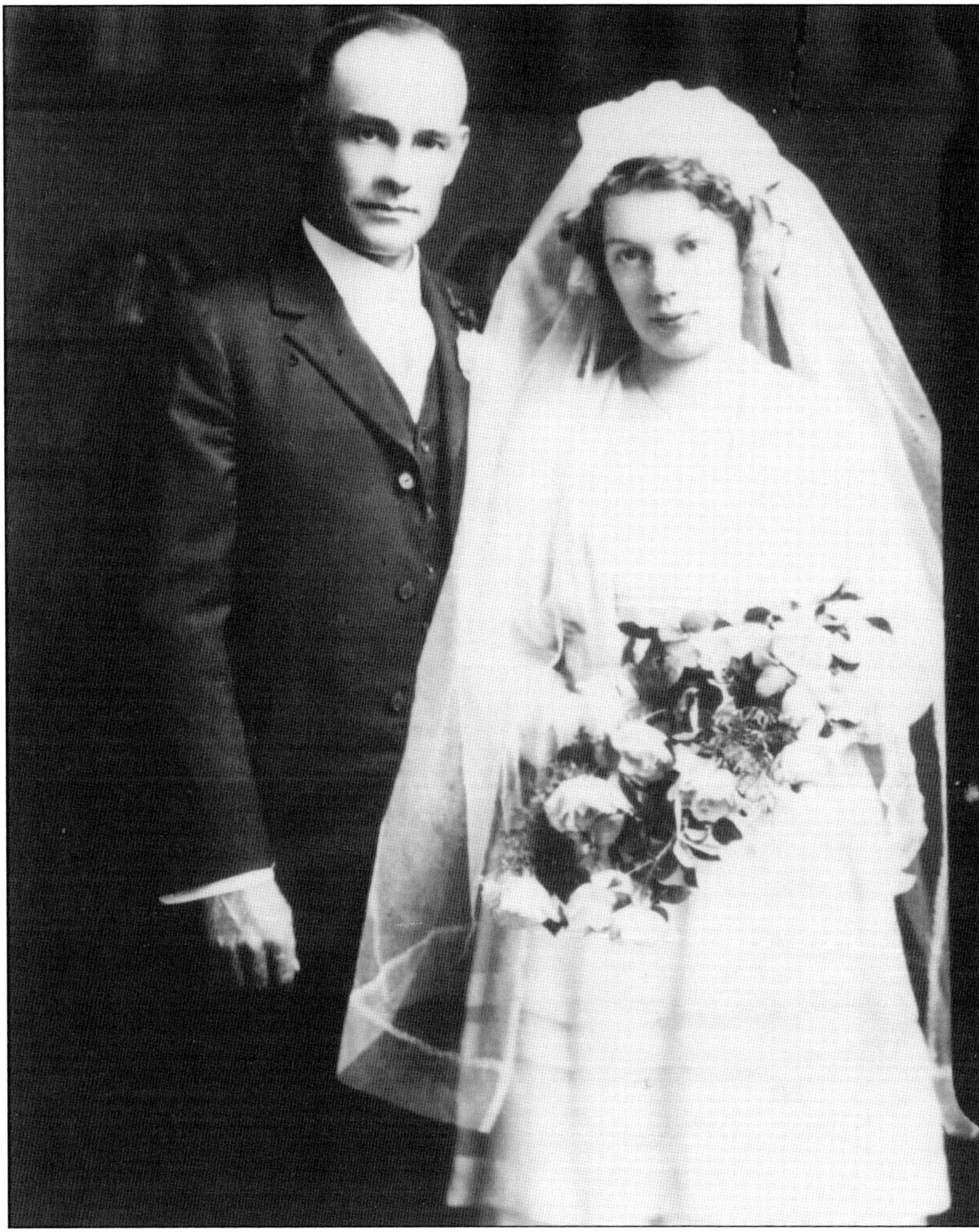

On June 7, 1886, John Steven Leisen was born in Wabasha County. He fought in World War I, and shortly after being discharged on November 25, 1918, he planned on marrying Mary Elnora Eischen, otherwise known as "Nora." The night before the wedding, disaster struck—their house broke out in flames and burned to the ground. The wedding went ahead anyway, and the two were married on June 3, 1919, in Kellogg, Minnesota. They had 11 children—Bernice (Franklin Stark), Joseph (Kathryn Spitzer), Harold (Eileen Ryan), Eleanora (John Henshaw), Mary, Leona (Raymond Patzner), Kenneth (Alice Felstead), Dorothy (Myrton Stoos), Rita (Morris Miller), Joan (Dwight Gavin), and Yvonne (Harold McMahon). (Courtesy Tammy Bronk.)

William J. DeZell was born in Wabasha in 1876 to William and Anna (Stone) DeZell. Anna was born here in 1853 to Philo and Adeline (Campbell) Stone, who were among the area's first settlers. William Jr. married Maud Weimerkirch and they had three children—William, Culliton (Marie Welch), and Robert. (Courtesy of Merle E. Campbell.)

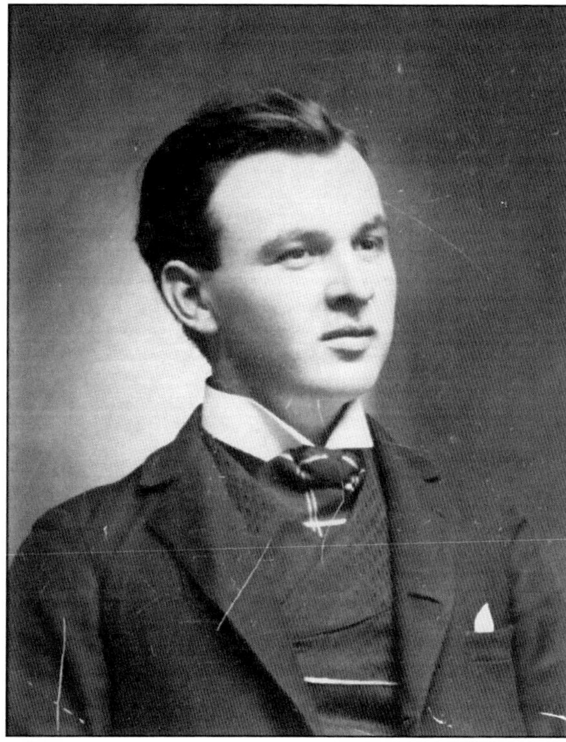

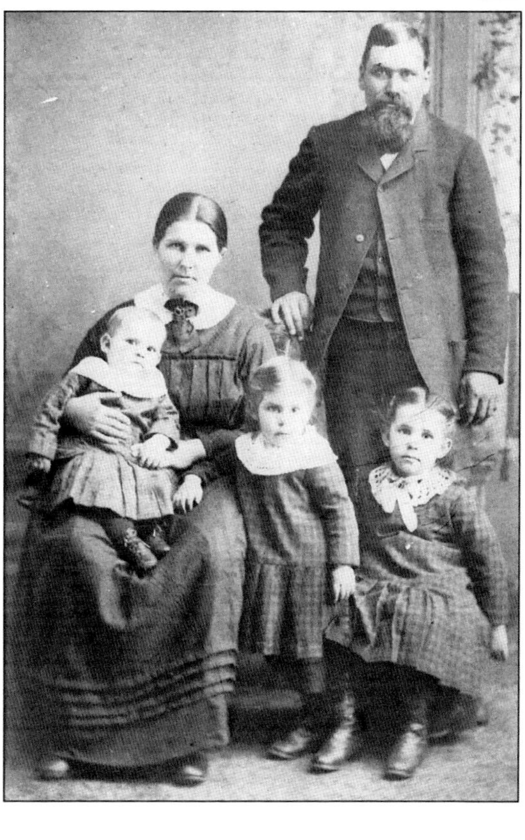

Joseph II and Sarah (Huber) Schurhammer are shown here in 1885 with three of their children—Emil (left), Caroline (center), and Wilhelmina (right). Joseph did farm work until 1906, when he moved to Kellogg and worked on the railroad. In 1908 he went into the saloon business. He served for years as supervisor and roadmaster of Greenfield Township, as a night watchman, and he belonged to the International Order of Odd Fellows in Wabasha.

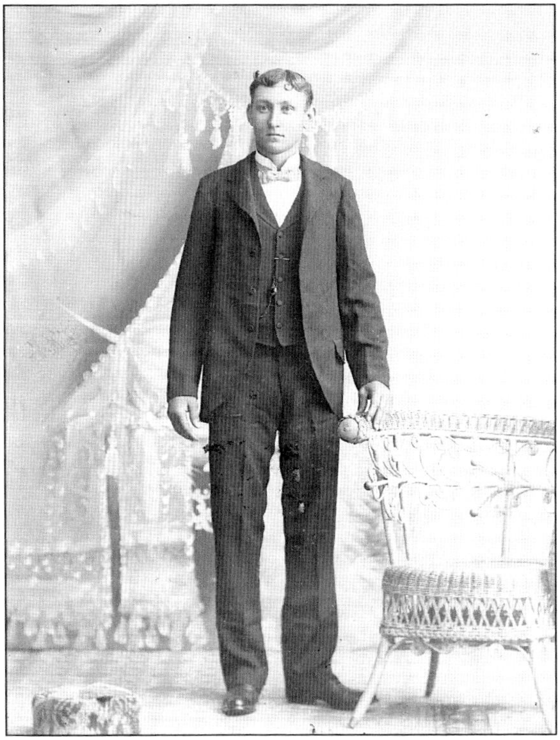

Henry Giem, the youngest child of Jacob and Margaret (Markadont) Giem, was born on January 29, 1879, in Wabasha. He was about three years old when his mother passed away. At the age of 23, he went to Virginia City, MT, where he met Ellen Pearl Cornforth. On March 27, 1905, they were married, and they had six children—Leo (Gladys Wilcox), Marguerite (Edward Lunger), James (Viola Mason), Laurence (Dorothy Couch), Viola (Lyle Burton-James Sullivan), and an infant who only lived 12 days.

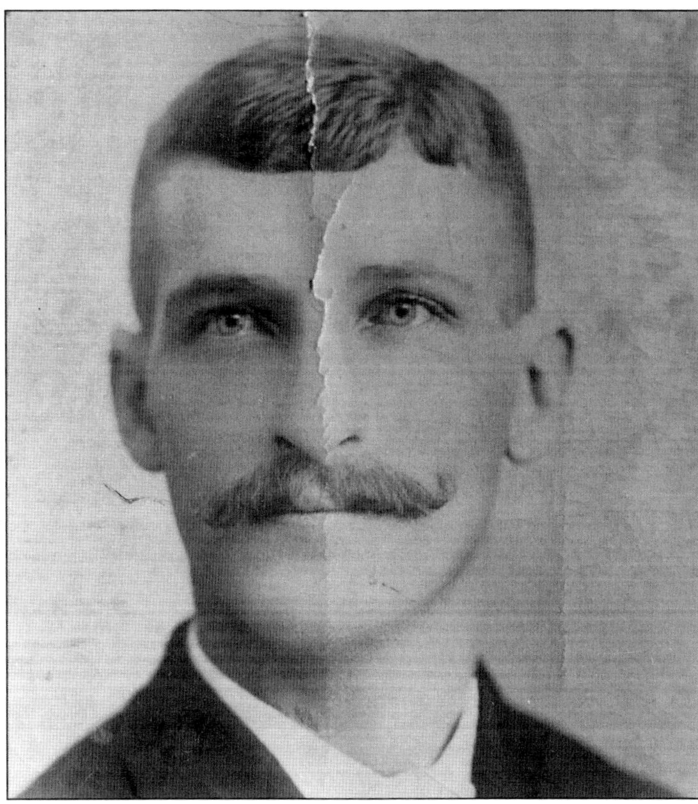

Frank Schouweiler was born on March 16, 1864, in Wabasha County. His parents are Michael and Catharine Schoueler.

August Schurhammer and Anna Jackson were married in August 1896. August was born in 1866 to Joseph and Magdalena Schurhammer, who settled in Greenfield Township in 1855. Anna was born 1875 in Greenfield Township to John and Jane Jackson.

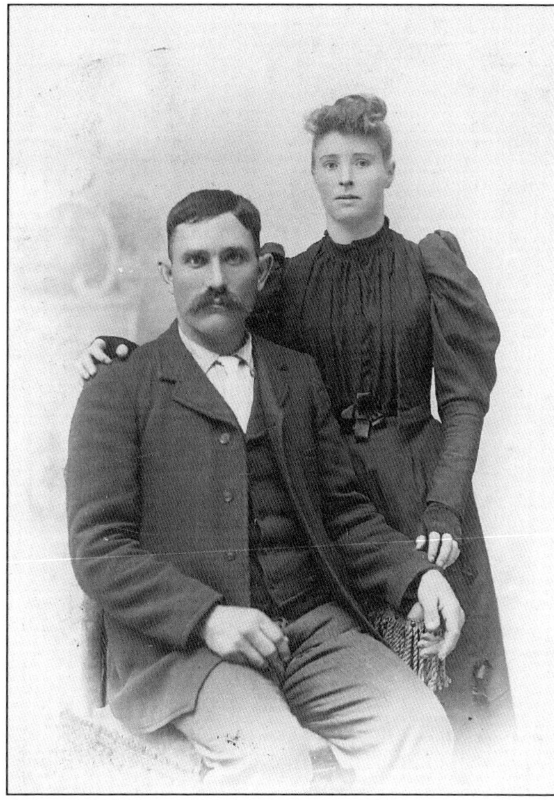

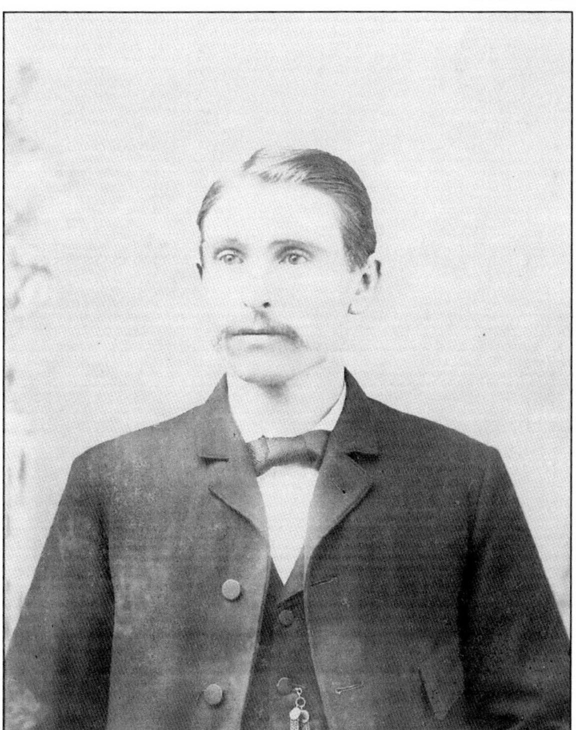

Samuel Jackson was born in 1870 to John and Jane (Griffis) Jackson. Like the Schurhammers, the Jacksons were among the early pioneers of Wabasha County. Sam's brothers and sisters were Mary LaBresh, Annie Schurhammer, and John, Bert, and Ethel Krull.

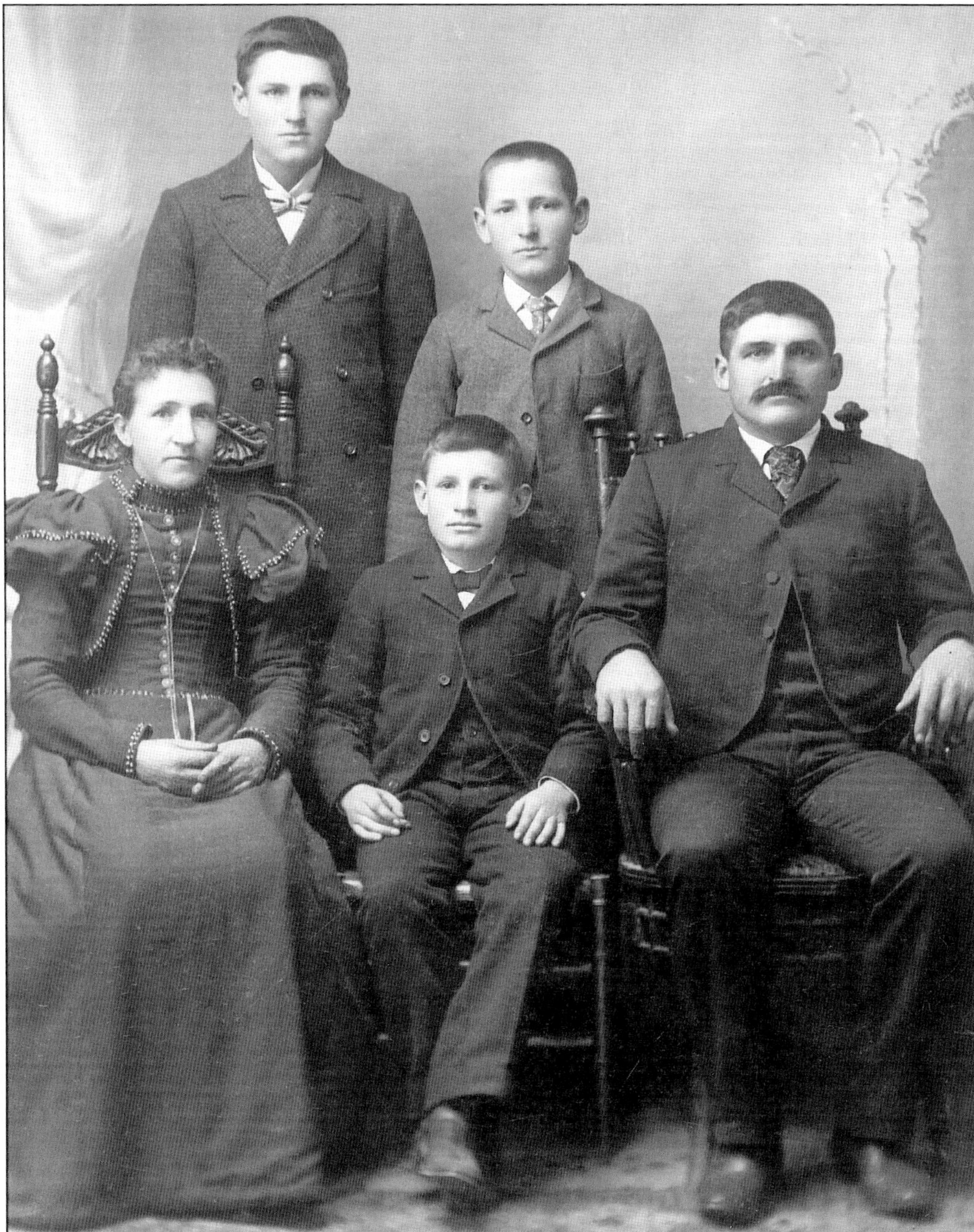

Henry and Elizabeth (Huber) St. Jacques pose with their sons Harry, Phillip, and Willie in St. Paul, MN, about 1898. Henry was born in Wabasha County in 1860 to Prosper and Philamina (LaPoint) St. Jacque. Elizabeth was born in 1859 to John and Caroline Huber. Henry and Elizabeth were well-known residents of Wabasha. In April 1892 they moved to North Dakota.

This photograph of Mrs. Jane (Griffis) Jackson and her children was taken about 1890 in Alma, WI. Jane was born in Malone, Franklin County, NY, on November 22, 1852. Her parents, Stephen and Elizabeth (Lampman) Griffis, were early pioneer settlers of Wabasha County. She married John Jackson on March 29, 1869, and had five children. Shown here are, from left to right, Alice, Mary, Anne, and John; Bert died when he was three, and is not pictured.

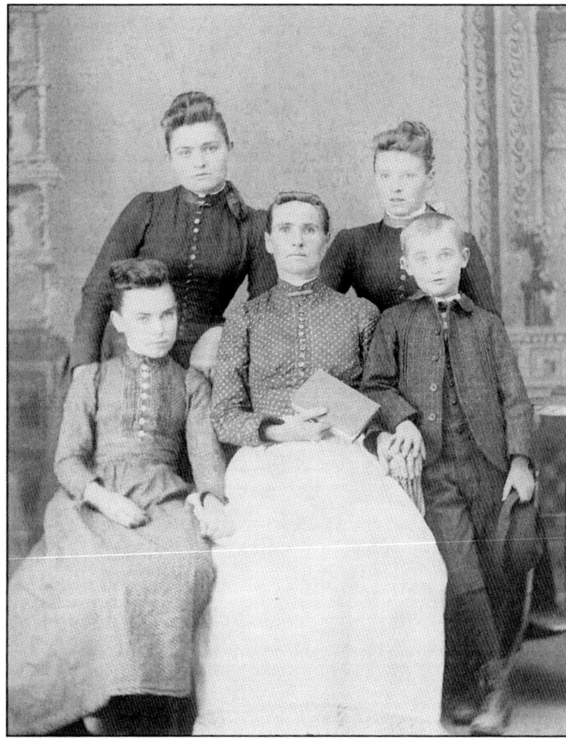

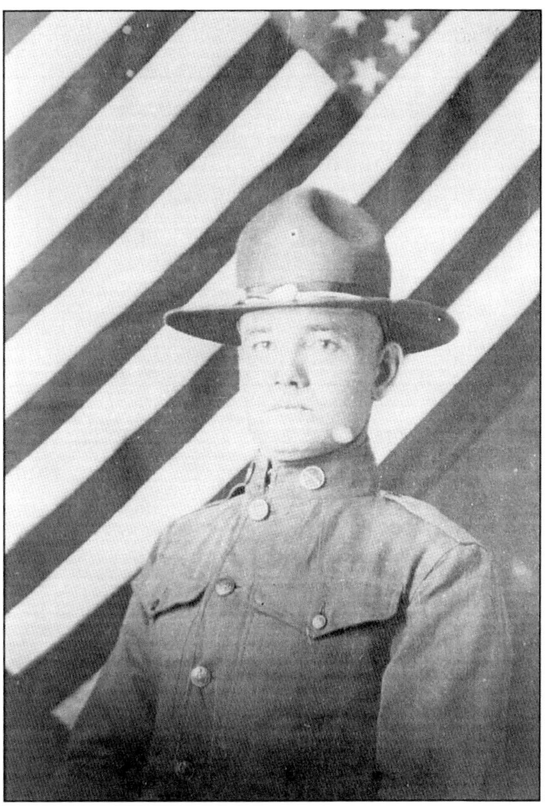

Another World War I veteran of Wabasha County is Mr. John Leisen, shown here in 1918. John was born on June 7, 1886, and he married Mary E. Eischen. His parents, Mathias and Kathryn Leisen, were among the early settlers of Wabasha County. (Courtesy of Dorothy Stoos.)

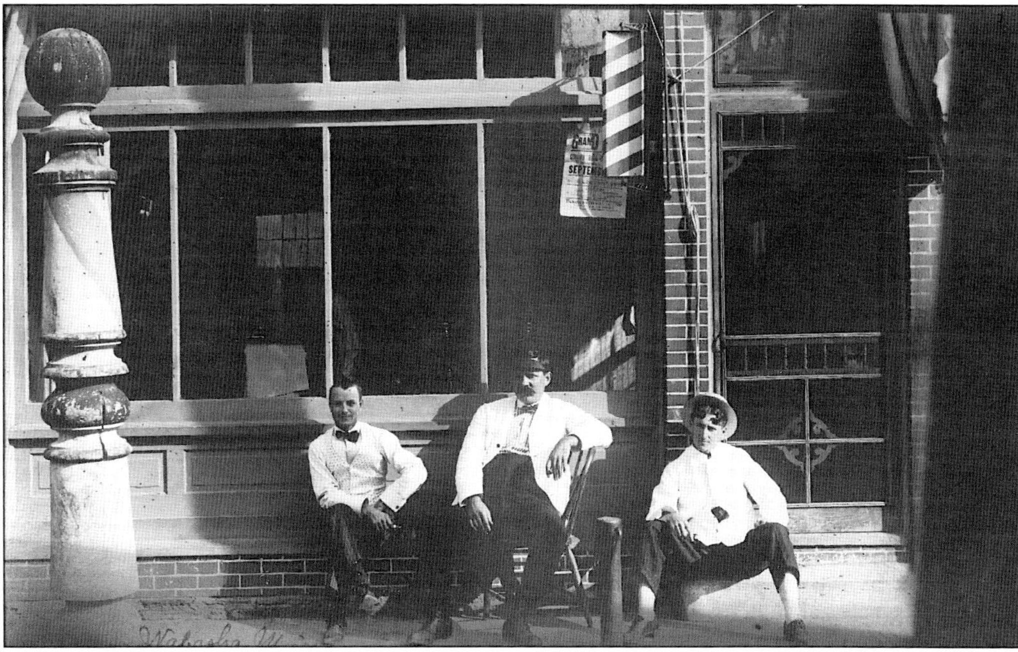

Lawrence Schurhammer (center) poses in front of the barber shop he operated for 25 years in Wabasha. He was associated with Farmer's and Merchant's Bank as vice president and president.

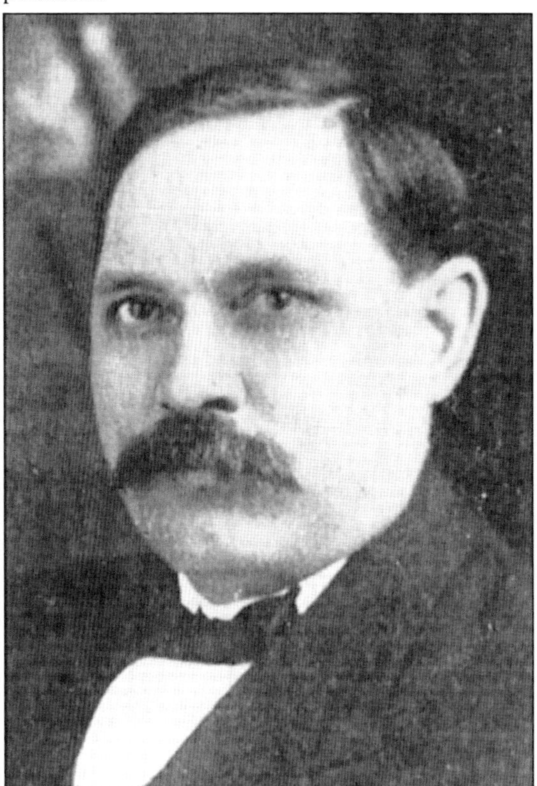

In addition to operating his barber shop for 25 years, Lawrence Schurhammer was a director in the Minnesota Beer Wholesales Distributing Association, chairman of the fuel depot project sponsored by the Wabasha Chamber of Commerce, and a member of the board of commissioners and the board of Buena Vista Sanatorium. He also was a distributor for Schmidt Brewery.

Sister M. Gerina Harrer poses with the Giem children in a photograph taken at St. Elizabeth's Hospital in Wabasha. Sister Gerina was born Walburga Harrer on August 22, 1911, in Eibach, Bavaria, Germany. She was the daughter of Ludwig and Walburga (Lenz) Harrer. In 1936, she came to Wabasha, residing and working at St. Elizabeth's Hospital. She passed away in 1996.

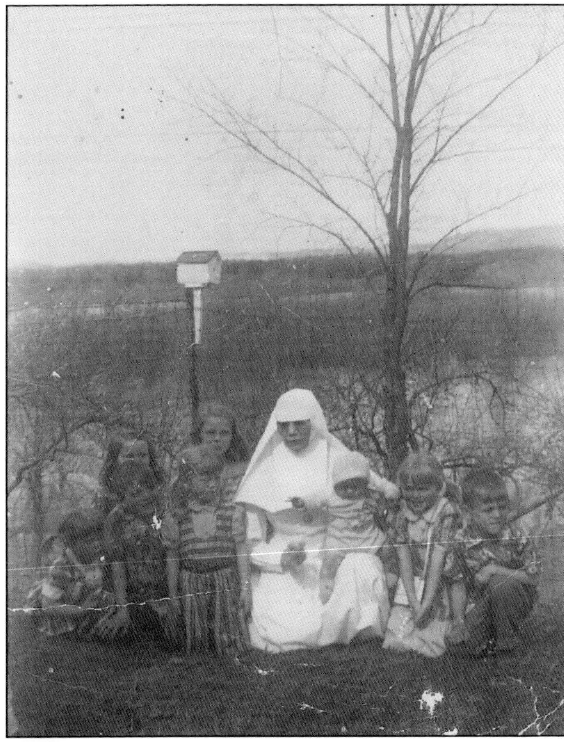

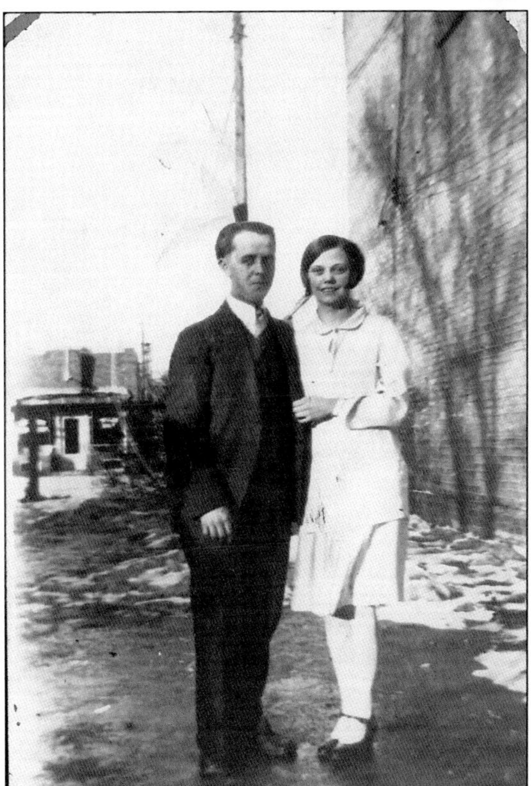

Ralph Deloss Curtis and Evadine J. Johnson were married on January 7, 1928. Ralph's parents are Fred and Caroline (Wright) Curtis. His grandparents, Orin Deloss and Rachel (Pepin) Curtis, were among the early pioneers of Wabasha County. Orin was a veteran of the Civil War. (Courtesy of Rachel Giem.)

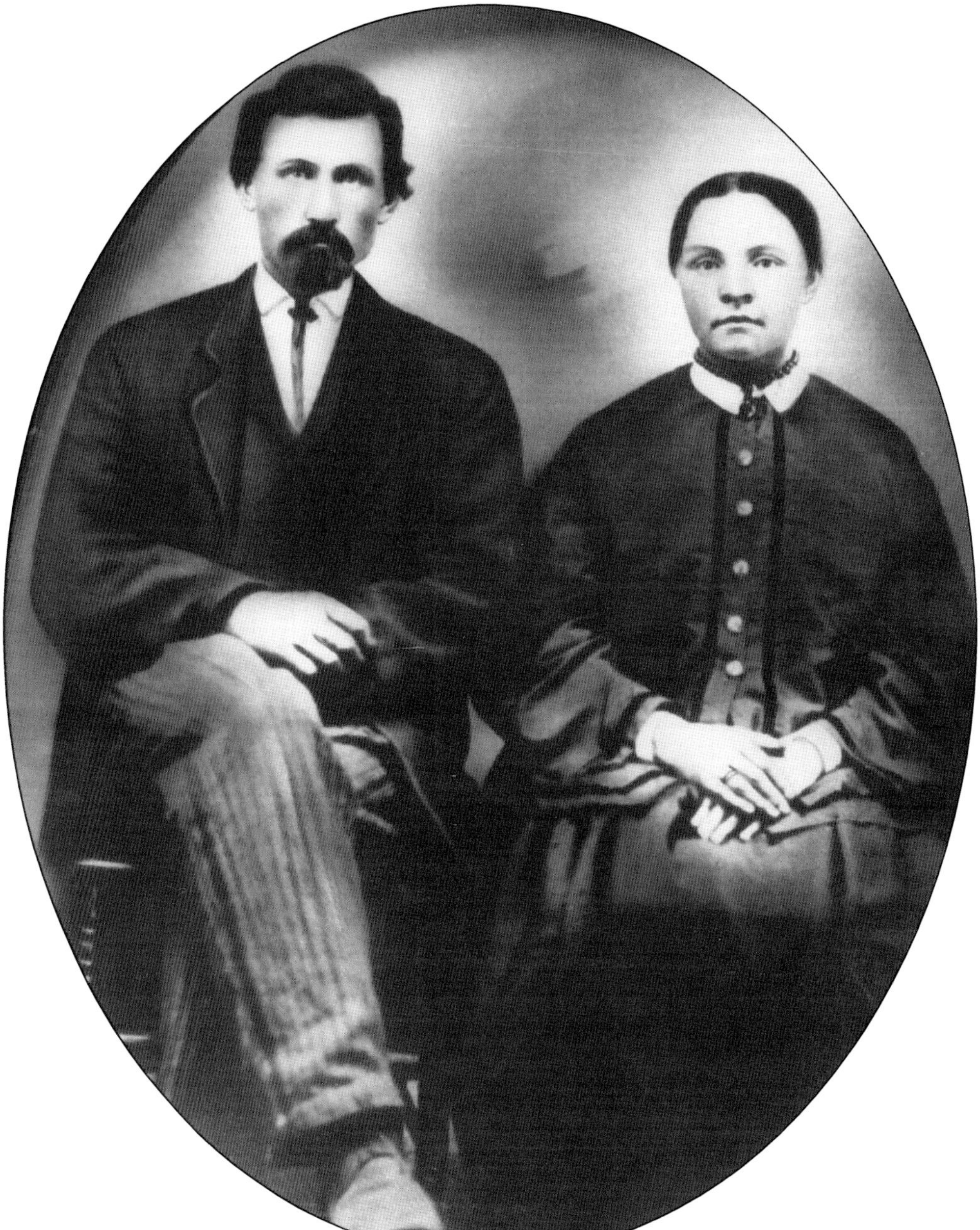

Jacob Giem and Margaret Markadont were married on June 12, 1868, in Wabasha. Jacob was born on September 21, 1839, in Tuscararas County, OH, to Johann C. and Elizabeth (Markofer) Giem-Giehm. He and his sister Elizabeth were raised by Johann's third wife, Lucinda (Brundberg) Giem. In 1856, his family settled in Elgin Township. In 1862, at the age of 23, he was mustered into Company K, 9th Regiment, at Fort Snelling under Colonel Henry Sibley. Jacob and Margaret had six children—John William (Ethel Redfern), Anna, Emma (Frank LaMont), Peter (Elizabeth Leisen), Jacob H. (Clara Harriman), and George Henry (Ellen Cornforth). Margaret died about 1882 in Wabasha, and Jacob died on July 18, 1913, in Kellogg, MN. Today they have descendants in Montana, Texas, and Washington!

This photo, taken in 1934, shows me, Gladys (Chadwick) Krusmark, at four years of age with my two-year-old brother Arthur. The chair pictured was made by my grandfather, William H. Chadwick, using buffalo horns and hooves for feet. I have kept the chair for all these years and recently donated it to the Reads Landing, Wabasha County Museum.

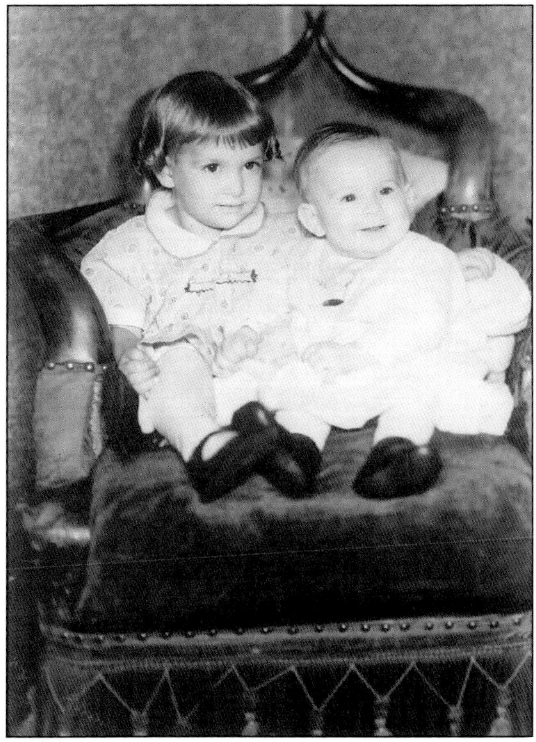

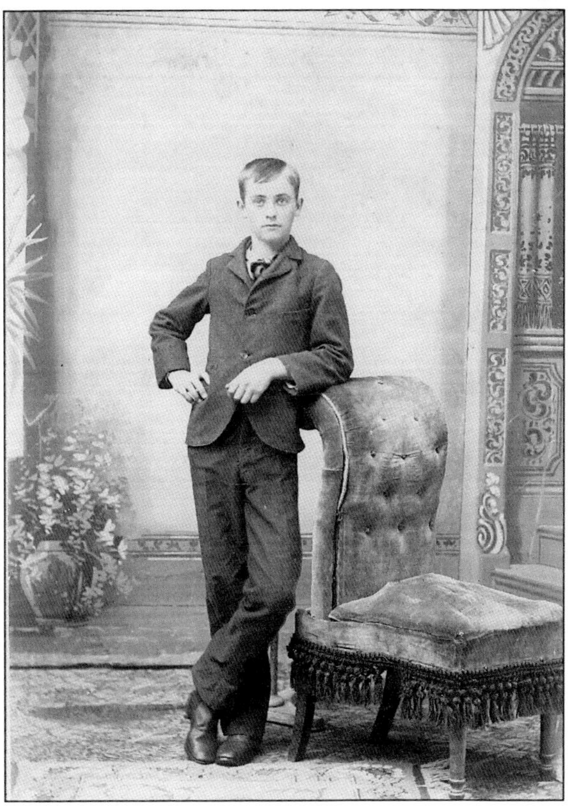

John Jackson Jr. (shown here) was the son of John and Jane (Griffis) Jackson. John Sr. came to Greenfield Township in the early 1860s with his parents, William and Mary Jackson. Jane Jackson, the daughter of Stephen and Elizabeth (Lampman) Griffis, was born in New York on November 22, 1852.

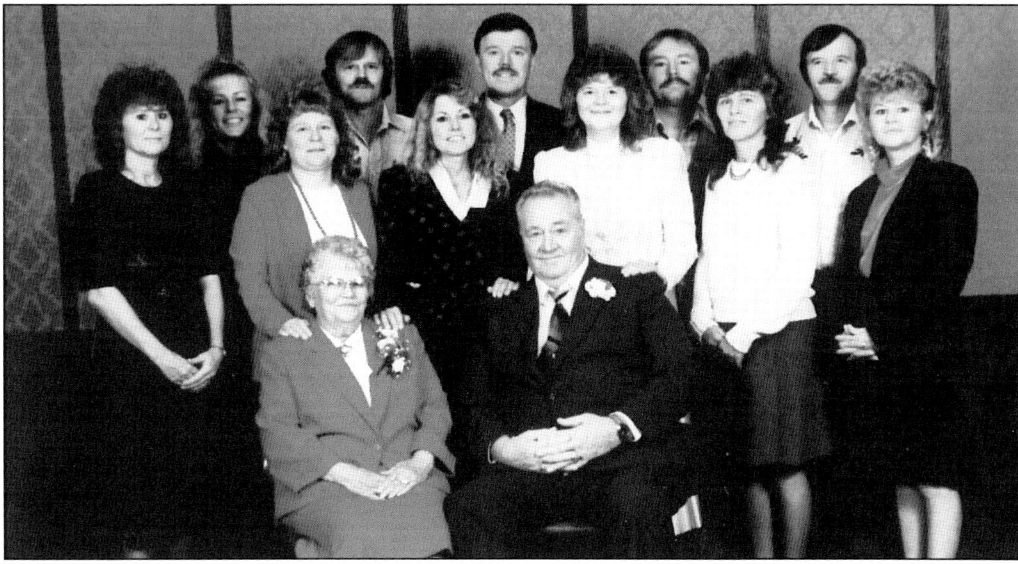

This 1991 photograph was taken at the 50th wedding anniversary of Leo and Rachel (Schurhammer) Giem. From left to right are as follows: (front row) Mary, Laura, Patricia, Kay, Judith, and Barbara; (back row) Joan, Gerald, Donald, Joseph, and Robert. The Giem family history in Wabasha County began in the fall of 1856, when Leo's great-grandfather, Johann Christian Giehm, settled in Elgin Township. Leo's grandfather, Jacob Giem, was a Civil War veteran. The Giems have lived in this county for 142 years, as of 1998. The Giem cemetery is located in Section 20 (Highway 2), Oakwood Township.

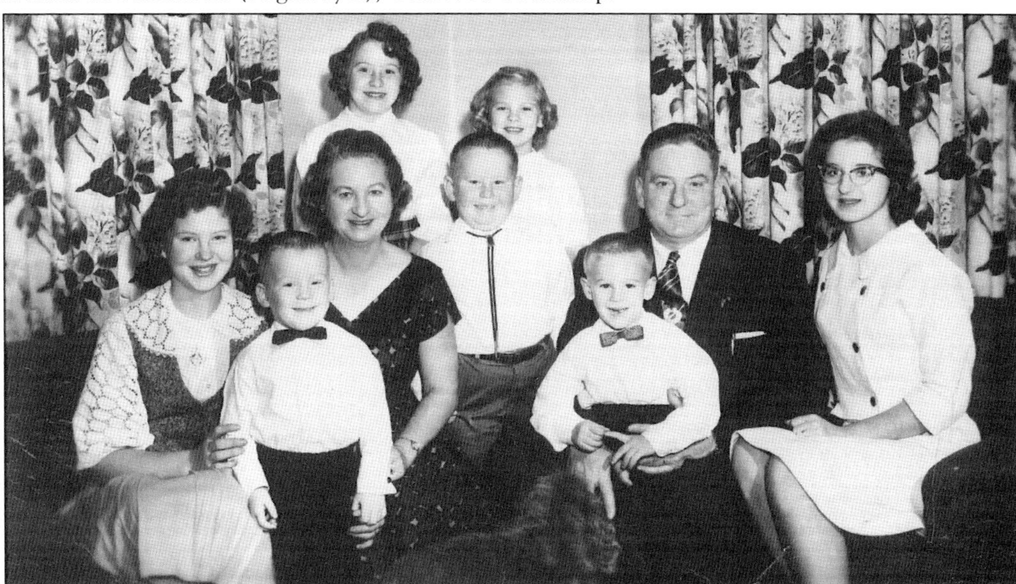

Members of the Eugene and Mildred (Hoffman) Deming family are shown here posing for a photograph. They are, from left to right, as follows: (front row) Robert and Michael; (middle row) Patricia, Mildred, Bill, Eugene, and Barbara; (back row) Joan and Dorothy. For 29 years, Eugene owned and operated the Deming Ford Agency in Kellogg. He is a World War II veteran, having served with the 60th SeaBee Battalion. Mildred passed away in 1973 and Eugene in 1985.

Eleven students were in the class of 1937 at the Kellogg School. From left to right, starting at the top, are Delilah Tentis, Catherine Klees, Eleanor Murphy, Rachel Tentis, R. Dooley (superintendent), Mary McEniry (principal), Wendel Woods (science), Mary Schurhammer, Marian Wolfe, Mildred Peters, Ervin Wehinger, Leo Hengtgen, Robert Schurhammer, and Jerry Keenan.

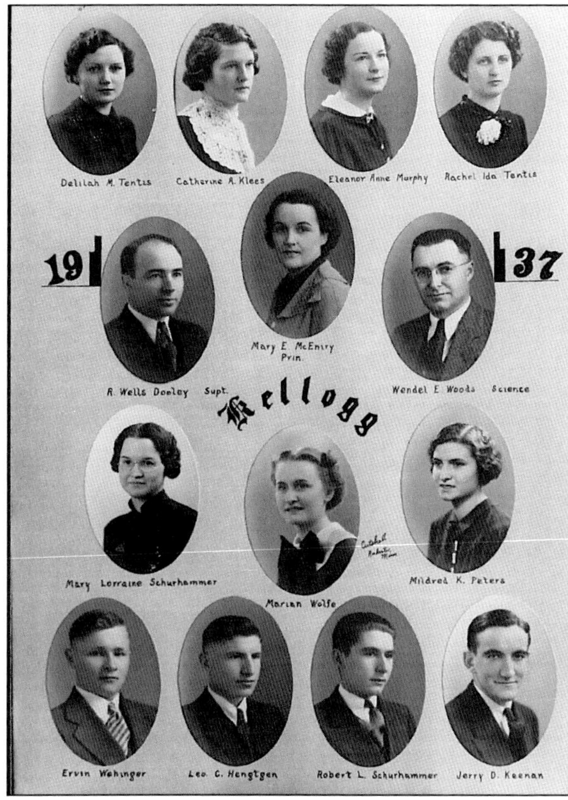

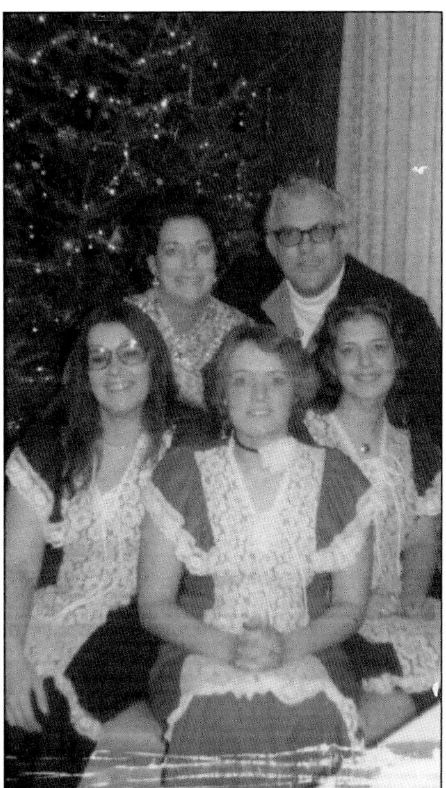

Richard and Gladys (Bootz) Krusmark are shown here with their three daughters—Cindy Halvorson, Vicky Belindir, and Nancy Flynn. Richard and Gladys live in Wabasha, where they built and have operated the Big Sioux Campground since 1972. Gladys's paternal lineage originates from John and Nathaniel Merrill, who came to Ipswich, MA, from Salisbury, Wilt County, England, and Wherestead Parish, England, in 1613.

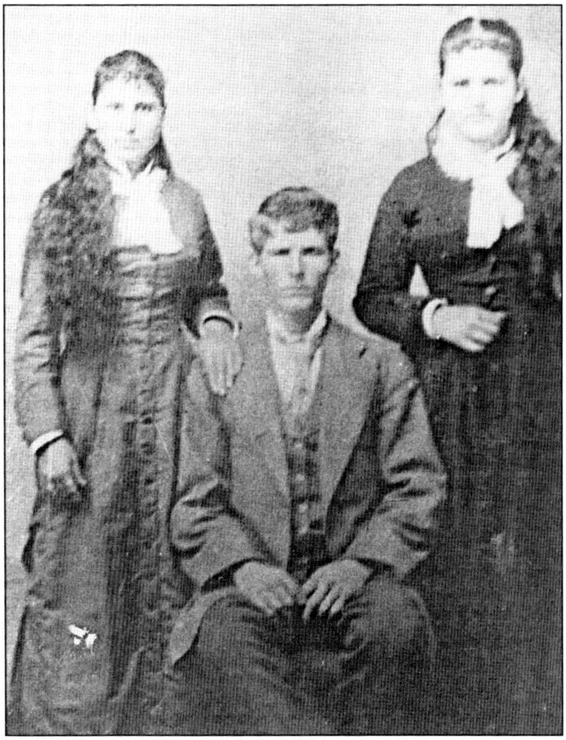

The wedding of Lorenzo and Laura (Harrell) Curtis took place on September 10, 1879. His sister, Alice Curtis, is on the right. Lorenzo's parents, Rachel and Orin Curtis, settled in Plainview Township in 1877. Laura's parents were George and Margaret Harrell. George was a riverboat pilot on the Mississippi River. There is a street named after his brother Pembrook in Wabasha.

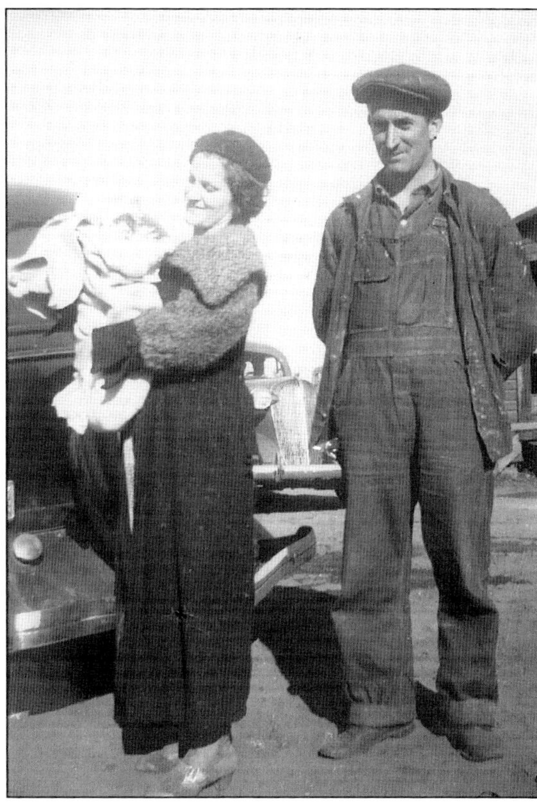

Andrew and Carnessa (Petroff) Schurhammer are shown here with their son Paul. Andrew (1904–1954) was born in Wabasha to August and Annie (Jackson) Schurhammer. He graduated from Wabasha High School, spent several years in the service, and married Carnessa. Many years later, he remarried and had two sons. His family has a very rich history in Wabasha County.

The wedding of Leonard and Alta (Curtis) Schurhammer took place in Wabasha on July 19, 1915. Leonard was born in Kellogg and Alta was born in Plainview. After their marriage, they lived in Chicago, IL, and then in Kellogg, MN, on a farm. In 1941, they moved to Stockton, CA, where he worked in the shipyards until 1947. They then moved to Chehalis, WA. The couple had three children—Elizabeth, Rachel (Leo Giem), and Robert.

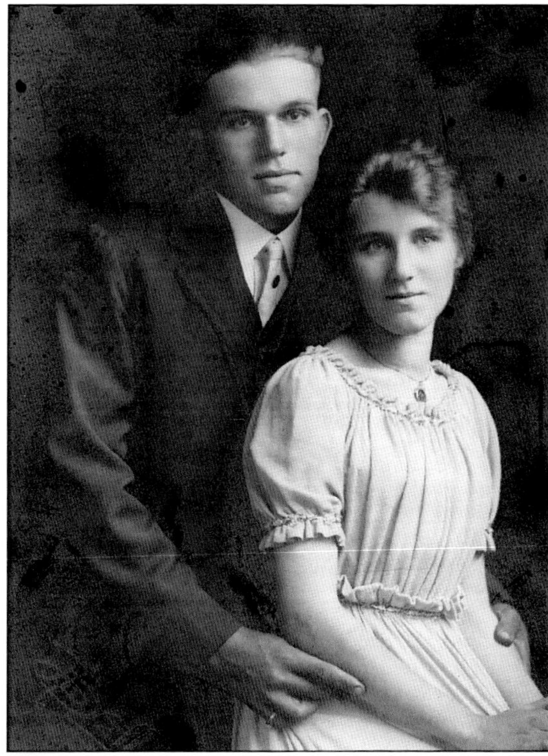

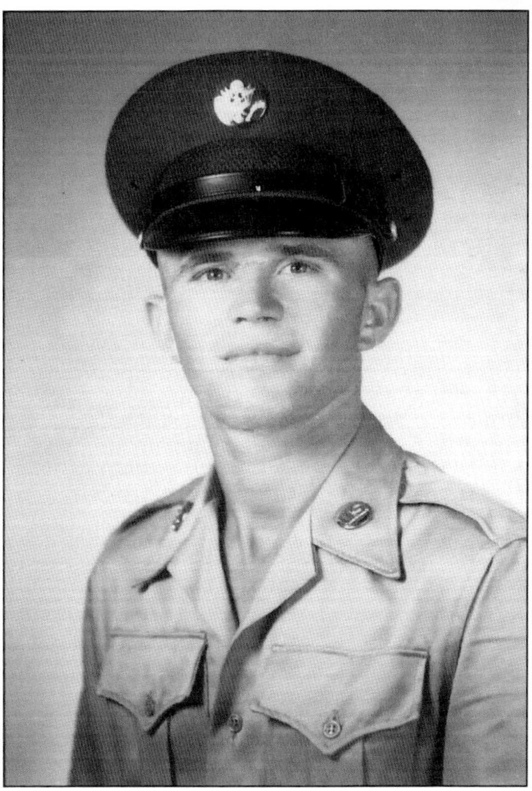

Robert Leonard Giem was born in Wabasha to Leo and Rachel Giem. He grew up in Kellogg, MN, and was educated in the Kellogg and Wabasha Public Schools. After graduating he worked at Deming Ford in Kellogg before entering the army. In 1966 he left for Fort Riley, KS, and on January 1, 1967, he left for Vietnam.

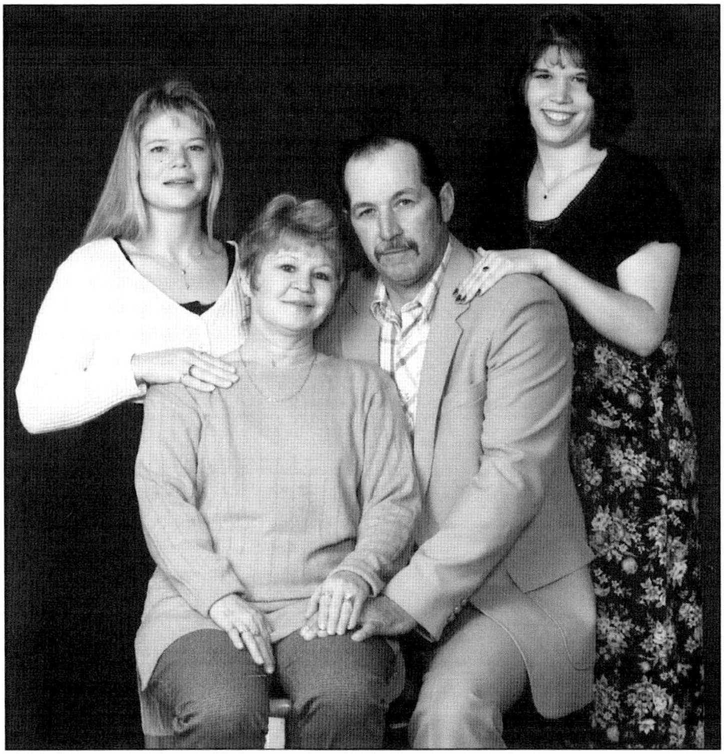

Shown here, from left to right, are Brenda Gave and Barb, Dale, and Dana Wagner. Dale was born to Adolph and Margaret (Wischow) Wagner. He grew up on a farm in Minneiska Township, Wabasha County, and fought in Vietnam. Barb's roots in Wabasha County history go back over 144 years on both her mother's and father's sides.

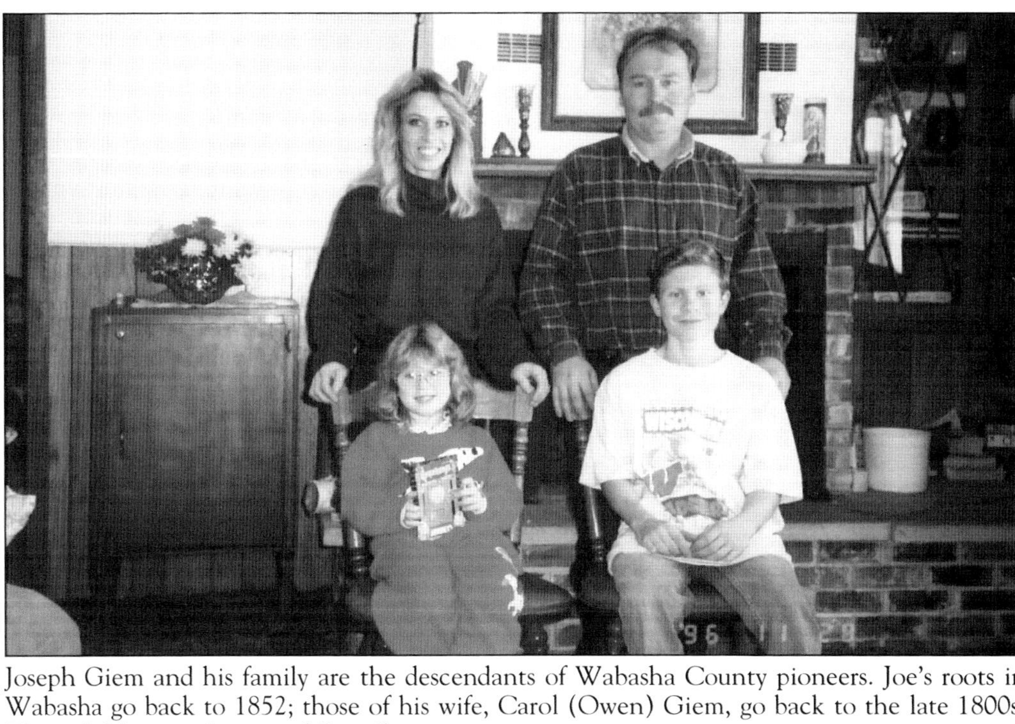

Joseph Giem and his family are the descendants of Wabasha County pioneers. Joe's roots in Wabasha go back to 1852; those of his wife, Carol (Owen) Giem, go back to the late 1800s. Their children are Jason and Sara Giem.

Wallace Whipple and Margaret Parkinson were married on August 12, 1896. Wallace was born in 1876 to Charles and Louise (Nichols) Whipple. Margaret's parents, William and Ellen (Knight) Parkinson, emigrated from England and settled in Zumbro Township, Wabasha County. Wallace and Margaret had four children—Wallace (Elda Tiedemann), Margaret (Henry Tiedemann), Elizabeth (Edward Books), and Charles. (Courtesy of Kenneth Tiedemann.)

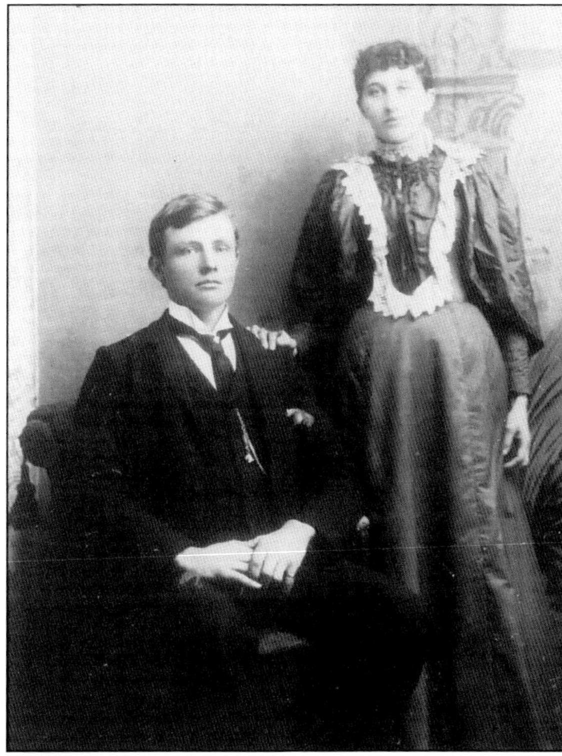

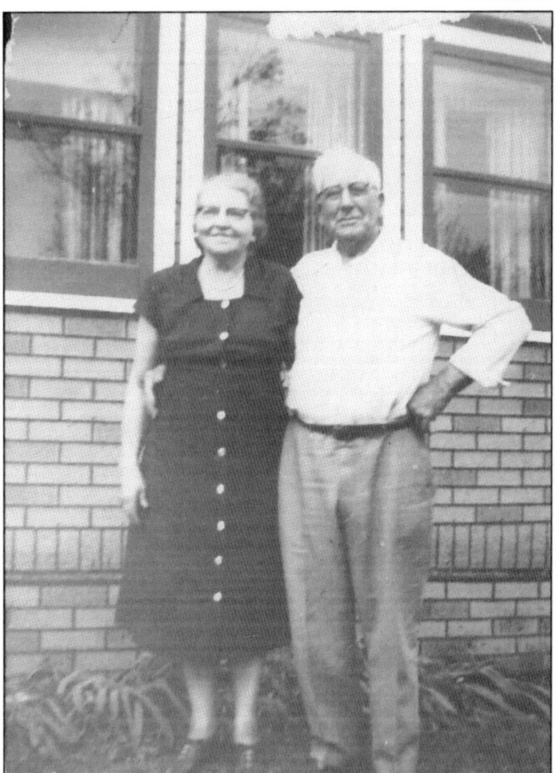

Claude and Margie (Curtis) Brownell pose outside their home in St. Paul. Margie's parents, Lorenzo and Laura (Harrell) Curtis, were born and raised in Wabasha County. Margie married Albert Nelson in 1906. The two had three children—Alton, Harleth, and Beulah (Dan Rush). Albert died in 1926, and Margie passed away in 1966.

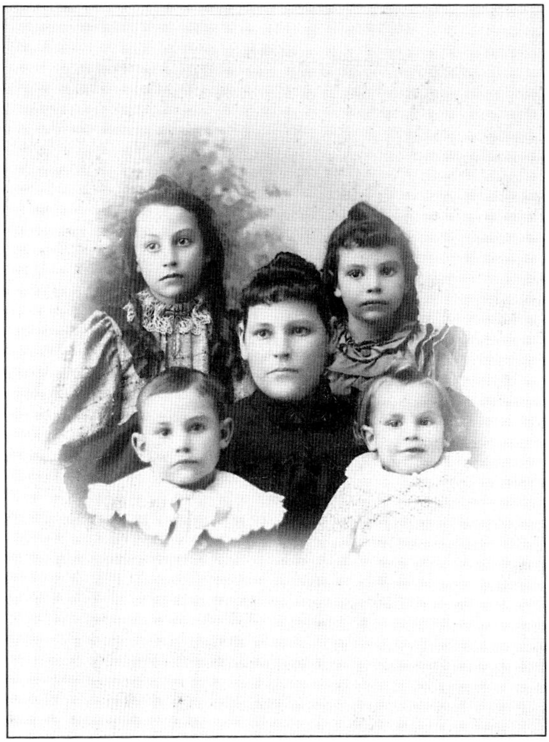

This is one of the county's pioneer families. Wilhelmina (Schurhammer) Herschberger is in the center; surrounding her are, from top to bottom, left to right, Aleda, Esmee, Elmer, and Thomas. They were counted in the 1860 census of the short-lived Tepeotah Settlement.

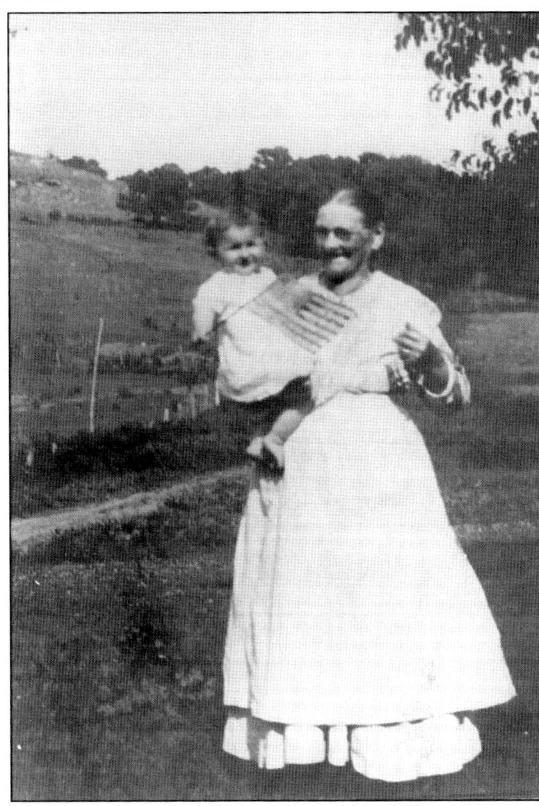

Katherine (Zeimetz) Leisen holds Elaine (Giem) Passe in her arms. Katherine's father immigrated to the United States in 1860. He settled in Chicago for two years before he and his family moved to LaCrosse, WI, where they lived until Mrs. Catherine Zeimetz died in 1870. Shortly after her death, the family moved to Wabasha. Katherine's brothers and sisters are Sebastian (Mary Connors), Thomas, Magdelena (Stephen Klees), Margaret (James Conroy), and Clara (John Kirchen). (Courtesy of Dorothy Stoos.)

Robert Leonard Schurhammer was born on February 5, 1918, in Greenfield Township, Wabasha County, to Leonard and Alta Schurhammer. He grew up on the family farm and graduated from Kellogg High School. After graduation he worked with his father on the farm until World War II, when he entered the military and served with the Army Corps of Engineers in Europe. After his discharge, he worked for Alice-Chalmers in Springfield, IL, as an inspector and trouble-shooter. He retired in 1976 and moved to Wabasha, where he joined the American Legion and Veterans of Foreign Wars Posts.

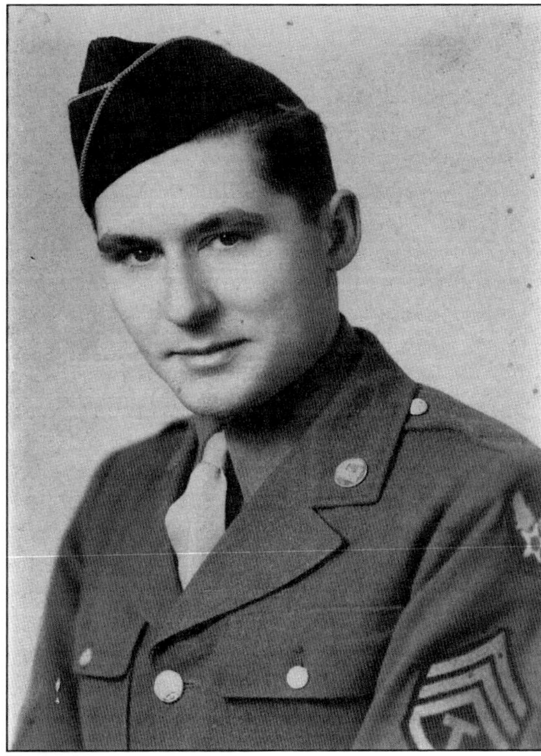

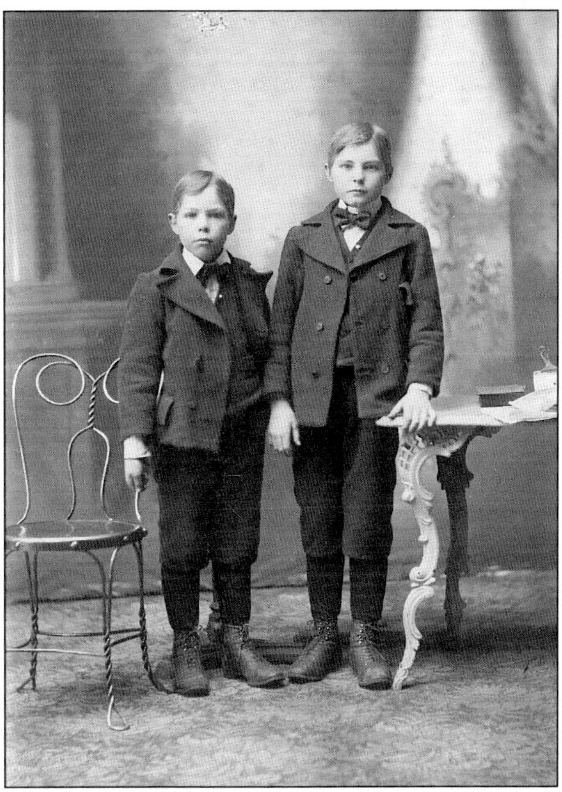

Leslie (left) and Ray LaBresh are the sons of Mrs. Mary LaBresh. Their grandparents, John and Jane (Griffis) Jackson, were early settlers in Greenfield Township. This photo was taken at Gesell Studio in Alma, WI.

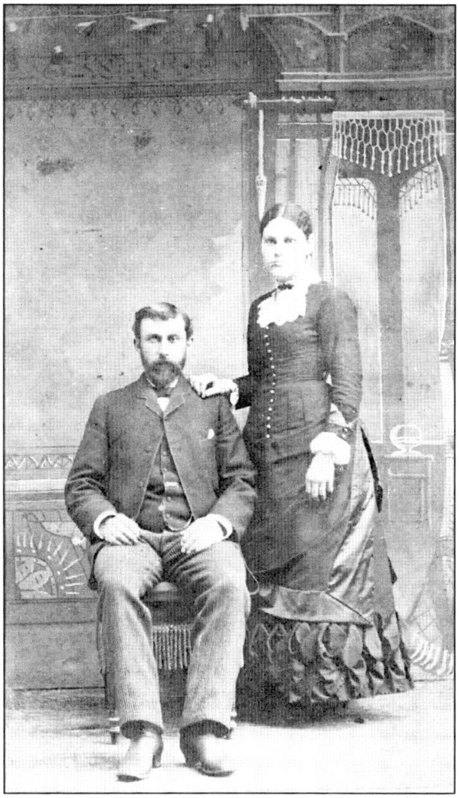

Thomas Park and Wilhelmina (Schurhammer) Hershberger were married in Wabasha in 1882. Thomas's parents, Jacob and Mary, came to Tepeeotah, Greenfield Township, in 1855. In 1871 Thomas helped prepare the land on which Duluth, MN, was built. He went to California in 1875 to mine gold and worked in the Black Bear quartz mills.

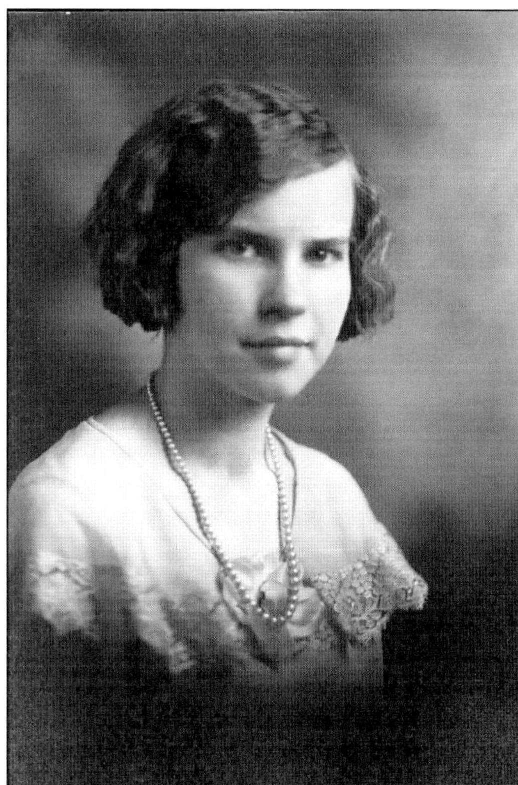

Lila Krull is the daughter of Richard and Ethel Krull. Her family history in Wabasha County began in the early 1860s, when John Jackson, who was born about 1848 in England, came to Greenfield Township with his parents, William and Mary Jackson. They cleared land here, built their home and out buildings, and began farming.

Arthur and Gladys (Pomeroy) Schurhammer are shown here in 1957 on their homestead in Greenfield Township. They were married in Wabasha in 1917. Art was a carpenter who often worked on bridges. The couple operated a tavern in Kellogg for 16 years, and their children are Marion (Lavern Deming), Arthur (Hilda Bennett), Harry, Harvey, and Ida May (Frank Hruza).

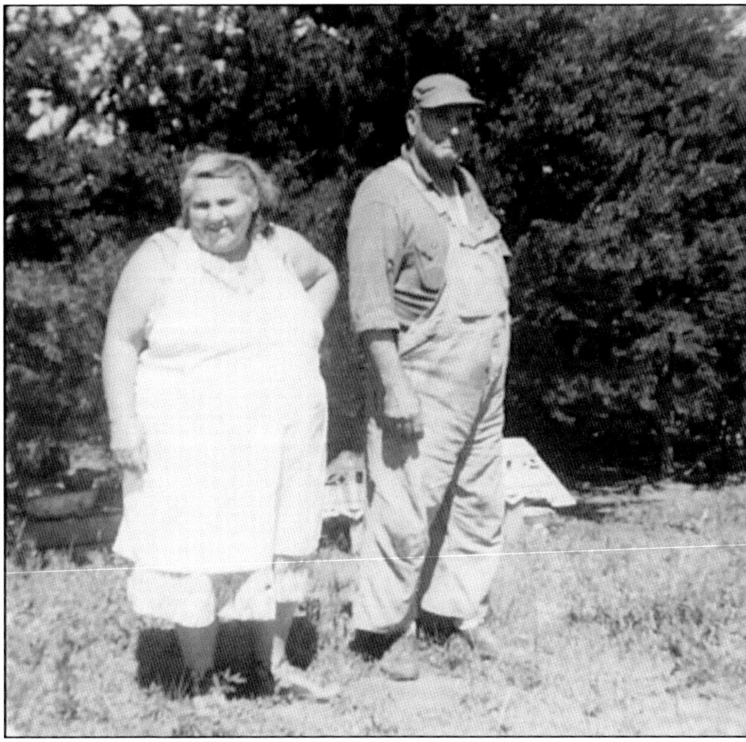

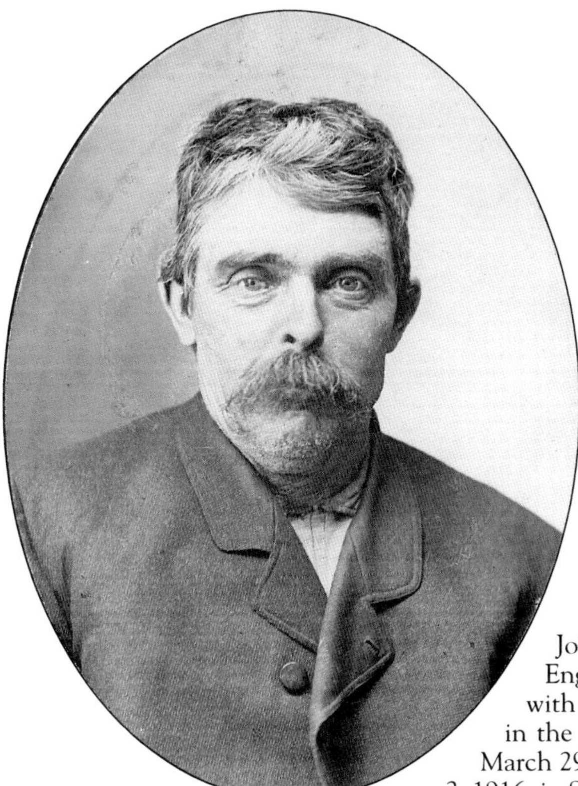

John Jackson was born about 1848 in England. He came to Greenfield Township with his parents, William and Mary Jackson, in the early 1860s, and married Jane Griffis on March 29, 1869, in Wabasha. He died on October 2, 1916, in St. Paul.

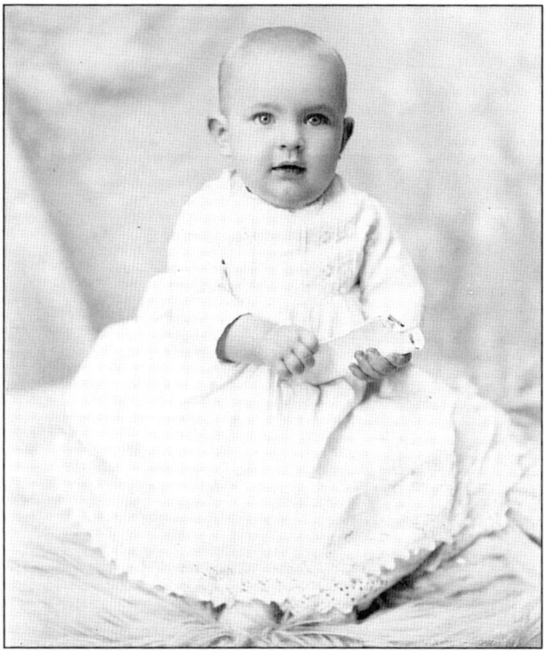

Lloyd Schurhammer, shown here while only five months old, lived his entire life in Wabasha County, Greenfield Township. He was born in 1894 to Christian and Alice (Jackson) Schurhammer, and his grandparents, Joseph and Magdalena Schurhammer, were among the earliest pioneers here.

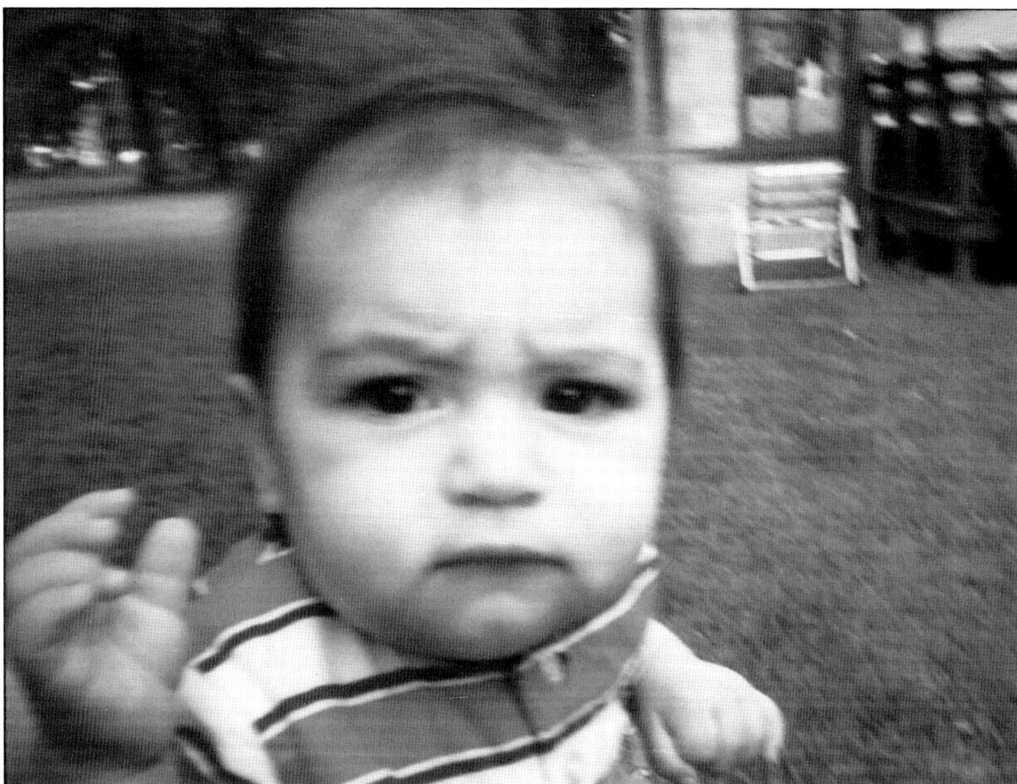

Dominic Dale Hoff was born on February 3, 1998, to Mark Hoff and Dana Wagner. Dominic's grandparents are Rick and Julie (Koopman) Hoff and Dale and Barbara (Giem) Wagner. He was born at the St. Elizabeth's Hospital in Wabasha, MN.

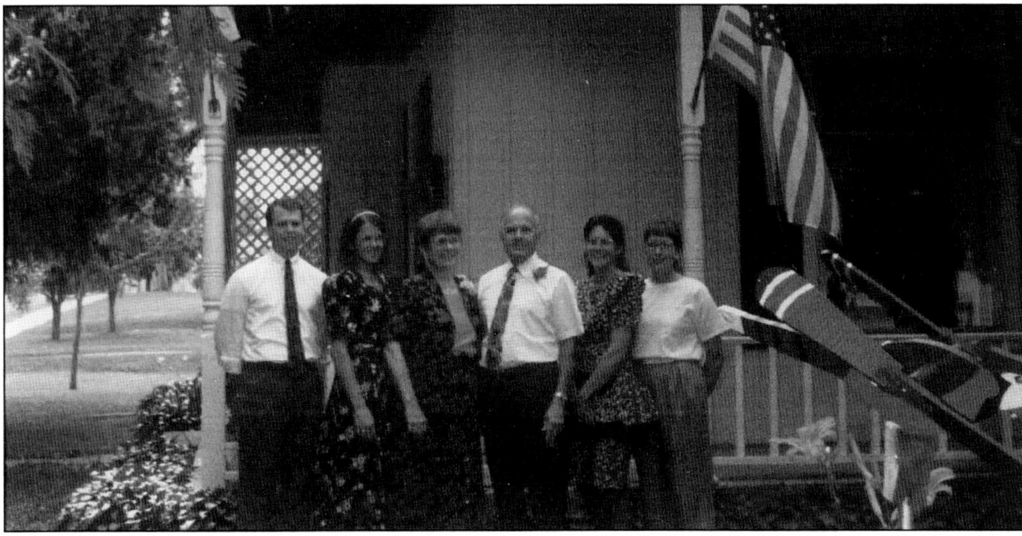

This Schurhammer family photograph was taken on the occasion of Donald and Laura (Lindmark) Schurhammer's 40th wedding anniversary. Pictured are, from left to right, Ronald, Karen, Laura, Don, Susan, and Diane. Don's parents were Valentine and Lorraine (Braun) Schurhammer and Laura's parents were Mauritz and Beatrice (Giem) Lindmark. Mauritz passed away recently, on July 25, 1991. Don and Laura had four children—Diane (Mark Peterson), Karen (Steven Arens), Susan (John Sheehan), and Ronnie (Diane Petit). (Courtesy of Rachel Giem.)

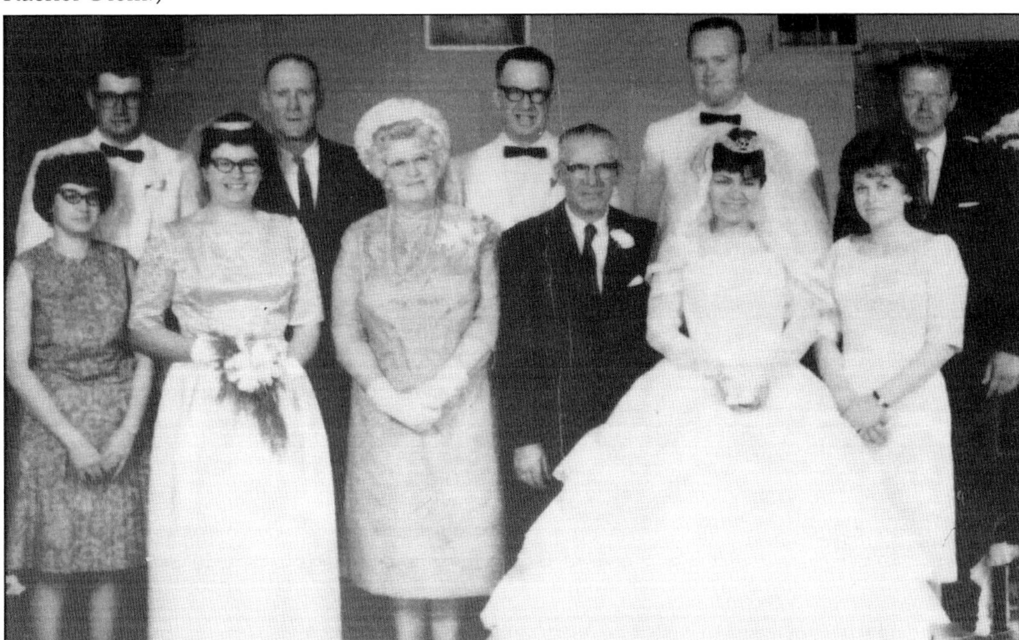

The wedding of Charles and Marlene (Olson) Lord took place on May 14, 1966. From left to right are as follows: (front row) Janice (McDonough) Olson, Thelma (Olson) Holland, Dorothy (Curtis) Olson, Gilmore Olson Sr., Marlene (Olson) Lord, and Elaine; (back row) Gilmore Olson Jr., Victor Holland, Bill Olson, Charles Lord, and Paul. Dorothy's parents were Andrew and Jeanette (Wright) Curtis.

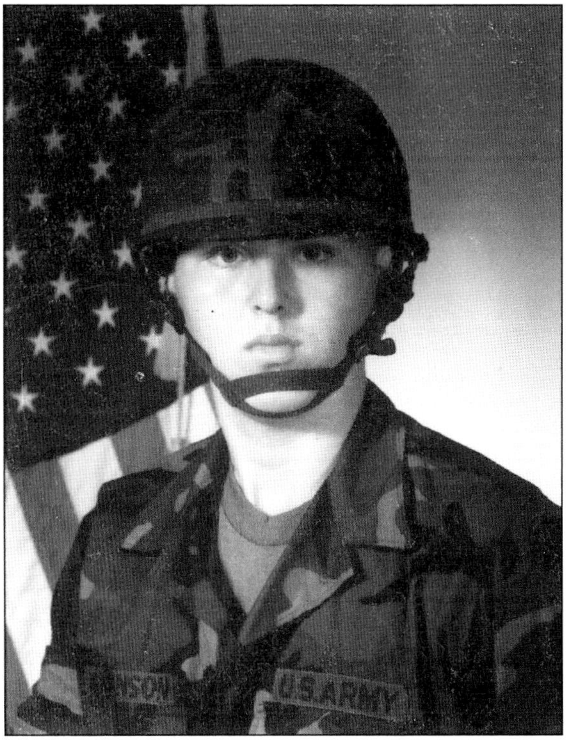

Another descendant of Wabasha County's pioneers is Lloyd Douglas Johnson, who was born in 1969 at Unity Hospital in Fridley, MN. Lloyd attended Wabasha-Kellogg High School. In 1986 he joined the Army National Guard, and received his basic training in Fort Benning, GA.

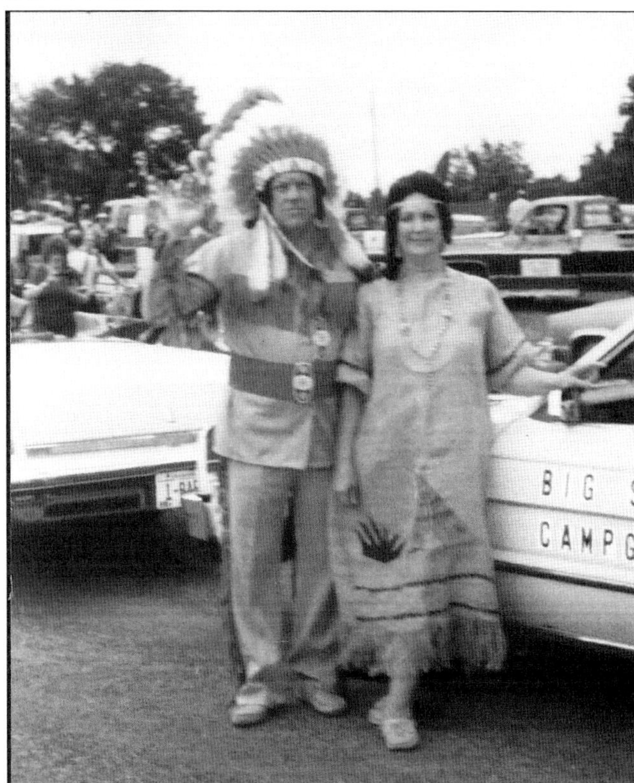

Richard and Gladys (Chadwick) Krusmark are shown here in 1984 at the Watermelon Festival in Kellogg. This was the first year Gladys dressed and rode in the parade with her husband. In 1972 they built the Big Sioux Campground in Wabasha, MN, and they have operated it ever since.

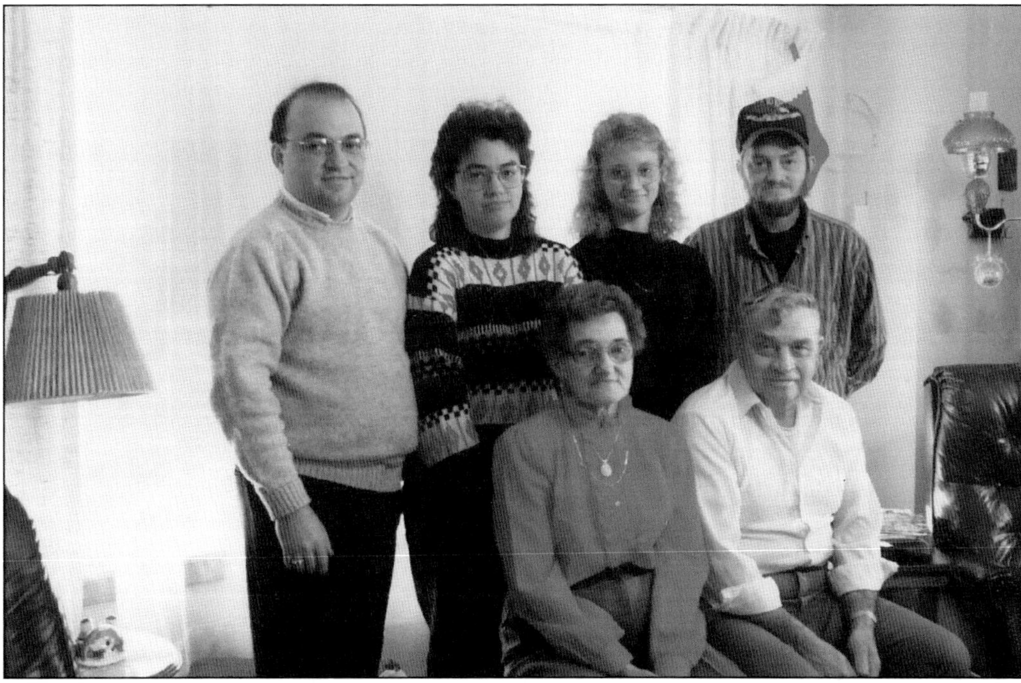

The Walter Tiedemann family posed for this photograph in 1995. They are, from left to right, as follows: (seated) Joan (Koenig) and Walter Tiedemann; (standing) Kenneth, Barbara, Nancy, and Russell. Walter and Joan farmed in Chester Township for over 25 years until moving to Mazeppa. Walter drove the school bus for the local school for several years and worked until retirement for the Wabasha County Highway Maintenance Department. (Courtesy of Kenneth Tidemann.)

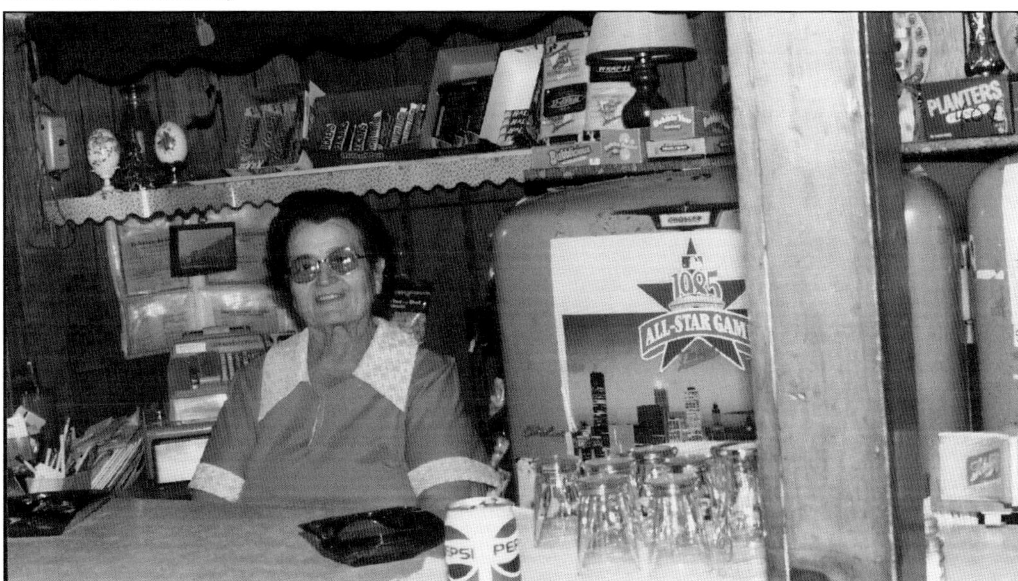

Berna Schwartzhoff is shown here at her place of business in 1987. Berna's parents owned this business until 1944, when Berna bought it. Her parents were Roy and Charlotte (Cruezer) Schurhammer.

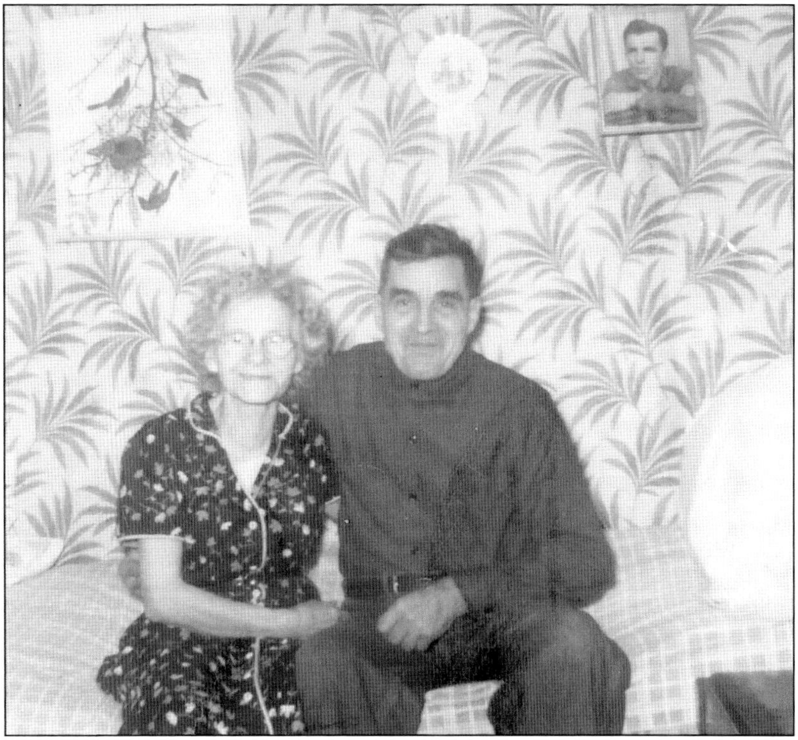

John Allen and Jesse Iona Curtis were married on February 11, 1911, and had three children—Irene, Stanley, and John William. Jesse and her twin, Jennie, were born on February 1, 1892, in Plainview, MN, to Len and Laura Curtis. Jessie passed away in 1957, and John Allen died in 1967. The two are buried in Chatfield, MN.

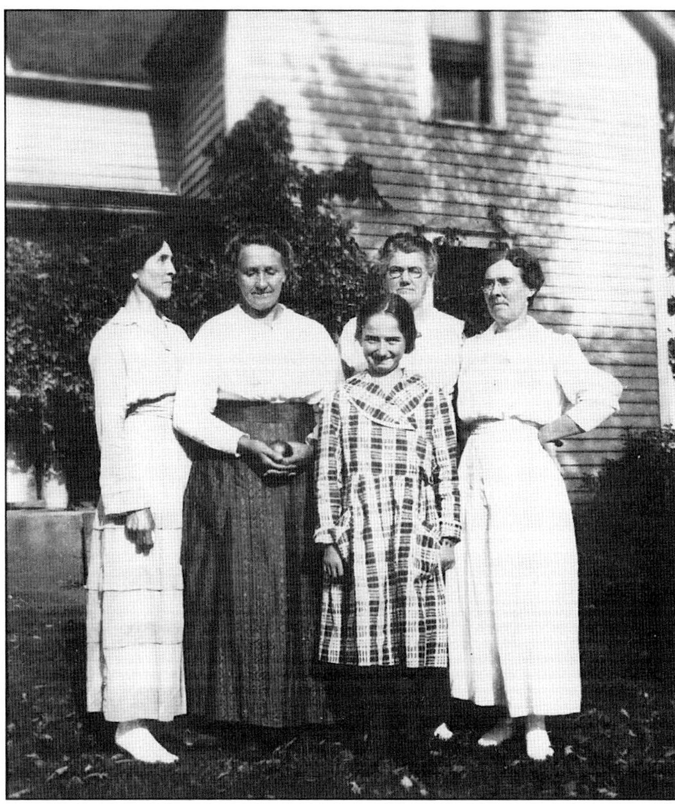

Josephine (Schurhammer) Sutter (left) poses for a photograph with Mrs. Balow, Mrs. Oachs, Mrs. Chris Schurhammer, and a neighboring girl, Audrey Erpelding. Josephine's parents were George and Anna (Braun) Schurhammer. In 1904 they had a son, Robert, who eventually married Ethel Witte.

Judith (Giem) Elliott's great-great-grandparents on her mother's side—Orin Deloss and Rachel (Pepin) Curtis, George and Margaret (McCollum) Harrell, Joseph and Magdalena (Tritchler) Schurhammer, and John and Carolina (Wacholtz) Huber—settled in Wabasha County. Her great-great-grandparents on her father's side are Johann C. Giem (Elizabeth Markofer died in Iowa), Peter and Christian Markadont, George and Elizabeth (Baker) Leisen, and Martin Zeimetz (Catherine died in Lacrosse, Wisconsin).

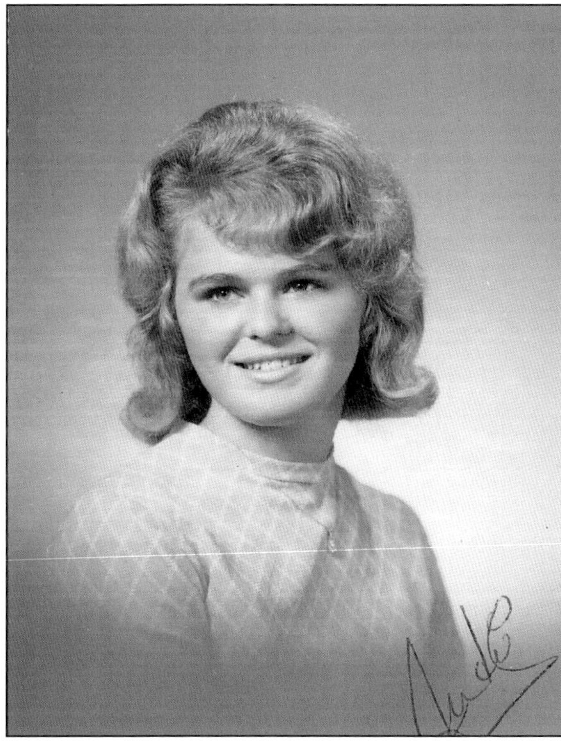

On November 13, 1993, Jerome Stein and Joan Giem were married. Jerome, the son of Joseph and Louella Stein, has two sons, Andy and Chris Stein, from a previous marriage. Joan is the daughter of Leo and Rachel Giem, well-known farmers in the county. Jerome and Joan have had two children—Brittany and Brandon Stein.

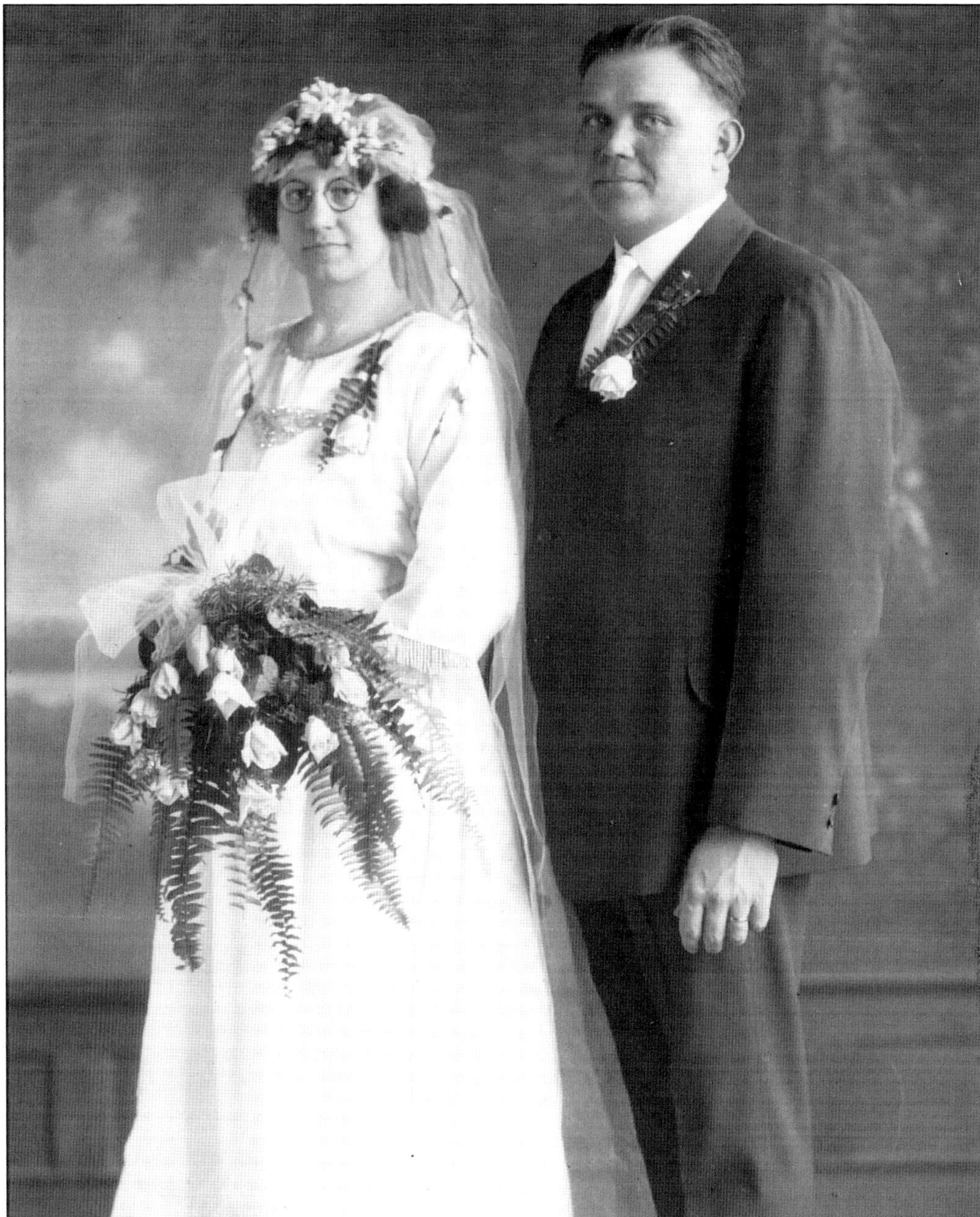

John and Frieda (Holst) Dahling are shown here on their wedding day, March 10, 1921. Frieda's parents were John and Margartha (Albers) Holst of rural Bellechester, MN, and John's parents were Frederick and Anna (Schact) Dahling. John worked on the Milwaukee Railroad while Frieda worked as a housewife, sometimes in other people's homes. The two were avid gardeners; they raised a good amount of fruit and vegetable produce each year, much of which Frieda preserved to be used in the winter months. On March 29, 1925, their only child, Donald John Dahling, was born (he eventually married Evelyn Deloris Copp). After John died in 1974, Frieda sold the family-owned home at 214 North 8th Street, Lake City, and lived for ten years at the Senior Apartment complex on the edge of town. (Courtesy of Evelyn Dahling.)

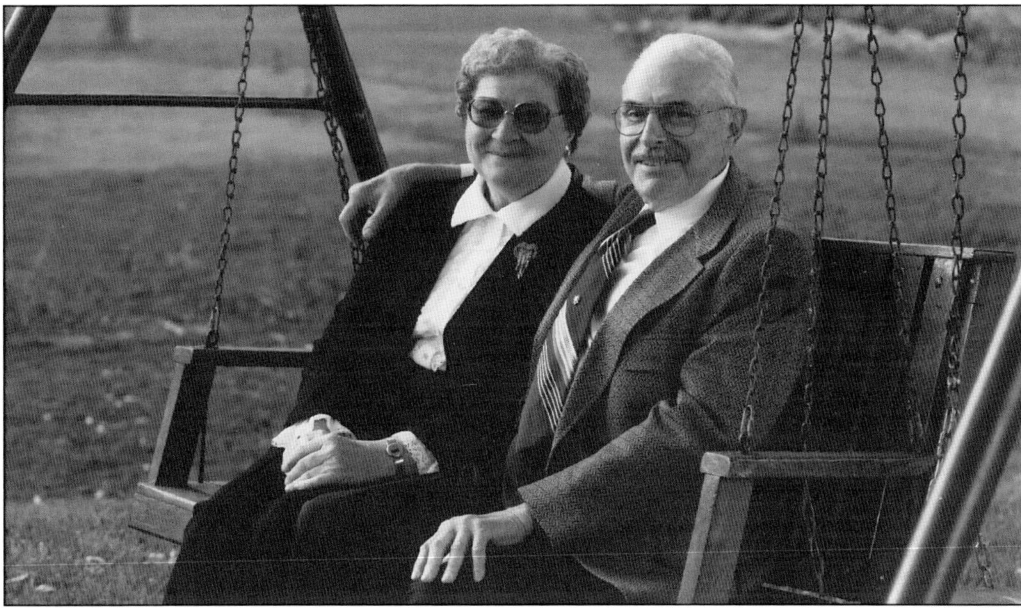

Alphonse John Kronebusch and Margaret Elizabeth Giem were married on May 10, 1939, and they farmed at Oak Ridge in Winona until 1947, when they moved to Kellogg. Their children are Jeanette (John Dynes), Lawrence (Shirley Zabel), Kathleen (Dennis Speltz), Patricia (Wayne Zabel), Alphonse (Lauri Senn), Clifford (Debra Zabel), Victoria (Laurence Lemke), and Marcella Kay (Edward Schneider). Mr. Kronebsch passed away in 1987. (Courtesy of Rachel Giem.)

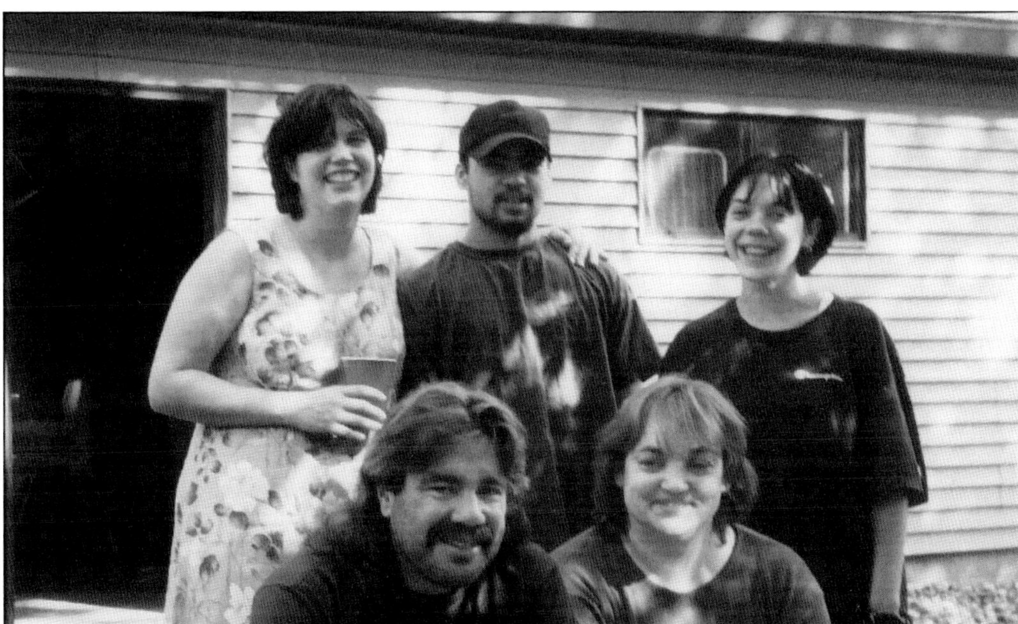

Rick and Julie (Koopman) Hoff's family has been in Wabasha County for many years. Pictured here are, from left to right, as follows: (front) Rick and Julie (Koopman) Hoff; (back) Dana Wagner, Mark Hoff, and Leslie Hoff. Julie is the daughter of Mavis Koopman.

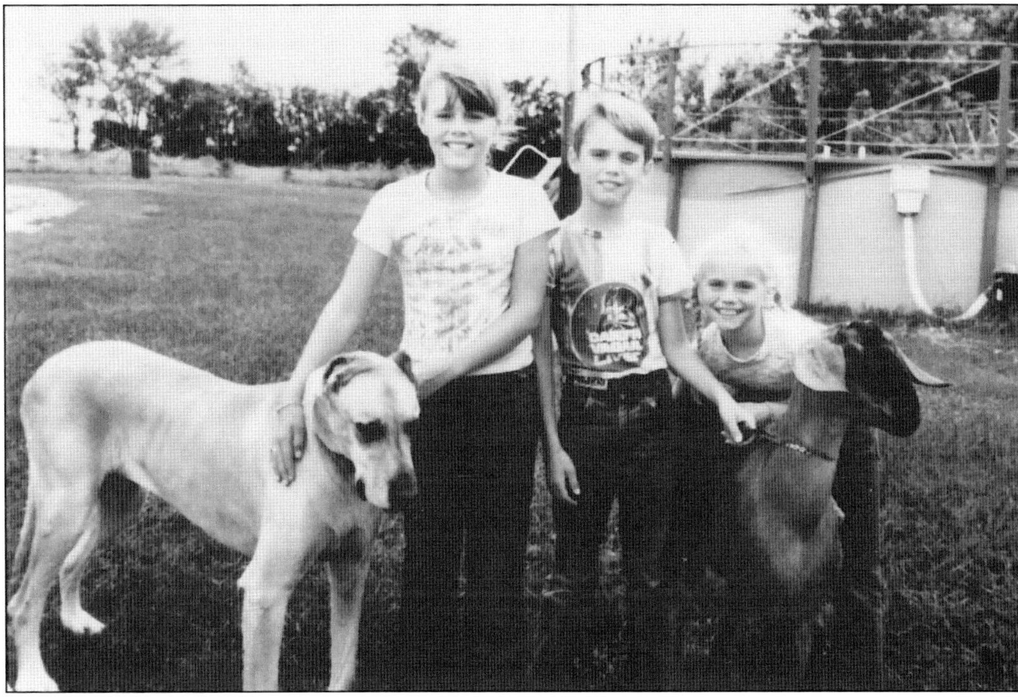

Jeannie, Robert, and Linda Giem, the children of Robert and Janalee (Packer) Giem, can trace their lineage back to 1653 on the side of their grandmother, Rachel (Schurhammer) Giem. They can trace the lineage of their grandfather, Leo Giem, back to the 1770s from Konnern, Saxony, Germany.

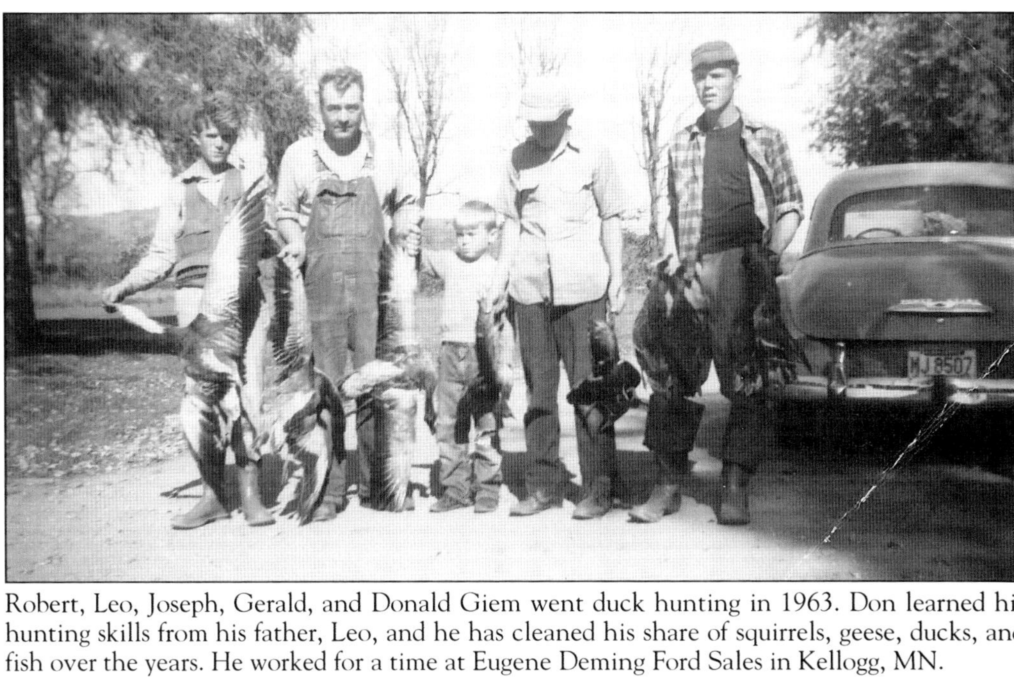

Robert, Leo, Joseph, Gerald, and Donald Giem went duck hunting in 1963. Don learned his hunting skills from his father, Leo, and he has cleaned his share of squirrels, geese, ducks, and fish over the years. He worked for a time at Eugene Deming Ford Sales in Kellogg, MN.

Lawrence "Larry" Kronebusch, the son of Al and Margaret (Giem) Kronebusch, has lived in Wabasha County all of his life. He and his wife, Shirley A. Zabel Kronebusch, live in Greenfield Township. Larry has a rich history in this county. His great-great-grandfather, John C. Giem, arrived in Oakwood Township in 1856. Larry and Shirley have three children—Robert, Terrance, and Karen.

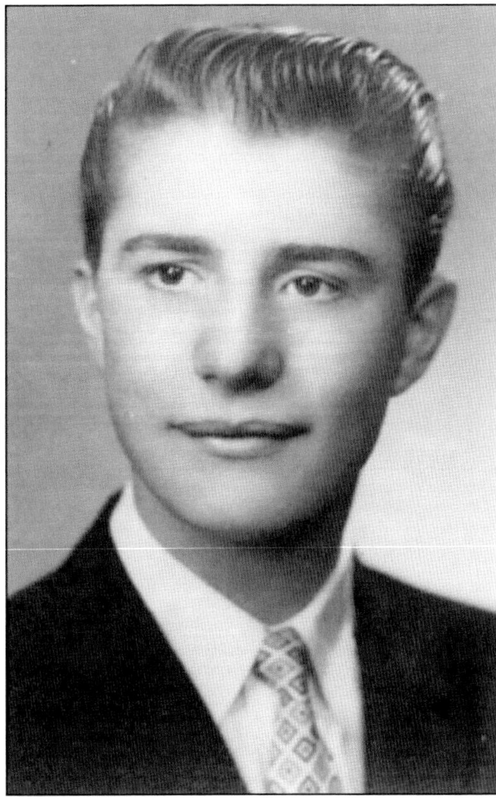

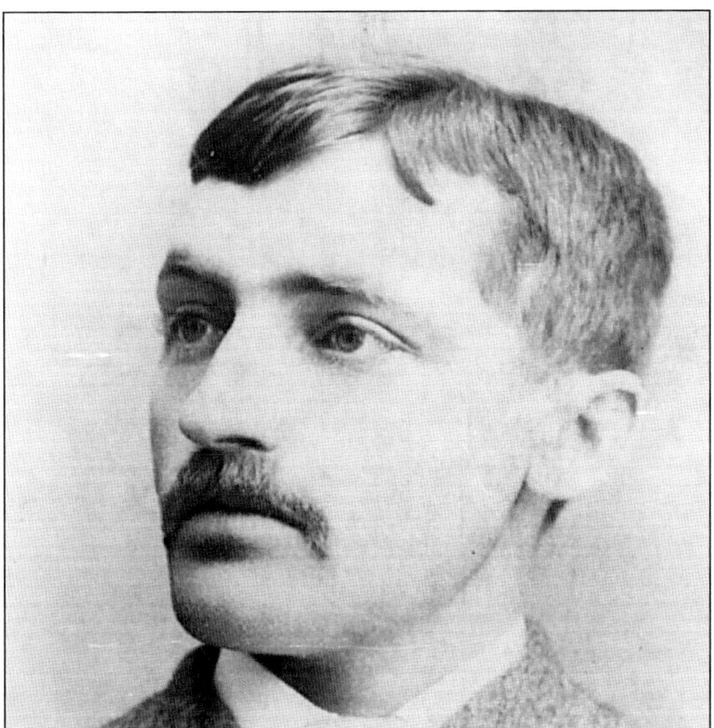

Nicholas Schouweiler was born in Wabasha County on November 24, 1862, to Michael and Catharine Schouweiler.

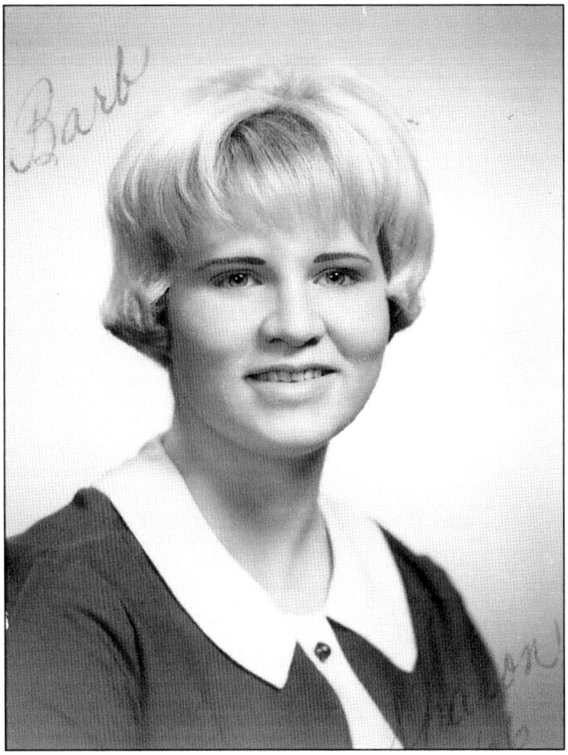

Sharon Peterson was born in Wabasha to Andrew and Margaret (Ziebell) Peterson. The Peterson family history in Wabasha County goes back to the early 1800s. Sharon married Larry Stromness on December 19, 1966, and has three children—Dean, Lori, and Schelby. She is the sister of Betty Peterson. (Courtesy of Barb Wagner.)

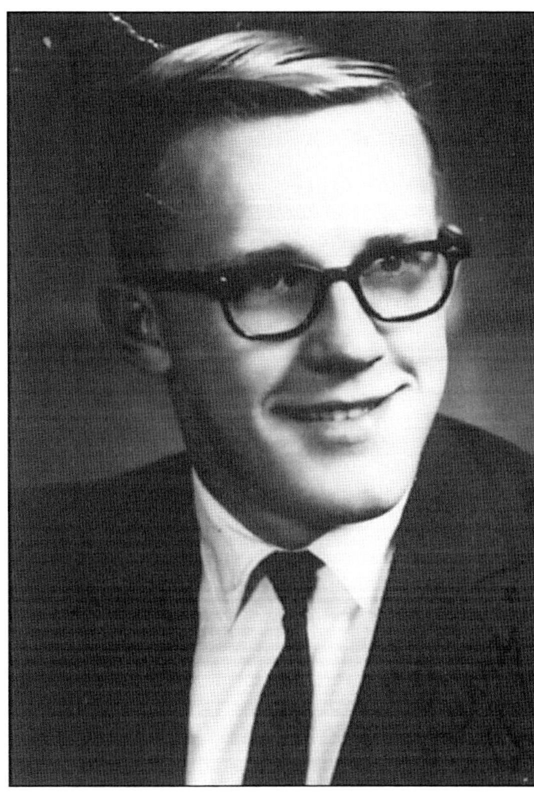

Larry Stromness was born in Wabasha to Alton and Esther Bernice (Austin) Stromness. The Stromness family has been in Wabasha County for well over 60 years. Larry's brothers and sisters are Shirley, Diane, Phyllis, Karen, Linda, Richard, and Leonard. (Courtesy of Barb Wagner.)

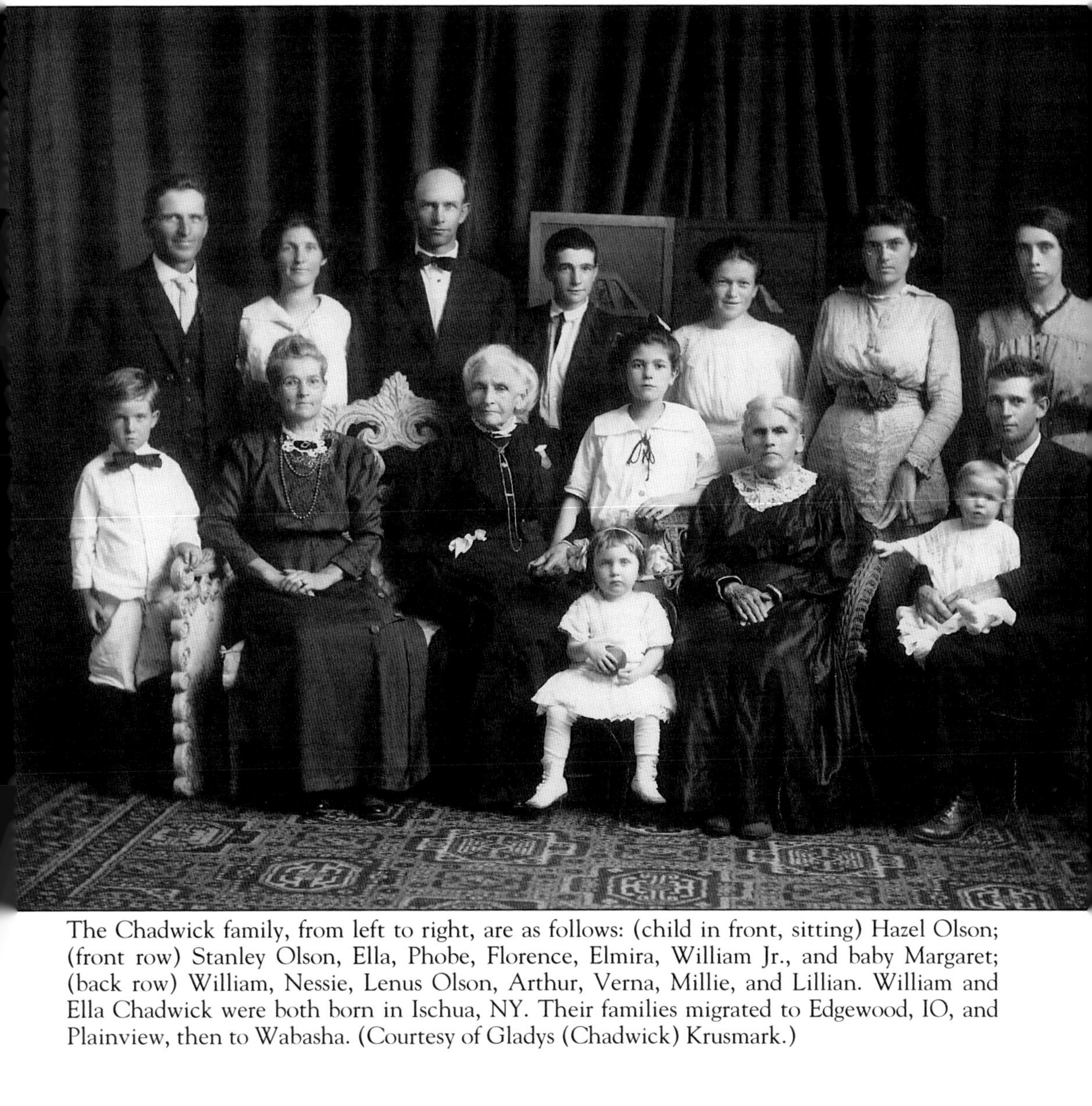

The Chadwick family, from left to right, are as follows: (child in front, sitting) Hazel Olson; (front row) Stanley Olson, Ella, Phobe, Florence, Elmira, William Jr., and baby Margaret; (back row) William, Nessie, Lenus Olson, Arthur, Verna, Millie, and Lillian. William and Ella Chadwick were both born in Ischua, NY. Their families migrated to Edgewood, IO, and Plainview, then to Wabasha. (Courtesy of Gladys (Chadwick) Krusmark.)

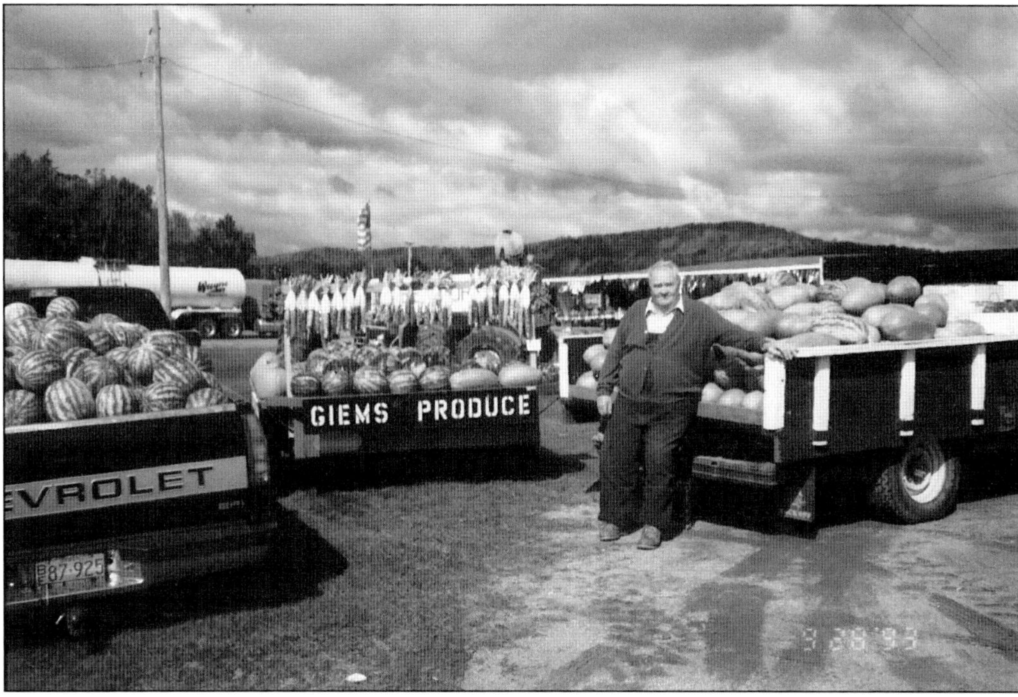

Leo A. Giem stands by the business, Giem's Produce, that he started with his father, Peter Giem. In 1998, the city of Kellogg donated some colorful flags to the stand in recognition of its 69 years of history. It is now one of the oldest landmarks in Kellogg. Leo is married to Rachel Schurhammer, who raised watermelons with her parents, Leo and Alta (Curtis) Schurhammer.

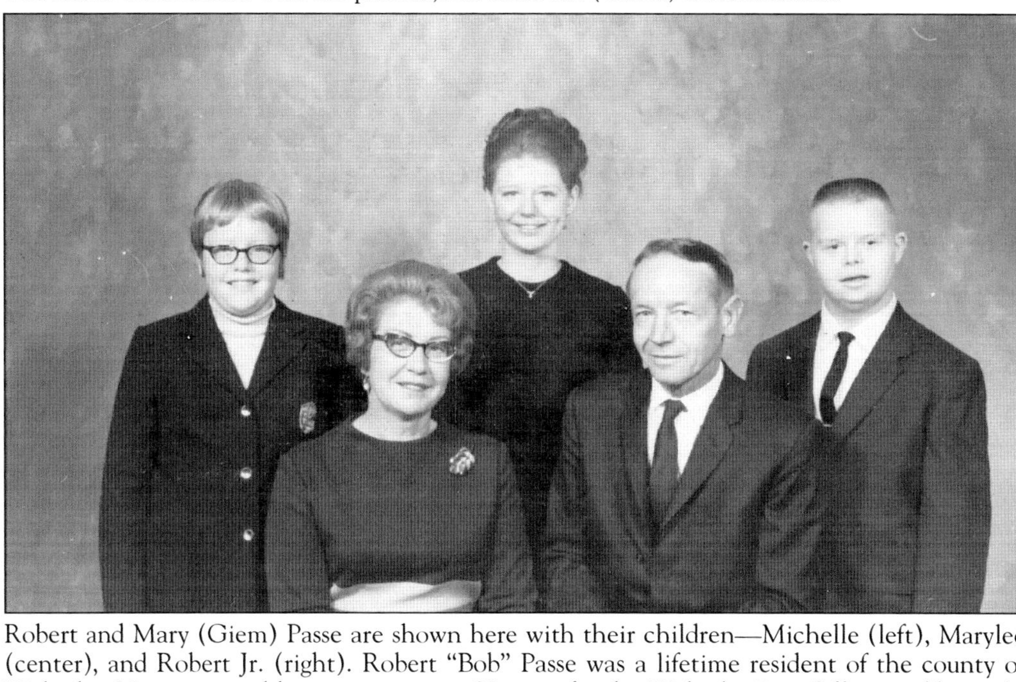

Robert and Mary (Giem) Passe are shown here with their children—Michelle (left), Marylee (center), and Robert Jr. (right). Robert "Bob" Passe was a lifetime resident of the county of Wabasha. He was a rural letter carrier over 32 years for the Wabasha Post Office, and his wife, Mary, served as director of the Wabasha County Civil Defense Program for over 14 years.

Daniel, Kelly, and Greg (the youngest) are the children of Darryl and Laura (Giem) Webster. Their family history in Elgin Township can be traced back to 1856, when their great-great-great-grandfather, Johann C. Giehm, settled there (the "h" in Giehm was dropped when he and his brother came to America).

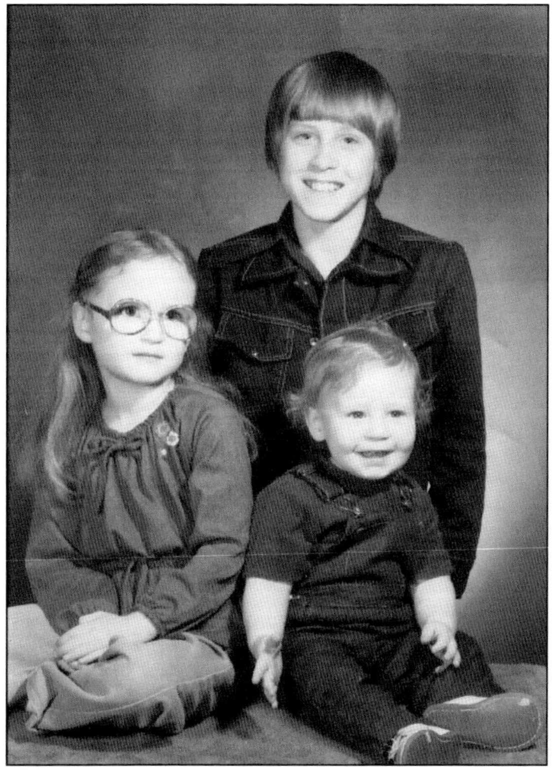

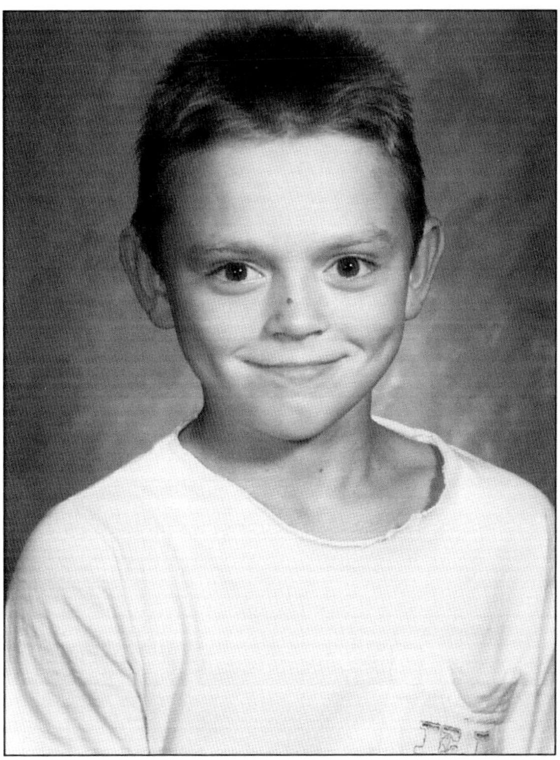

Jared L. Elliott, the son of Harold and Judith (Giem) Elliott, was born in Wabasha at St. Elizabeth Hospital. He attended the Wabasha-Kellogg School and the Galesville-Ettrick-Trempealeau High School in Wisconsin. His grandparents are Leo and Rachel (Schurhammer) Giem and Julia Juanita (Pellett) Elliott, and his step-grandfather is Robert Manka.

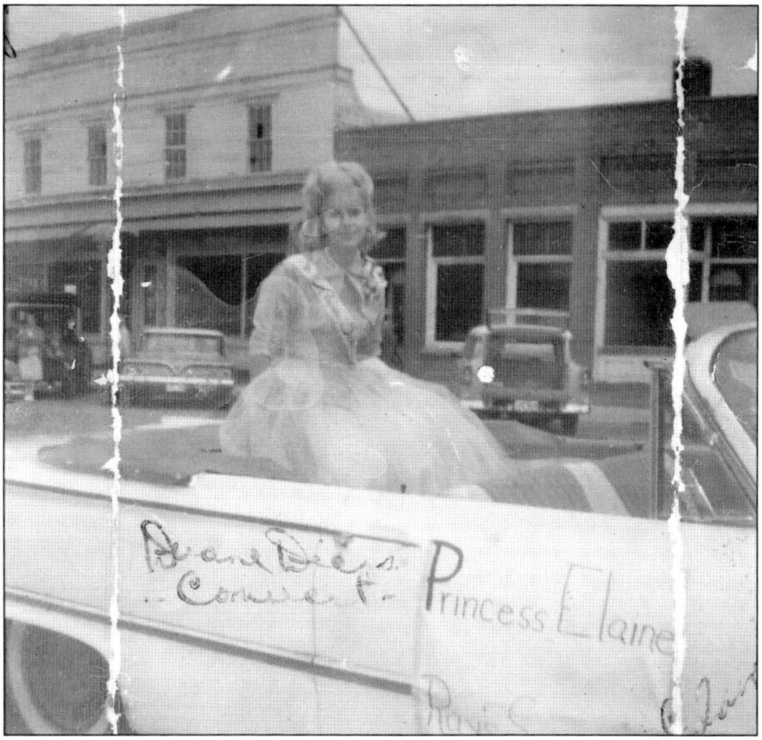

Elaine Kruger is shown here at the 1965 Kellogg Watermelon Festival. Her family has been in Greenfield County, Wabasha County, for over a century, and her mother, Muriel Kruger, had a business for many years in Kellogg. Elaine's brothers and sisters are Sally Hoffman, Bridget Rodrigues, Mary Lou, Allen, Ronald, Albert, David, and John. She married Donald Huth, who also has an extended family history here.

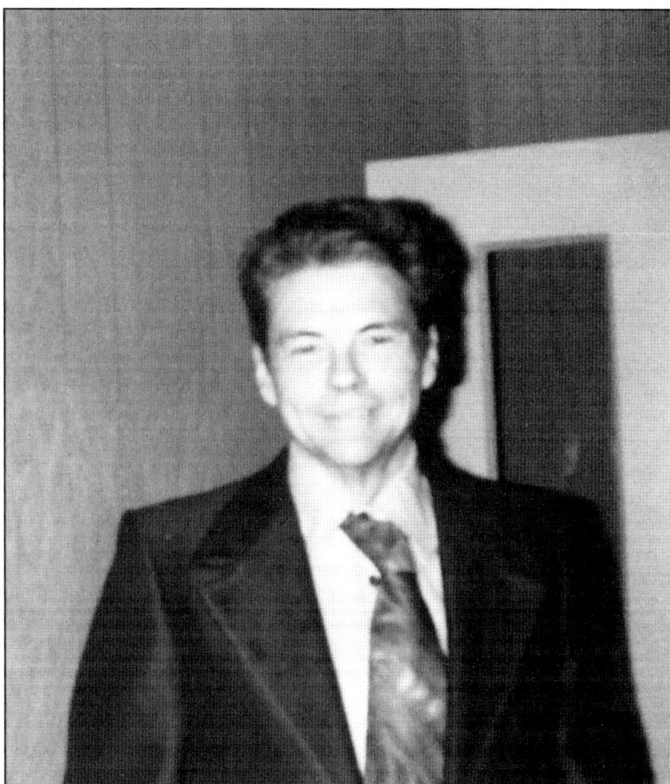

Carl Lindmark's family history goes back to 1775, when Johann Gottlieb Giehm was born in Germany. In 1790 Johann married Dorthea Elizabeth Michael in Konnern, Germany, and the couple had a son, Johann Christian, on September 1, 1803. Johann Jr. eventually came to the United States, first settling in Tuscarawas, OH, where he married Elizabeth Markofer. The two had a son (Jacob) and a daughter (Elizabeth) before Elizabeth Sr. died at a young age. Johann remarried, to Lucinda Brundberg, and moved the family to Wabasha County, MN, in 1855.

James Curtis and Kathleen Ann Middleton were married in Flint, MI, on January 5, 1968, and they had three children—Scott (top), Danny, and Claudene (not pictured). James is a Vietnam veteran. His parents were Donald and Rosemary (Sorenson) Curtis, and he has a brother, Mike Curtis.

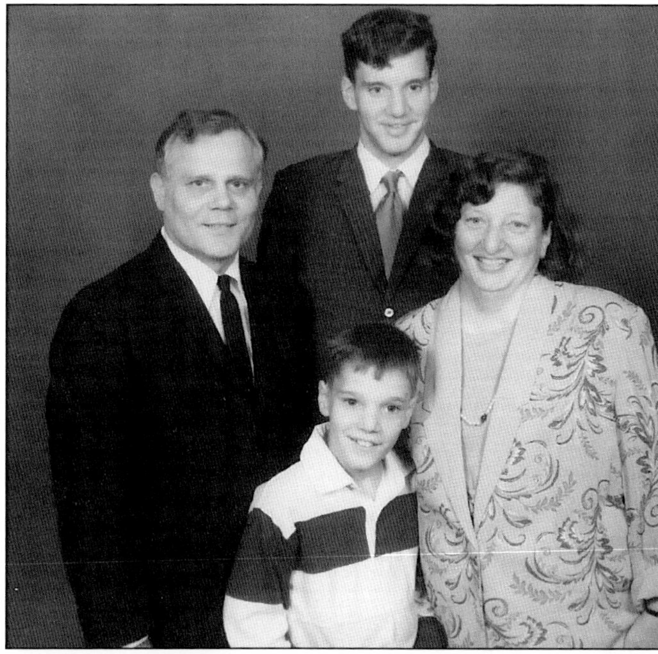

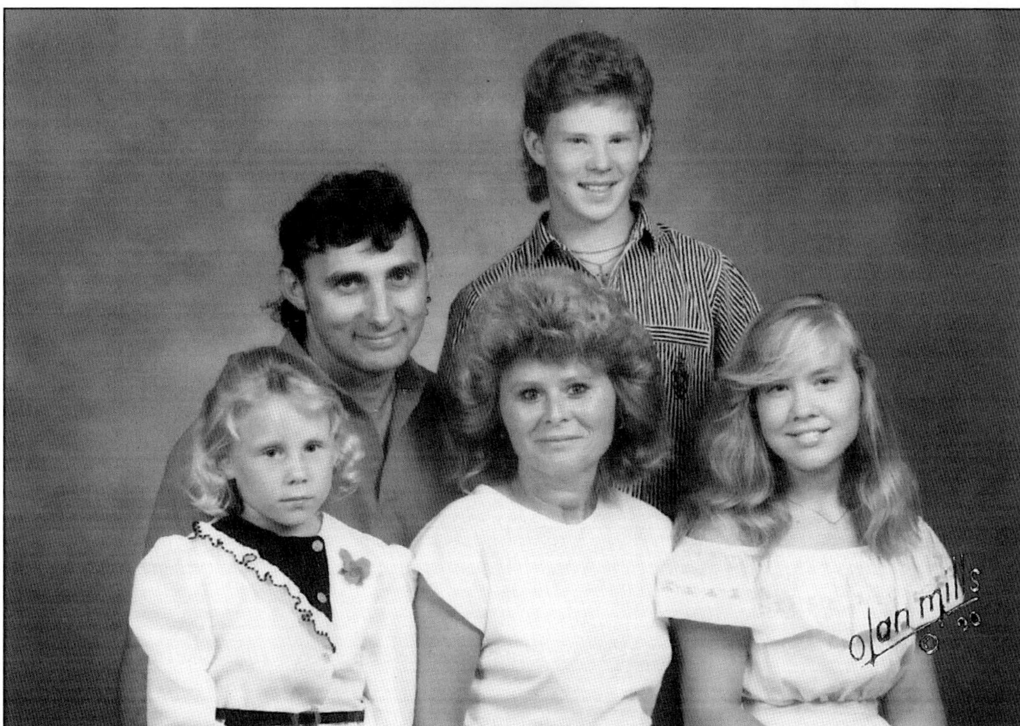

Herman "Butch" and Mary (Giem) Gady are shown here with their daughter Crystal (left), Mary's daughter Tina, and son Peter (Mary's son Dennis is not pictured). Mary was raised in Kellogg, MN, and received her education in the Kellogg Public School and Wabasha High School. Her family history can be traced back to 1852, when two riverboat pilots arrived in Wabasha and built the first hotel here. It was called "Harrell's Exchange."

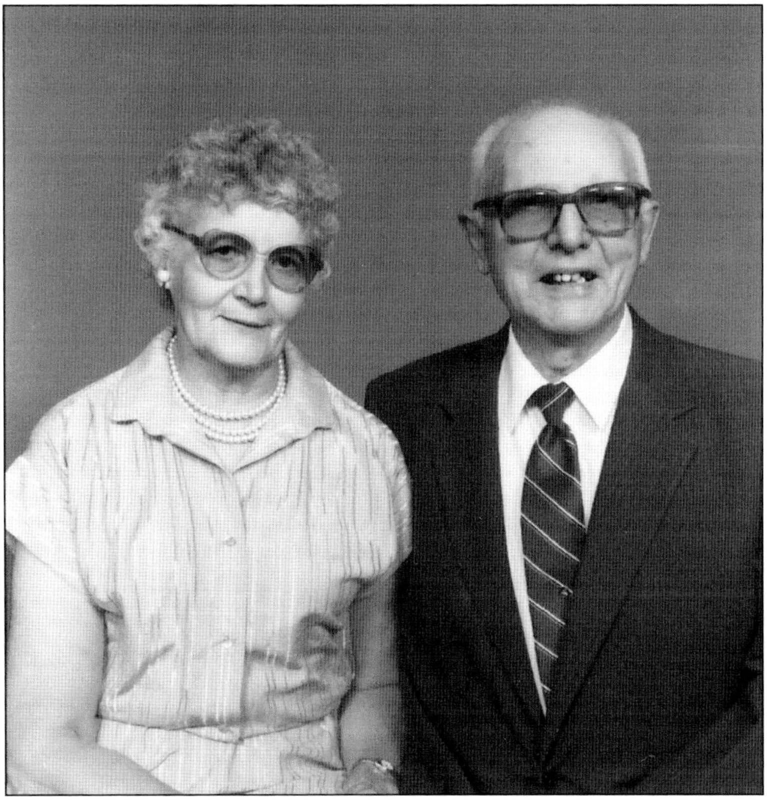

Herbert and Bertha (Evers) Dankwart were married on June 24, 1946, at St. Felix Church in Wabasha. Bertha taught in rural schools for eight years. She was the 10th of August and Augusta (Passe) Evers's 18 children; the others were Leo, Martha Blee, Laura Blee, Agnes Meyer, Marian Goihl, Marcella Larsen, Albertina Eiynck, Clara Graner, Julius, Ervin, Lucille, Lawrence, Harry, Gertrude, Lindgren, Myrtle Hawkins, and Walter.

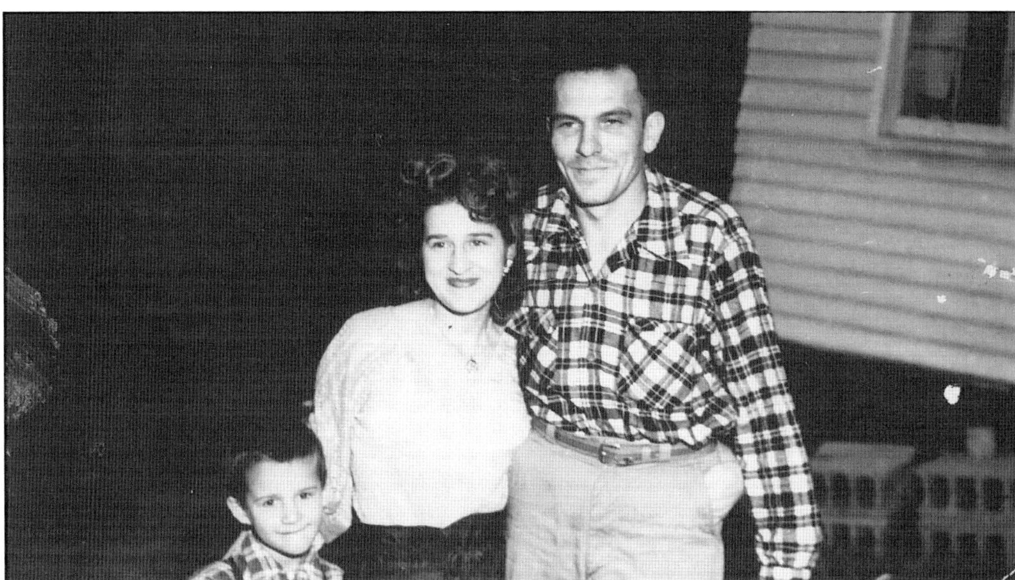

John and Marion (Sagissor) Allen and their son Robert are descendants of early Wabasha County pioneers. John's grandparents are Lorenzo and Laura (Harrell) Curtis. His parents, John and Jessie (Curtis) Allen, had three children—John, Irene (Harold Sivula-Harold Young), and Stanley. They lived in Plainview, MN.

Herbert Danckwart poses with his three-year-old daughter Judy, his dog "Pal," and a baby calf, *c.* 1949. Born in West Albany Township on June 12, 1920, to William and Margaret (Gilles) Danckwart, Herbert had an older brother, Robert, and a younger sister, Margarey. In February 1942 he was inducted in the Army, and he served four years during World War II. He and his wife, Bertha (Evers) Danckwart, had three children (Judy, Diane, and William) and two foster children (Tom and Debbie).

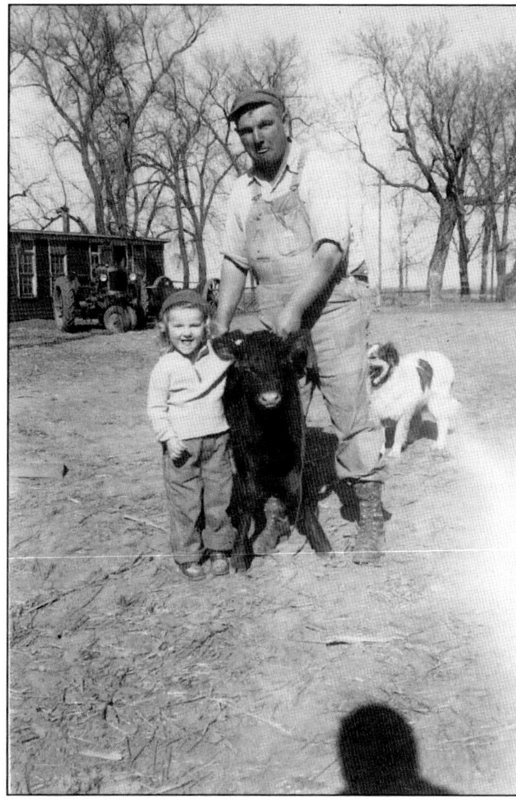

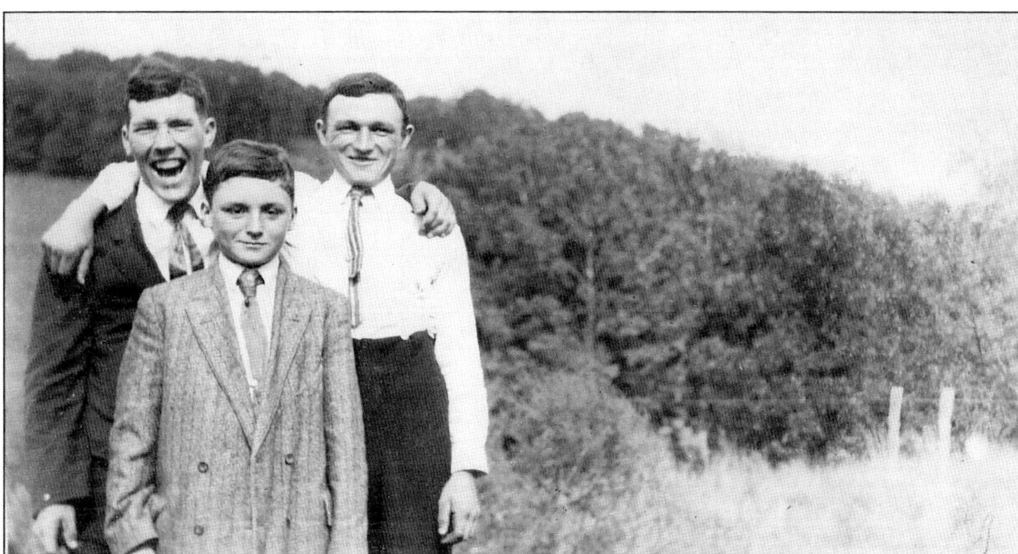

Walter Schurhammer (left), Bartly Buol (center), and Chris Buol (right) pose for a photograph. The Buol family history can be traced back to Switzerland with Christ and Katherine (Loitscher) Buol. They had seven children—Peter, Bartley, John, Andrew, Barbara, Dora, and Valentine. Peter came to America in 1880 and settled in the village of Wabasha. In 1883, he married Louisa Birkly, the daughter of Mr. and Mrs. Lawrence Birckley. Louisa's parents were born in Baden, Germany, came to America in 1856, and settled in Wabasha in 1857.

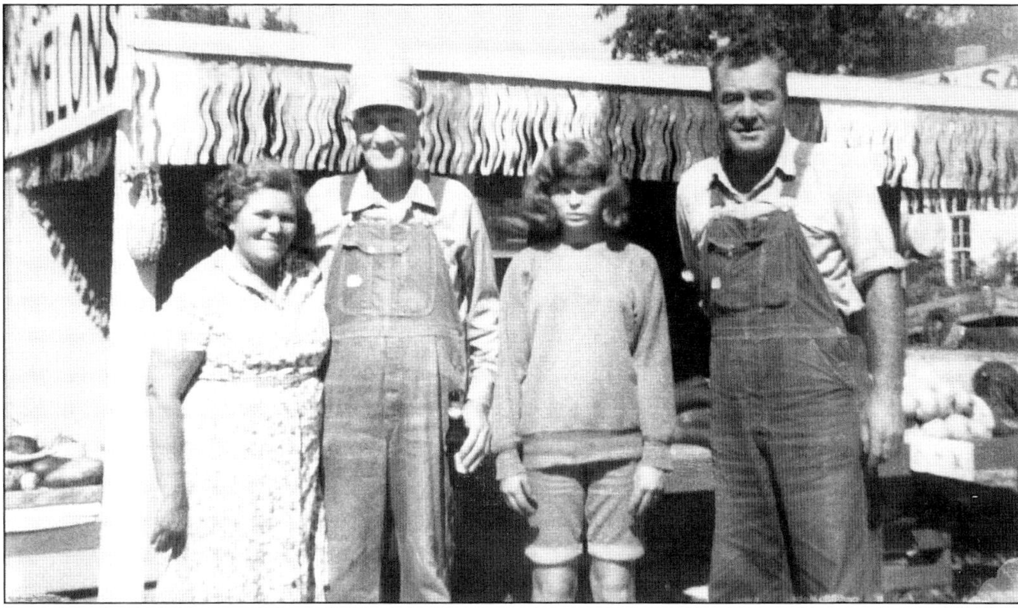

Bill Bennett (second from the left) is pictured here with Rachel and Leo Giem and their daughter Mary. On August 26, 1911, he married Laura Hannawell in Richland Center, WI. In 1921 they moved to Wabasha, and they later moved to Kellogg. The couple had nine children—Buelah Rieck, Dorthea (Sam Jones), Virgil, Dean, William, Hilda (Arthur Schurhammer), Pearl (Ira Putnam), Margaret (Ed Mickels), and Beverly (Quentin Schmitz).

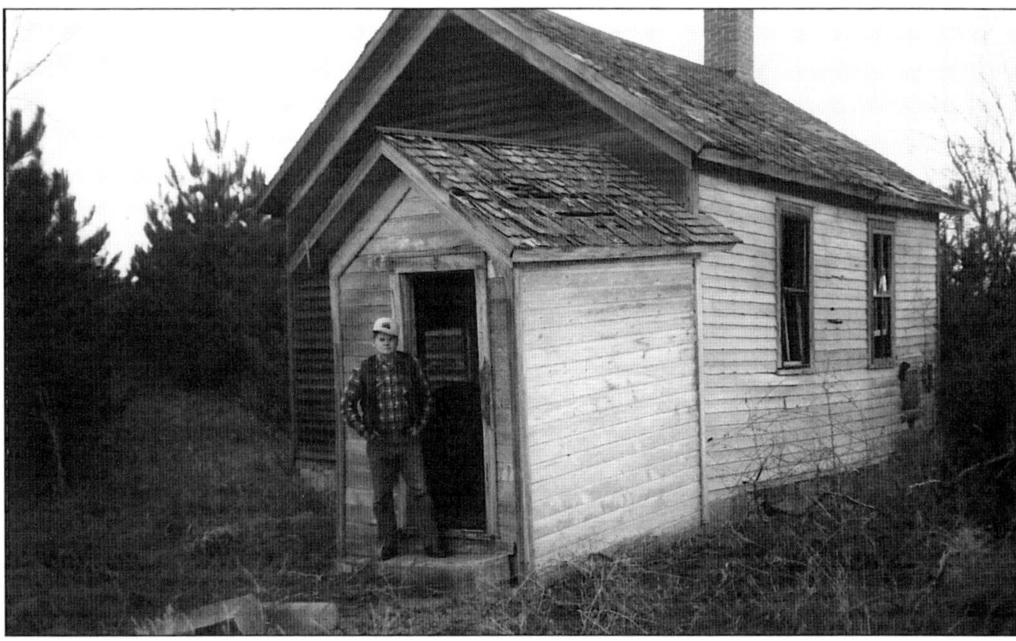

Eugene Lamey stands by the old district schoolhouse in Wabasha County that he attended when he was young. The Lamey's have been in Wabasha County for over a century now, since 1860. It would be nice to see this fixed up with a fresh coat of paint, new windows, etc., to be used as a tourist attraction. However, it probably will be torn down.

Richard Olson and Kay Giem were married in 1964 in Kellogg, and this photo was taken on their 25th wedding anniversary. Kay is the oldest daughter of Leo and Rachel Giem. She received her education in the Kellogg Public School for eight years and graduated from the Wabasha Public School. Richard was born in Arlington, IO, to Mr. and Mrs. Gordon Olson. They have four children—Debbie, Diane, Donna, and David. Their family history goes back over 140 years in Wabasha County.

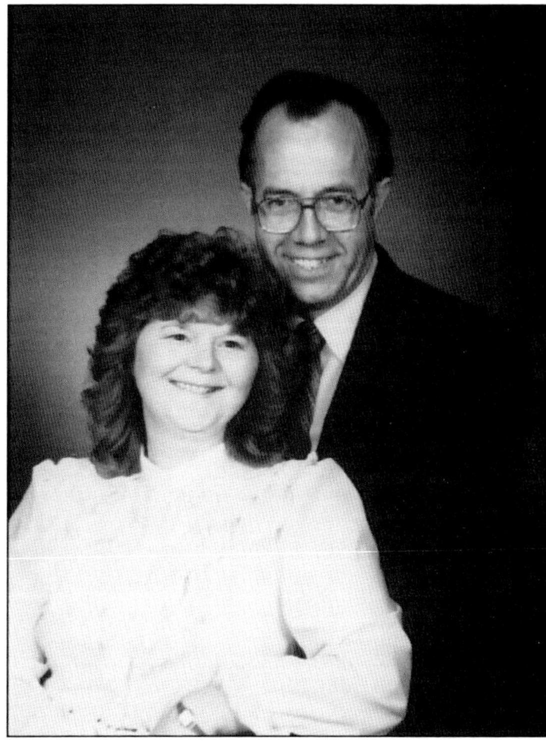

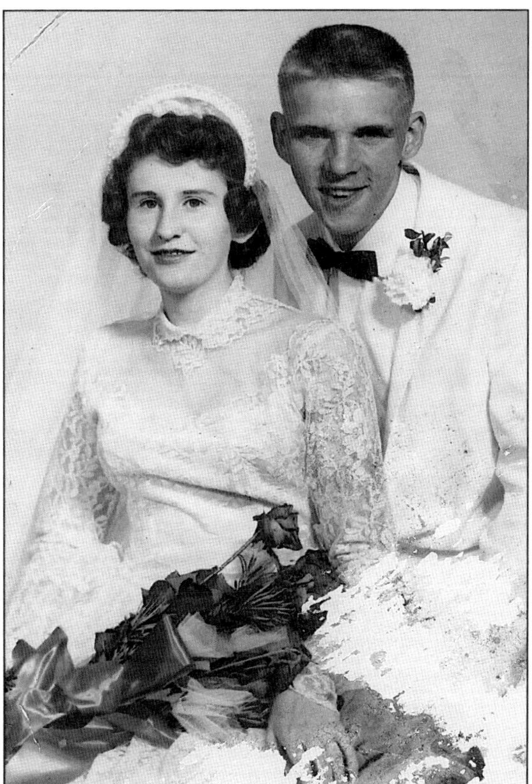

Frank and Ida May (Schurhammer) are shown here on their wedding day. Ida, the daughter of Arthur and Gladys (Pomeroy) Schurhammer, has a family history in Wabasha County that can be traced back to 1855, when her great-great-grandparents, Joseph and Magdelena (Tritschler) Schurhammer, settled here. Frank and Ida had four children—Donald, Diane, Debbie, and Dale.

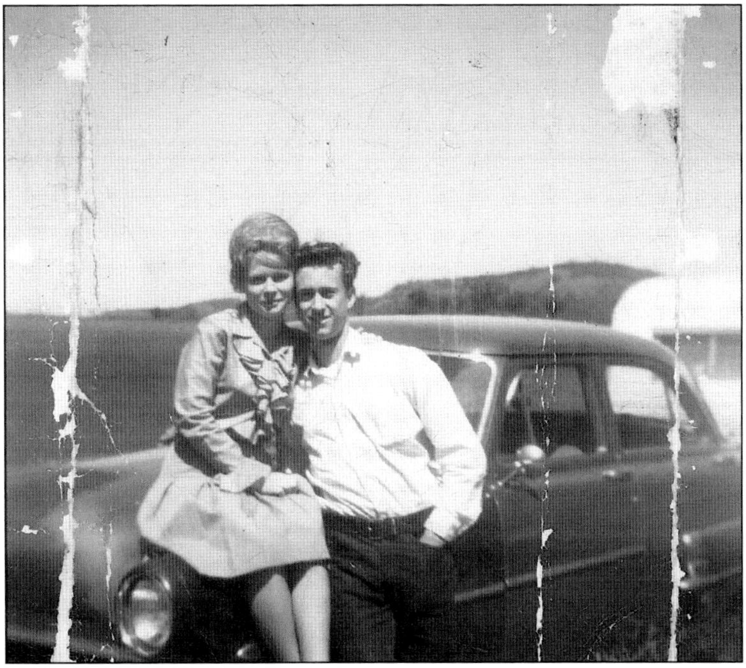

Darryl and Laura (Giem) Webster pose for a photograph in 1964. Laura's family history in Wabasha County began when her great-great-grandfather, George Harrell, and his brother Pembrook arrived in the village of Wabasha in 1852. They erected the first hotel here, which burned in 1858, the same year Minnesota became a state. Darryl's and Laura's children are Danny, Kelly, and Greg. Danny is deceased.

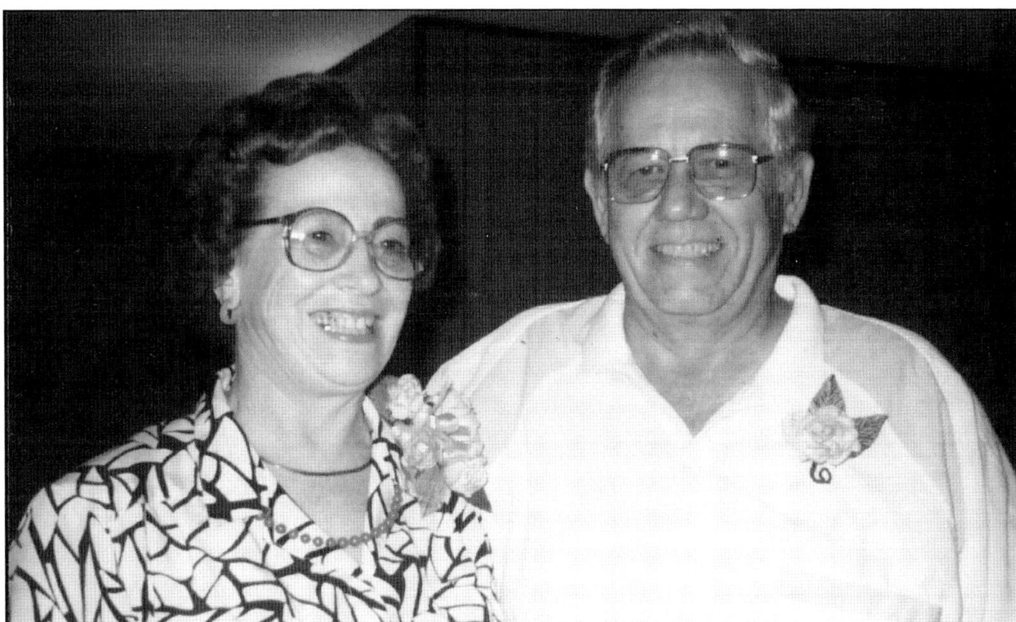

The 40th wedding anniversary of Donald Dahling and Evlyn Copp took place on August 2, 1989. The two were married at St. John's Lutheran Church in Lake City, MN, and have lived in a number of places, including Red Wing, LaCrosse, and Marshfield, WI, before settling in back at Lake City in 1962. Donald was employed by the tire industry and, at one time, owned a small bus route. Evlyn has served on many boards throughout the years and presently is on the Advisory Board for the Public Health, the local Food Shelf Board, and the local Red Cross Board. She is also a volunteer and board member for the local branch of the Lutheran Brotherhood.

Charles T. and Eva Cratte smile for the camera while sailing on Lake Pepin in 1985. Charles was very proud of his ancestry (he was the descendant of Oliver Cratte and Chief Wahpasha II), and was married twice—first to Josephine Havens, who died in 1965, and then to Eva. He had no children from either marriage, but had two siblings: a brother, William, and a sister, Jane (who married Ralph Rice in Wabasha and had three children—Richard, Robert, and Jill). (Courtesy of Gladys (Bootz) Krusmark.)

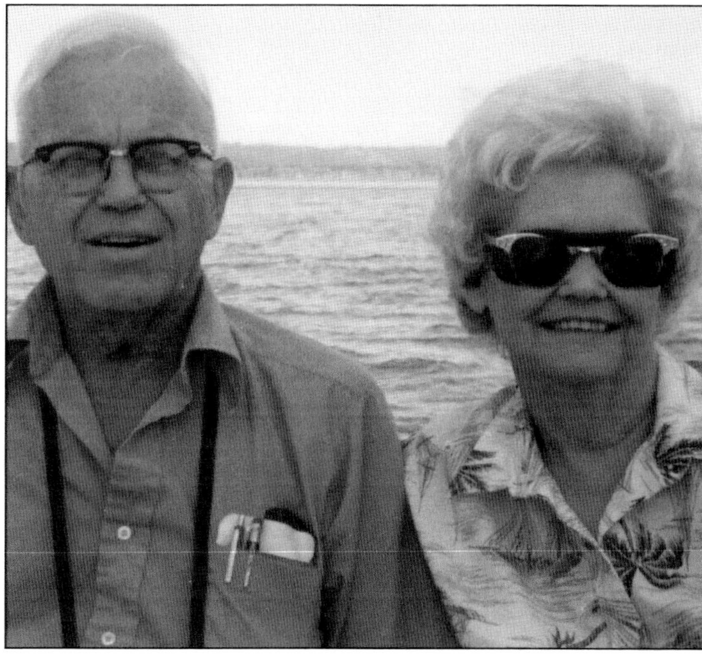

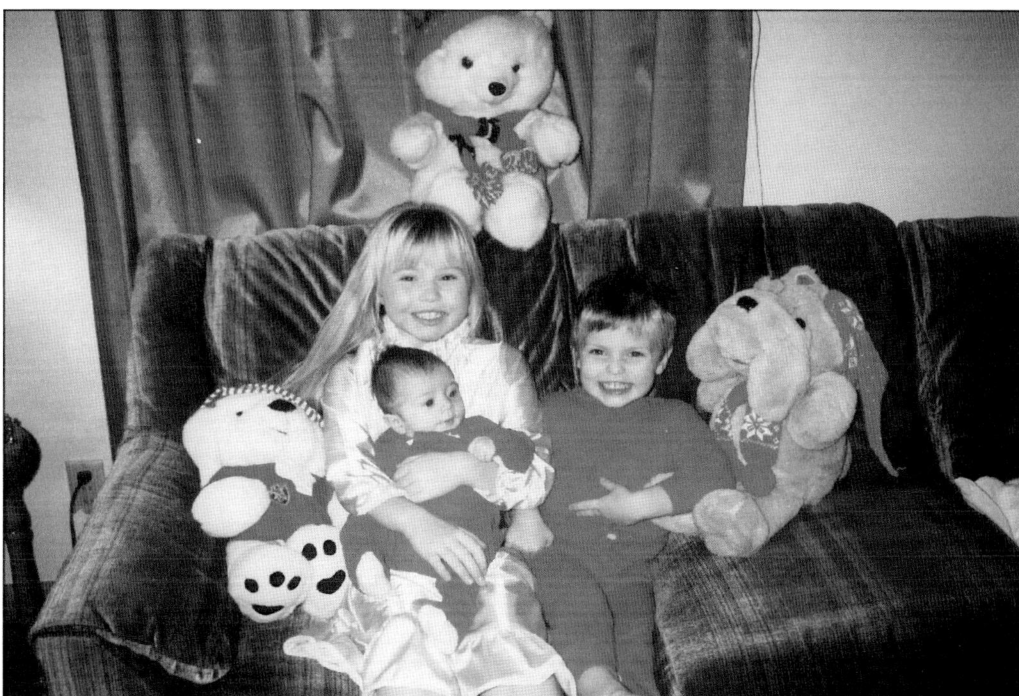

The children of Shawn and Donna (Olson) Duffing, from left to right, are Shauna, Tanner, and baby Trevor. Their family history in Wabasha County, on their mother's side, goes back 124 years now.

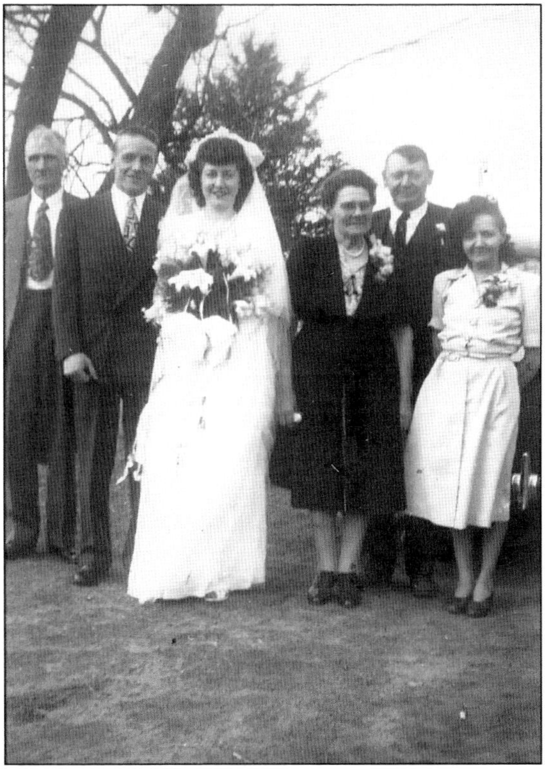

Shown here at the wedding of Robert and Mary (Giem) Passe are, from left to right, Peter Giem, Robert Passe, Mary Passe, Elizabeth Giem, Ben Passe, and Mary (Ender) Passe. The Passe families have lived in Wabasha County for many years. Robert has six brothers—Ray (Darlene Dornack), Harry, James, Daniel, Harold, and Arthur—and is the founder and first president of the Wabasha County Chapter for the Association for Retarded Citizens.

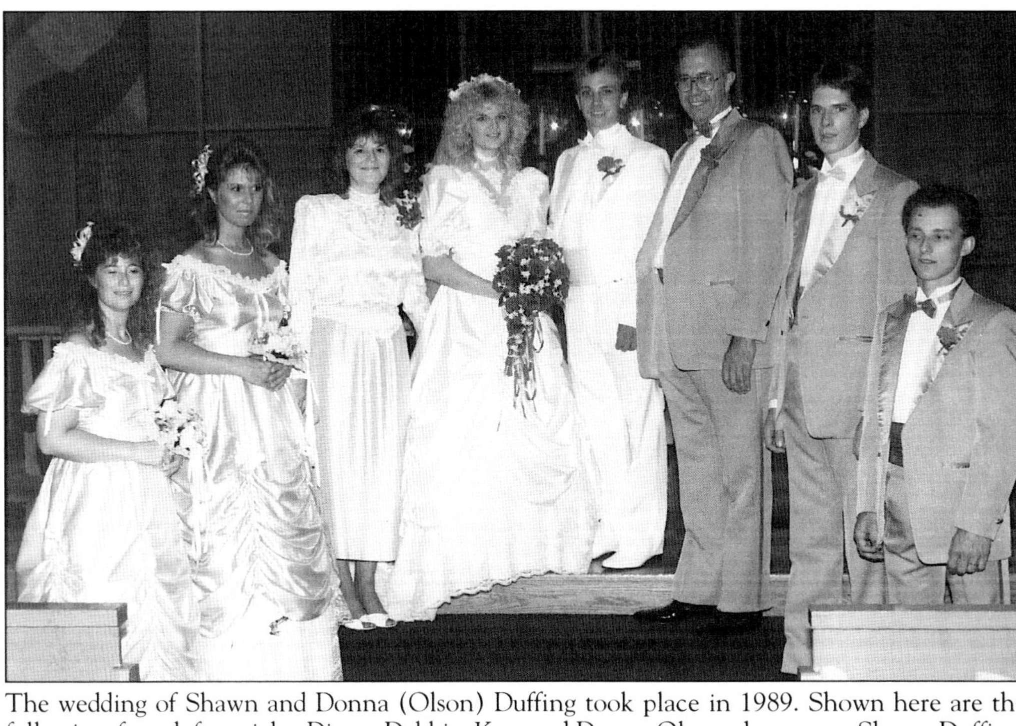

The wedding of Shawn and Donna (Olson) Duffing took place in 1989. Shown here are the following, from left to right: Diane, Debbie, Kay, and Donna Olson; the groom, Shawn Duffing; the bride's father, Richard Olson; David Olson; and Jeff Holland.

Albin "Jake" Konkel and Josephine Giem were married on February 19, 1977. Josephine's parents are Peter and Elizabeth (Leisen) Giem, and Albin's parents are John and Beneana (Ciersan) Konkle. Josephine's first marriage, to Gerald Paine in 1939, produced two children—Janice Balow-Steffen and Virginia (David Marien). (Courtesy of Rachel Giem.)

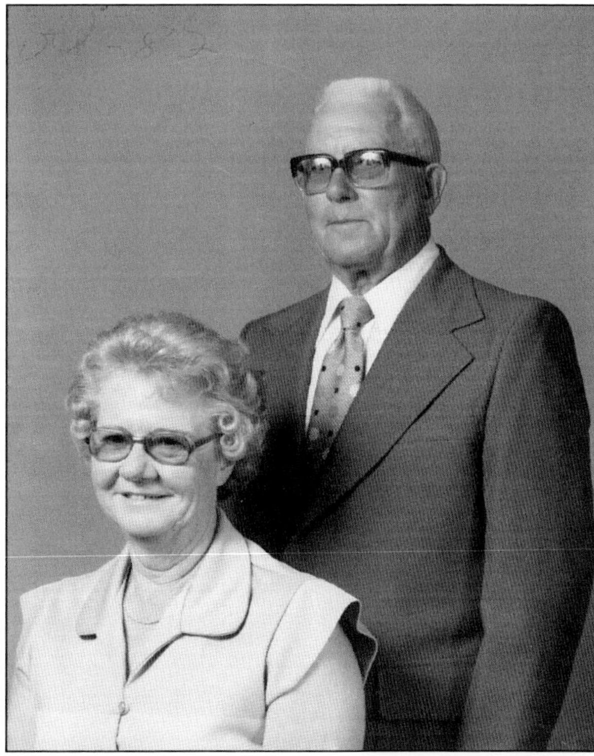

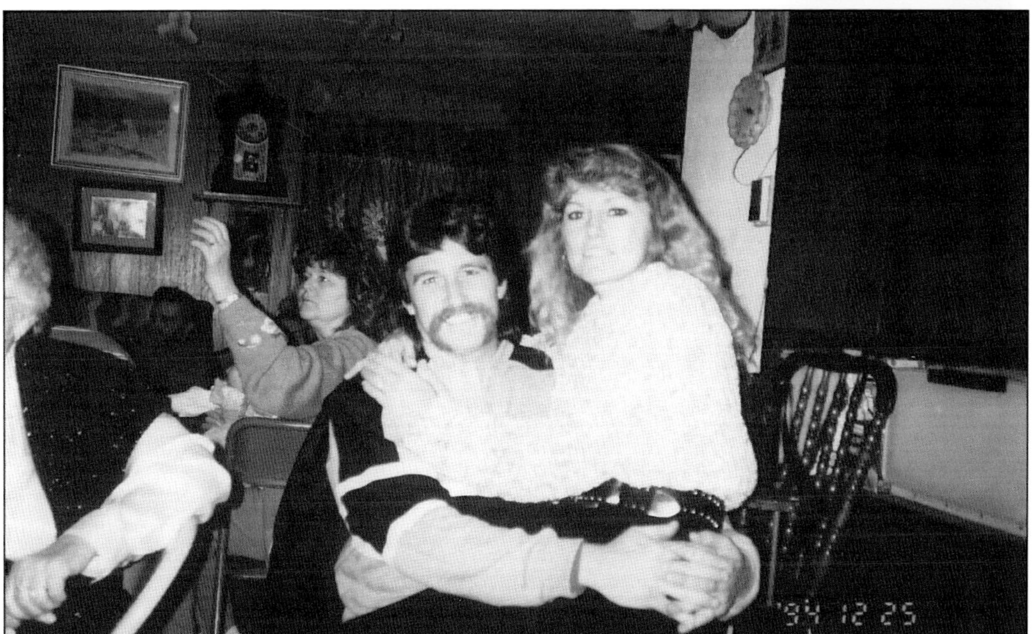

Tom Joyce and Patricia Giem celebrate Christmas in 1994. Patty received her education in the Kellogg and Wabasha Public Schools. She worked in the fields with her father, Leo, raising watermelons, tomatoes, and other produce. Tom and Patty reside in Greenfield Township, Wabasha County.

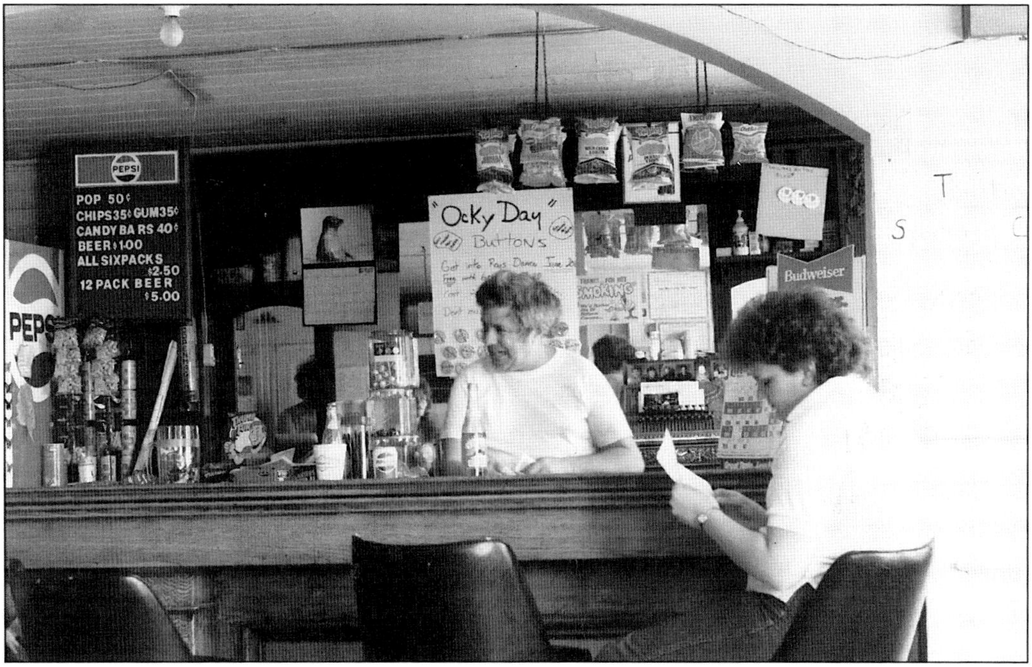

Another descendant of the early pioneers is Mr. Roy Eggenberger of Theilman, MN. This 1986 photo was taken inside Roy's Tavern, where he was born and raised. In 1987 the building was razed and a new one was erected in its place.

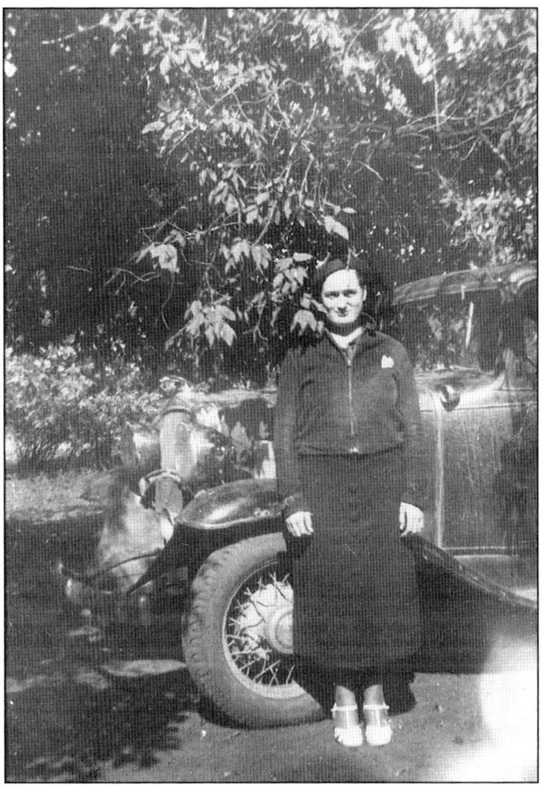

Clara Louise Schurhammer, the daughter of Roy and Charlette Schurhammer, was born in Wabasha County in 1917. She married Ben Yarolimek on February 12, 1951. Her sisters are Berna (Vincent Schwartzhoff) and Marjorie (Joseph Niswander), and her brother Walter (Mary Getschmann) was killed in action in World War I.

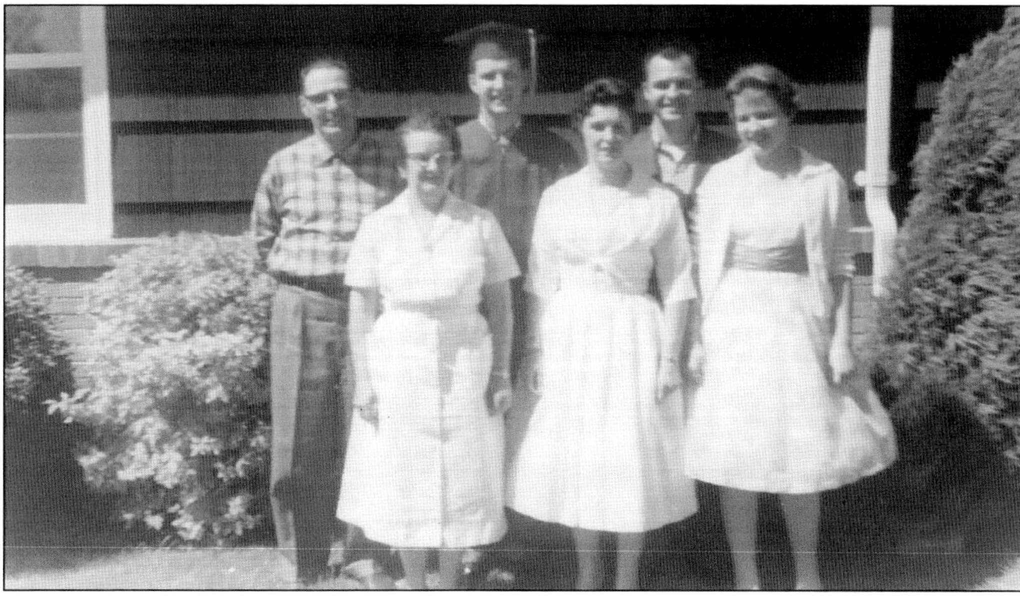

The Larry and Stella (Eischen) Giem family, shown here in 1960, is descended from Wabasha County pioneers. From left to right are Lawrence, Stella, William, Elaine, Clyde, and Sharon. Larry and Stella's son Ronald Lawrence died in 1954.

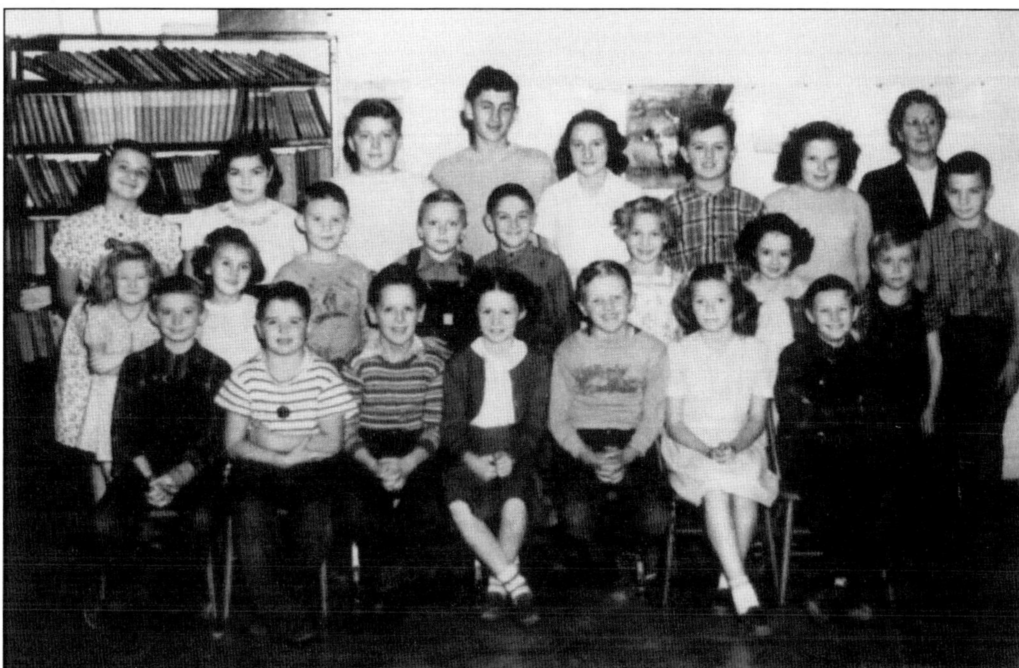

These Minneiska schoolchildren are, from left to right, as follows: (front row) Jim Morey, Bill Schultz, Dave Keller, Janice Paine, Don Peshon, Marilyn Arbuckle, and Walter Martin; (middle row) Joan Morey, Darlene Streich, Jackie Faye, Larry Merchelwitz, Len Husser, Gloria Brueske, Ginger Paine, Dave Merchelwitz, and Roscoe Buresketop; (back row) Greta Heaser, Lois Arbuckle, Jerry Swanson, Joe Hartert, Ellen Martin, Leigh Hartert, and Pat Swanson. Mrs. Gilchrist is the farthest right in the back row.

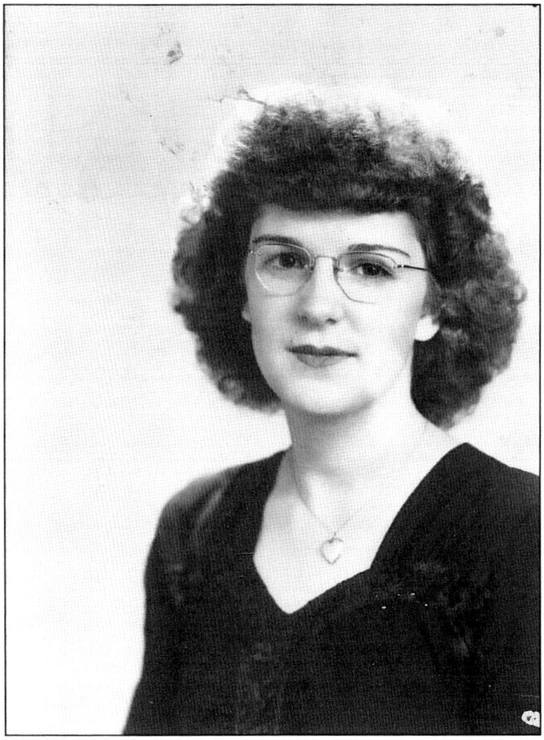

Elaine Mary (Giem) Passe is the daughter of Lawrence and Stella (Eischen) Giem. Giem family history in Wabasha County can be traced back to Johann C. Giehm, who settled here in 1856. Elaine married Mr. George H. Passe and they have two children—Marcia (Robert Krummel) and Jeff (Marion Spychalla). Elaine's brothers and sisters are Ronald, Clyde, William, and Sharon.

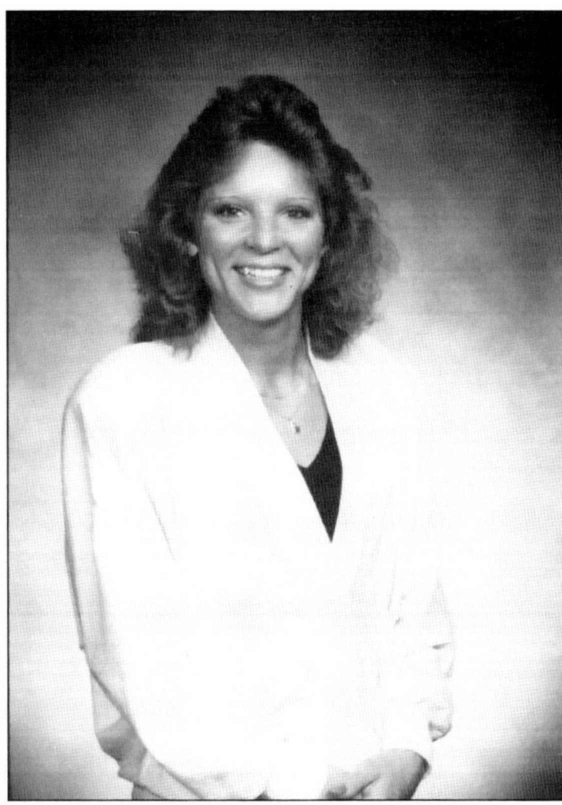

Jane (Giem) Mudder has a rich family history in Wabasha County—all 16 of her great-great-great-grandparents moved here in the early 1800s (two of them died on the journey). Jane lived in St. Paul with her husband, Rick Mudder.

Gerald Peter Giem was born on July 5, 1946, to Leo and Rachel Giem. He attended Kellogg Elementary and Wabasha Public Schools, worked a few years raising watermelons with his father, and eventually moved to Minneapolis, where he was employed by the Columbis Mills Incorporated. He later joined the Army and was trained at Fort Leonard Wood, MO, to fight off night attacks, conduct raids on "enemy" villages, remove booby traps, and set ambushes. He married Diane Irish (a native of Rochester, MN) on June 28, 1969, and they had two children—Angie and Jerry.

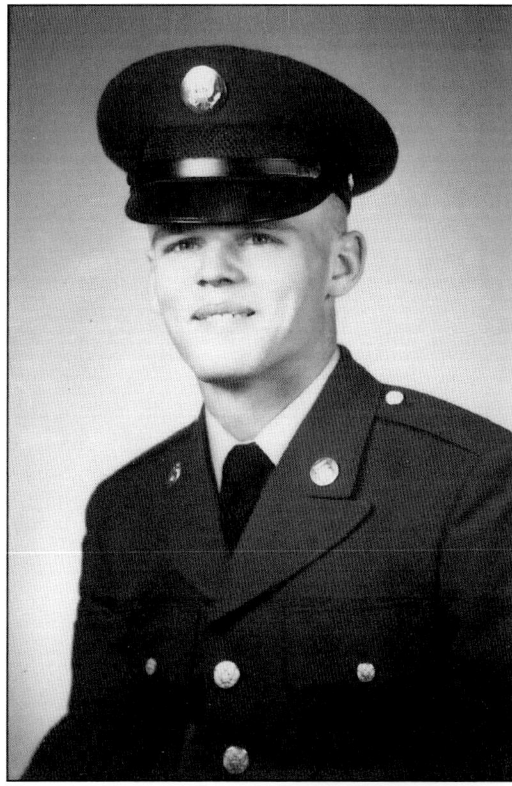

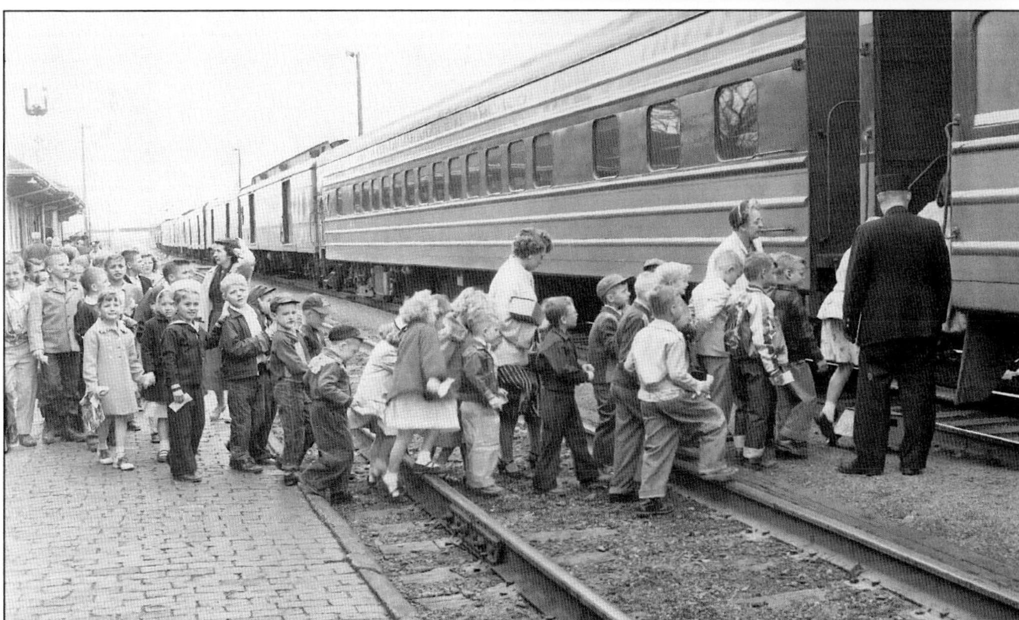

Leona Davidson is taking her third grade class on their first train ride in 1956. They went to Winona on a tour and came back on the scenic dome cars of the Hiawatha. Some of the children are Jerry Giem, Ronald Schouweiler, Larry Peters, Dennis Wayne, Judi Giem, Gerald Lien, JoAnn Deming, and Dennis Hall.

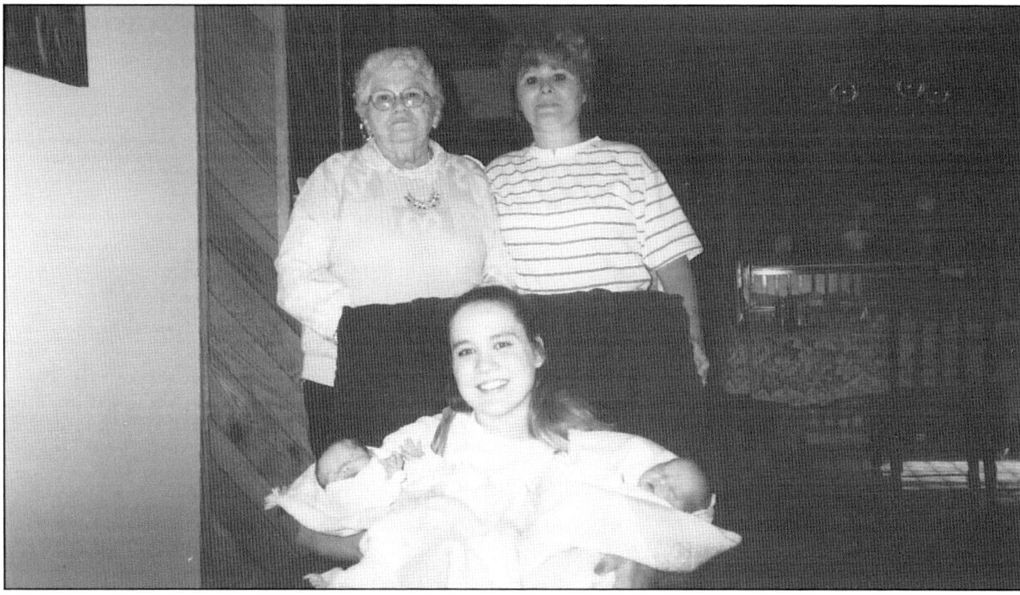

Shown here are, from left to right, as follows: (front) Tina Henderson and twins Kimberly and Samantha; (back) Great-Grandmother Rachel Giem and Grandmother Mary Gady. The image spans four generations, and the twin's family history on their great-grandmother's side can be traced back to 1653 in Germany.

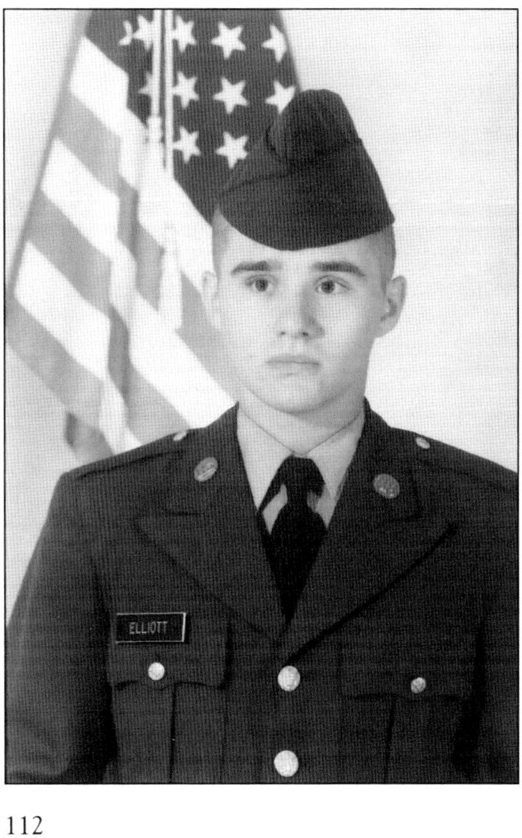

Casey H. Elliott was born in Wabasha, MN. He attended the Wabasha Public School and G.E.T. in Galesville, WI, before entering the Army in November 1993. In June 1994, he went to Fort Leonard, MO, for eight weeks of Basic Infantry Training. On September 26, 1995, he left for the Aberdeen Proving Grounds in Maryland, where he spent five months and three weeks working on tank turrets.

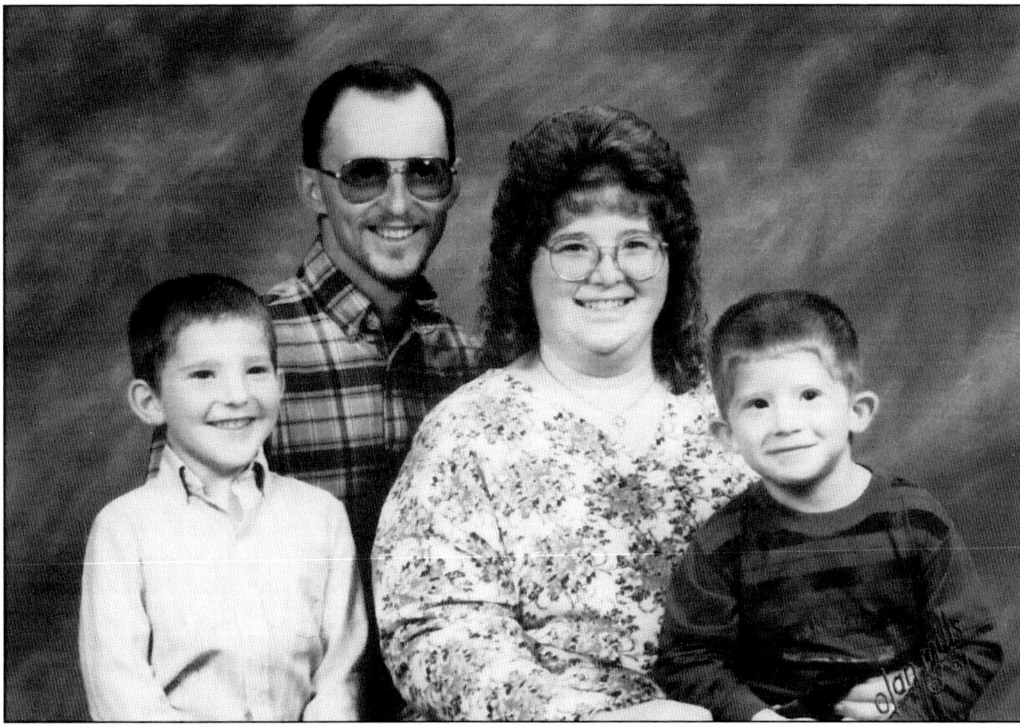

Jeff and Diane (Olson) Holland pose with their sons Jonathan (left) and Joseph (right). The Hollands live in Maden Rock, WI. Diane's family history in Wabasha County can be traced back for over 100 years. She is the daughter of Richard and Kay (Giem) Olson.

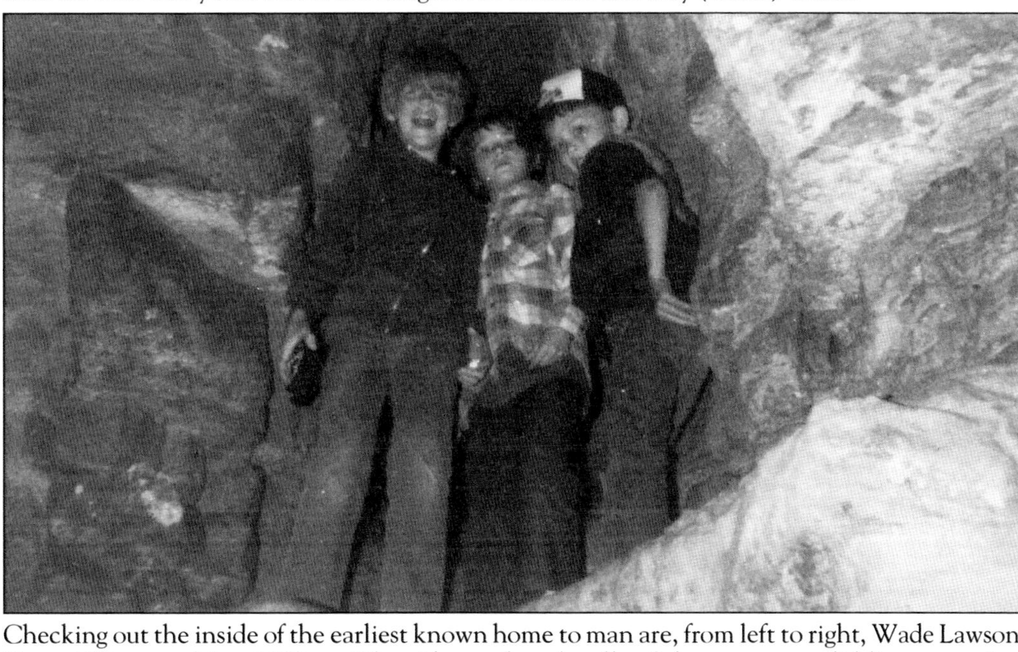

Checking out the inside of the earliest known home to man are, from left to right, Wade Lawson, Casey Elliott, and Jared Elliott. The side, roof, and walls of the cave are solid limestone. Just beyond it is Trout Brook, which empties into the Zumbro River. The boys enjoyed "getting wet" in the brook after this photo was taken in 1986.

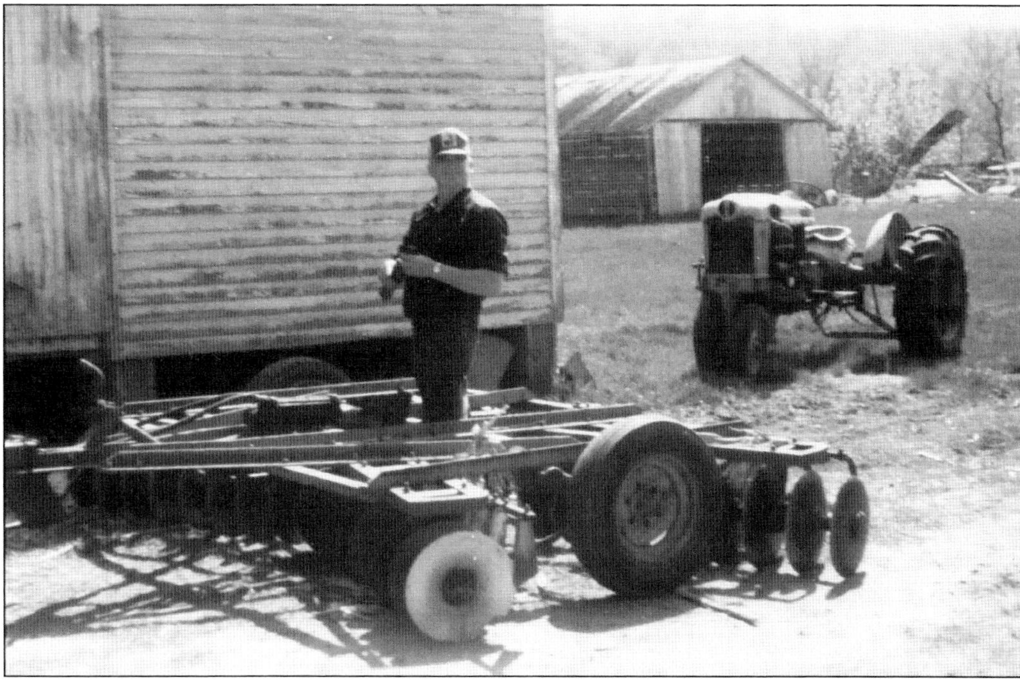

Fritz Dose is getting ready to plow in Mazeppa Township. Dose families have lived in Wabasha County for many years. The famous "Mazeppa Cave" is right across the road from Fritz's residence.

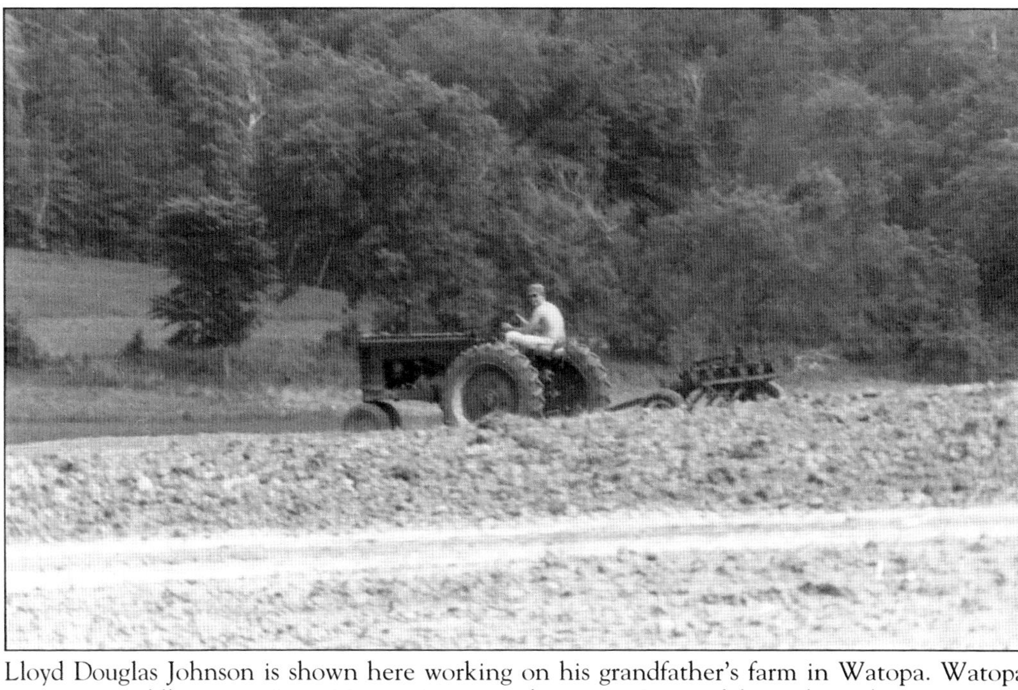

Lloyd Douglas Johnson is shown here working on his grandfather's farm in Watopa. Watopa means "to paddle a canoe" in a Native American language. Some of the early settlers in Watopa were John Gage, Frank Gage, Andrew Johnson, and Nels Westling. Lloyd's grandfather, Lloyd A., owned and operated the Johnson Sawmill in Weaver.

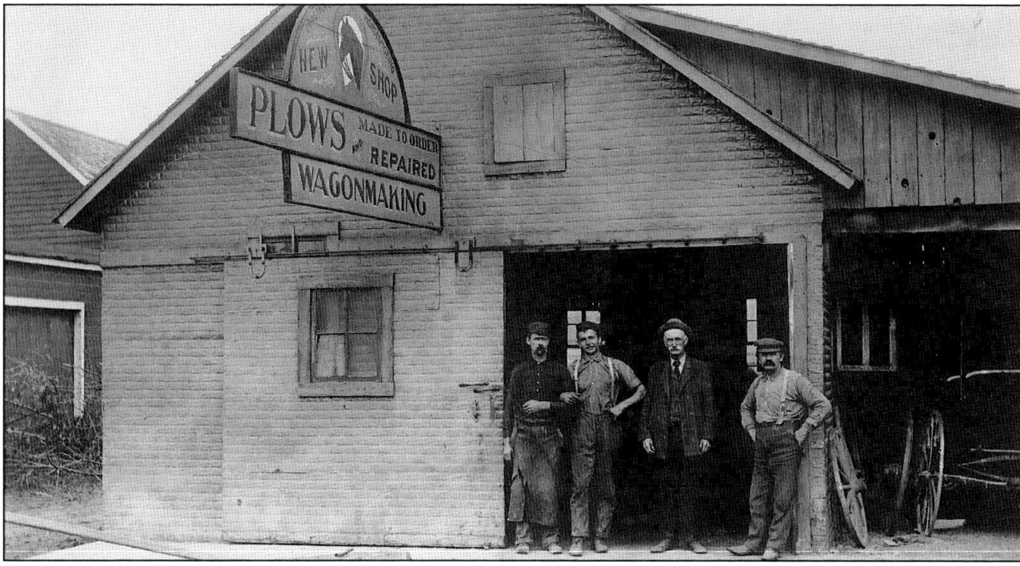

From left to right are William Hanson, Tony Trottner, George Hayes, and an unidentified man. This building was located on Alleghany Street in Wabasha near the library. It was owned by Tony Trottner, and was used as a blacksmith and machine shop. Tony married Helen Welp in 1912 at the St. Felix Church.

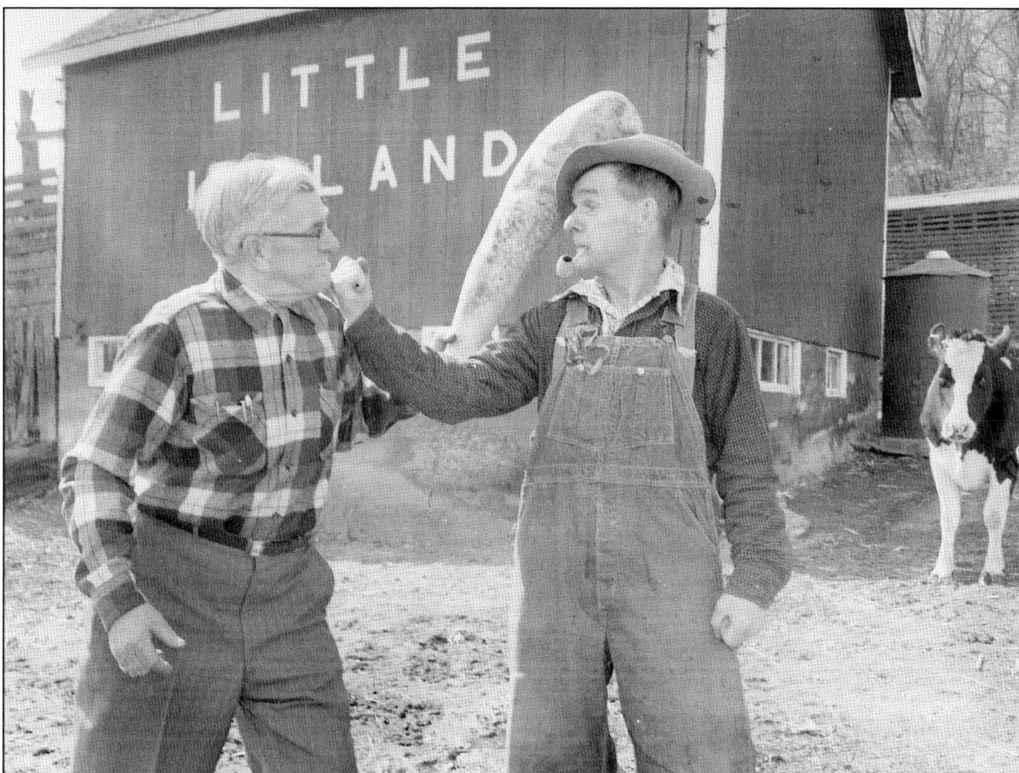

Ray (left) and Elmer Hall are shown here on March 17, 1957, on Elmer's farm, "Little Ireland," located in Greenfield Township.

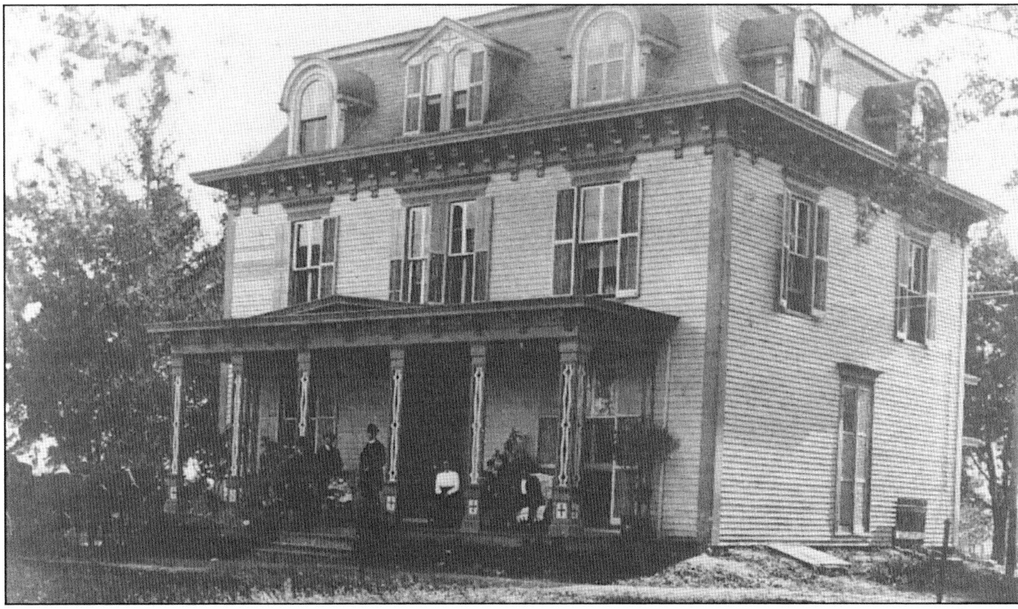

Dr. Francis H. Milligan came to Wabasha in 1853 as a practicing physician. He bought this residence, built on the site of a French fort, from Judge John Van Dyke, and after being inspired by the natural beauty of its trees, shrubs, and flowers, he and his wife named it "Fernbank." Following Dr. Milligan's death, the property was sold to Reverend Maximilian Wurst, who turned it into a hospital. The first patient was admitted on July 25, 1898. The site is now the location of St. Elizabeth's Hospital, which Father Koch named in memory of his mother and Mother M. Johann (Elizabeth Ankenbrand).

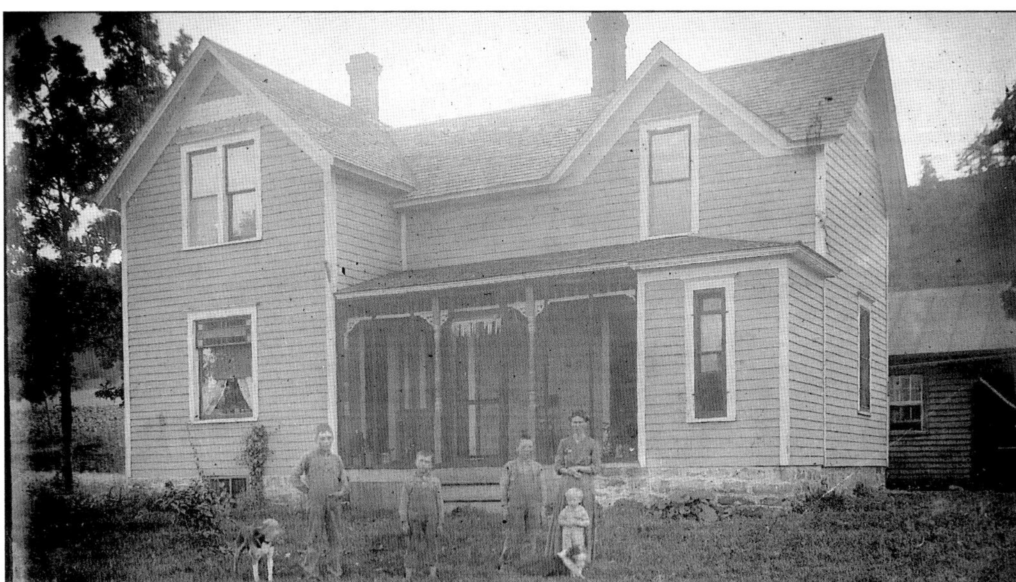

Mrs. Alice (Jackson) Schurhammer and her sons stand next to their homestead, which was originally owned by Thomas and Hannah Walcholtz, the great-grandparents of Gordy and Darlene Schurhammer. The building has been in the Schurhammer family longer than Minnesota has been a state, and is still standing today in Section 9 of Greenfield Township.

Four

BUILDINGS AND THEIR HISTORY

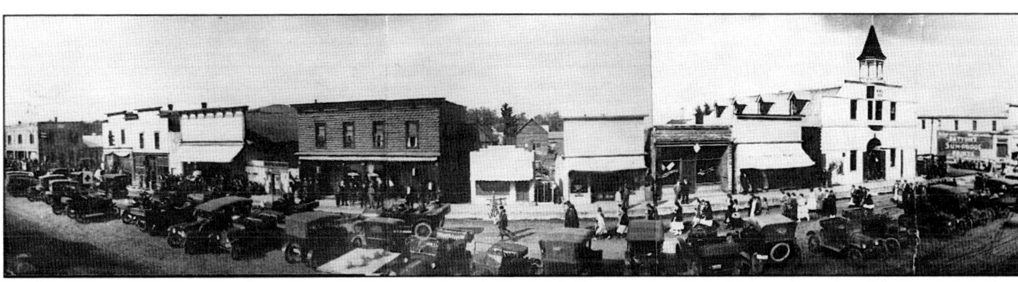

Kellogg had its beginning in 1840, when John Huddleston erected the first building. In 1871, Clement Brass built and opened a hotel, and in the fall of that year John Mealey opened a blacksmith shop nearby. The railroad adopted the name of Kellogg for the station in honor of a Milwaukee gentleman who furnished the station's signs, and the village took the same cognomen. Every September, Kellogg has a watermelon festival (the watermelons are donated by farmers). Some of the farmers who have donated have been members of the Giem, Lien, Lamey, and Kelly families.

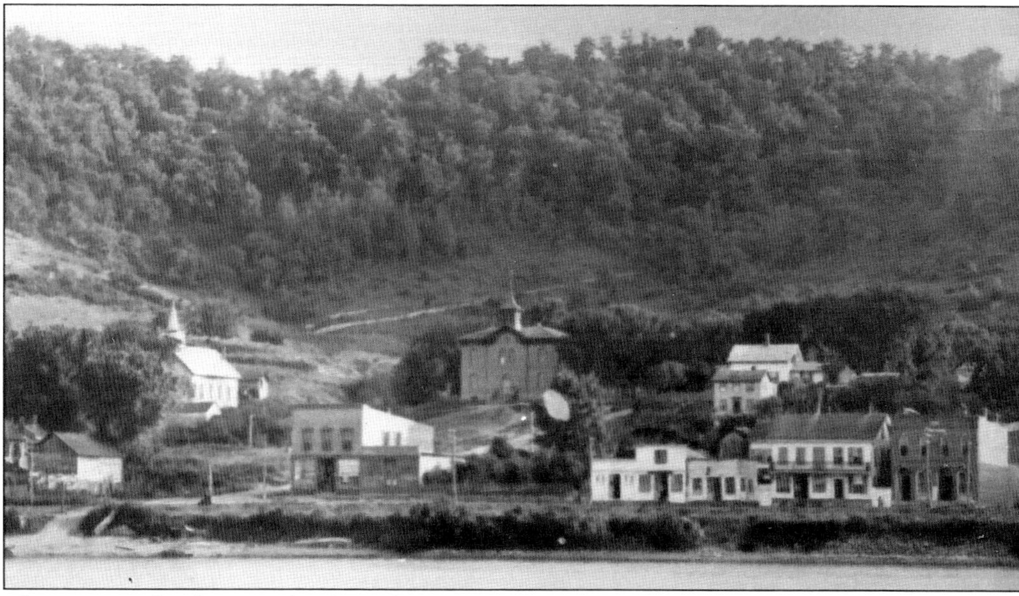

This is an early photograph of Read's Landing in Pepin Township. In 1841, Edward Hudson became the first Englishman to settle here. He erected a warehouse and stored supplies shipped up the Mississippi for the Chippewa Lumber trade. Following his death in 1843, Mrs. Hudson married Louis Rocque and continued the warehouse business, known as "Hudson Landing." John Campbell and his family arrived here in 1843, and in 1847 Charles Read, a trader from Nelson Landing (a steamboat landing across the river in Wisconsin), settled in the area.

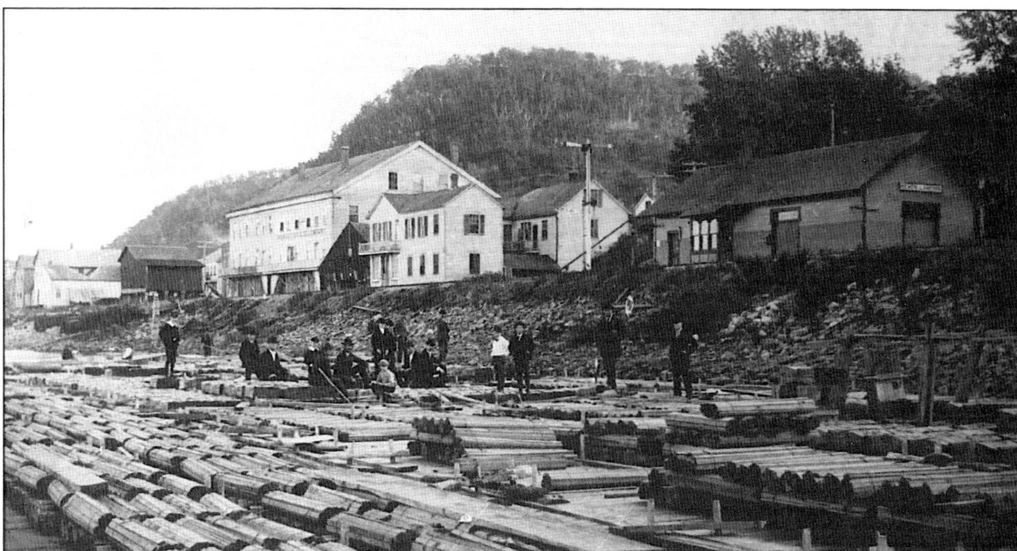

This photograph of lumber rafting in Read's Landing, MN, was taken about 1890. The large building on your left belonged to Knapp, Stout, and Company. The first building on the right is the Chicago, Milwaukee, and St. Paul Railroad Station. The village was incorporated on March 5, 1868, after it became "the largest point of trade on the Upper Mississippi River." This "boom" in business was weakened by the arrival of the railroad at Eau Claire, WI, in 1870, but recovered with a surge with the lumber and logging industry. When this business was lost, incorporation was abandoned.

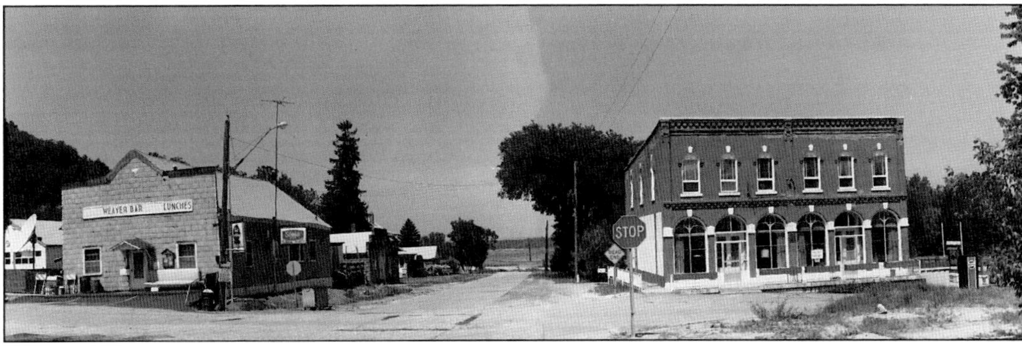

The first settler in Weaver, Minneiska Township, was Andrew Olson, who arrived in his early fifties. He was followed by George and Christopher Abbott. In 1857, William Weaver arrived and bought land from Harriet Bennett. The village of Weaver was laid out on a part of Mr. Weaver's land in 1870. Mr. Weaver erected a hotel and W.H. Hopkins erected a store and was appointed postmaster.

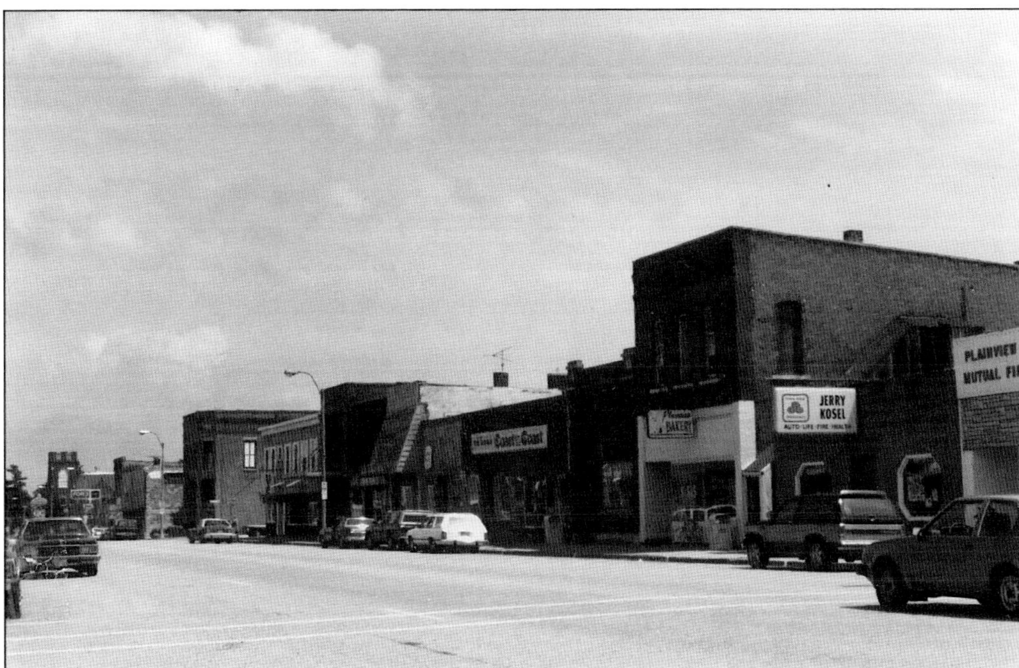

Plainview, MN, is shown here as it looked in 1987. Oliver Olson and Andrew and Christena Helgreen, natives of Norway, settled in Plainview Township in 1854. In the spring of 1855, Ezra and Jane Eddy, General A.T. Sharp, David Campbell, and Thomas Todd arrived. By 1857, this village had been laid out and named Centerville (the name was later changed to Plainview).

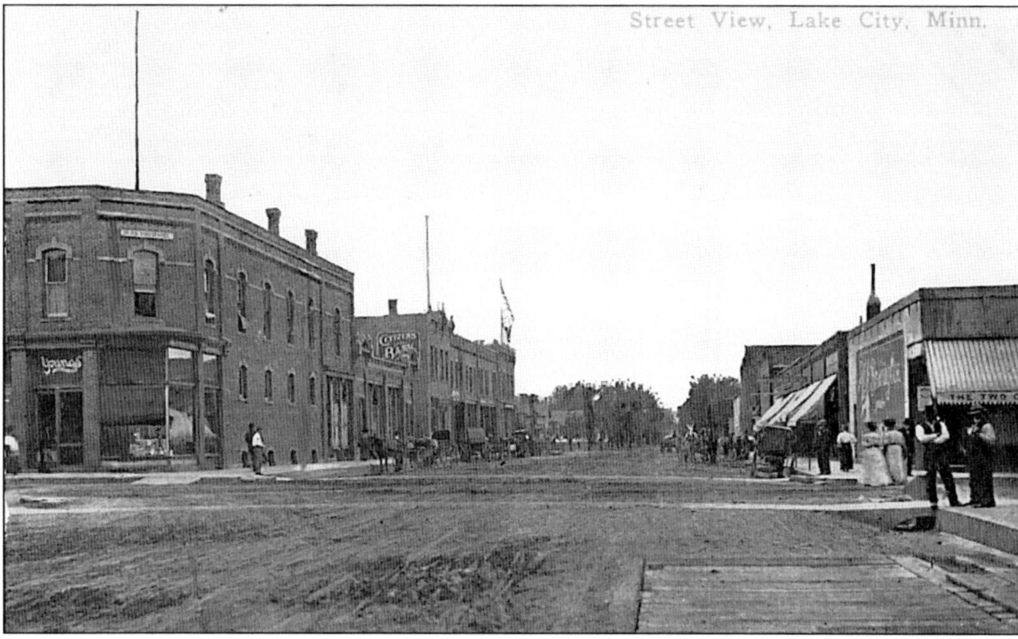

In the autumn of 1853, Jacob Boody arrived in what is known today as Lake City and claimed 328 acres of land. In June 1854, Phillip John Boody (Jacob's brother), Jacob's cousin, and Mr. Abner Dwelle arrived and staked out their claim. Abner Dwelle's claim was in the lower part of Lake City. Patrick Conway and his two sons, James and William, arrived in the month of May. By the spring of 1855, quite a few settlers, including Abner Tibbets, William Berry, Seth Skinner, and Samuel Doughty, had arrived.

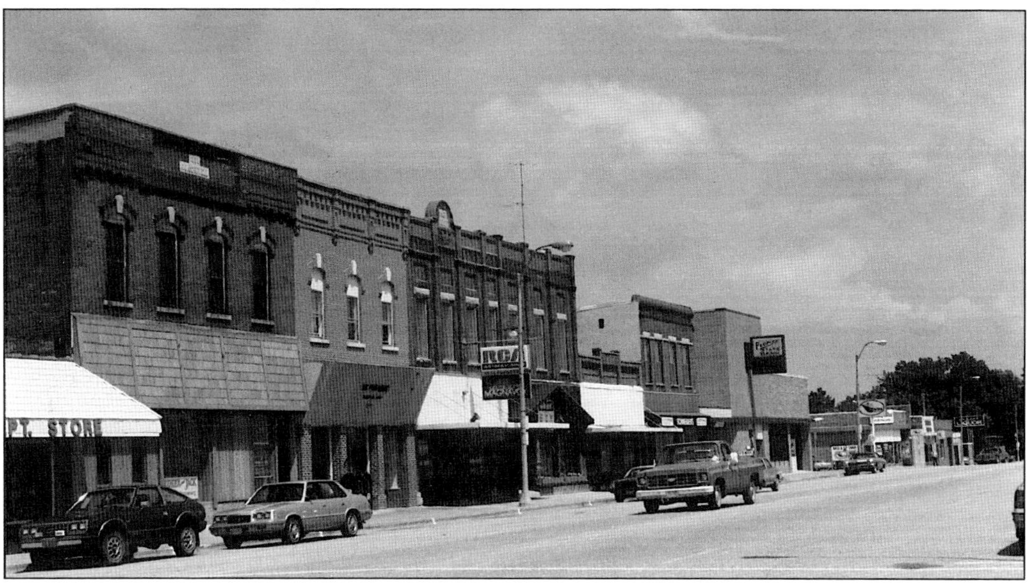

The earliest settlers in Elgin Township were George and Curtis Bryant, H.H. Arthurton, and George Farrar. They arrived April 7, 1855, and took claims upon Sections 27, 28, and 34. In May 1855, Leonard Laird and E.L. Clapp and his family arrived. Mrs. Clapp was the first female in this township. Other early settlers included Henry Stanchfield, Bryon Glines, Irving Rollins, and August William Giem.

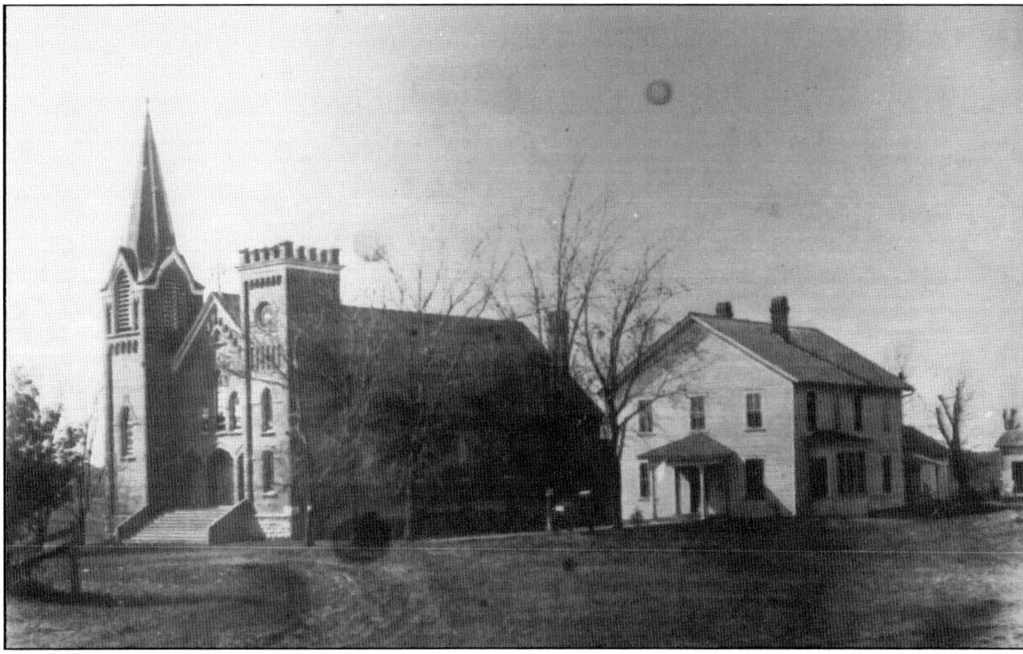

The first Catholic services in the town of Conception, located in Highland Township, were held at Mrs. Timothy Ryan's residence. In 1865, a church building was constructed on the former site of Mrs. Ryan's house. The building was enlarged in 1866 by Father James Trobec, the pastor at Wabasha, who at the time had charge of Conception. The parsonage cost $1,600 to build in 1881 and stood across the street from the church, which was eventually named Immaculate Conception. The cemetery, called St. Peter and Paul's, was donated by Mrs. Ryan. The other religious denominations in town held their services in the log schoolhouse.

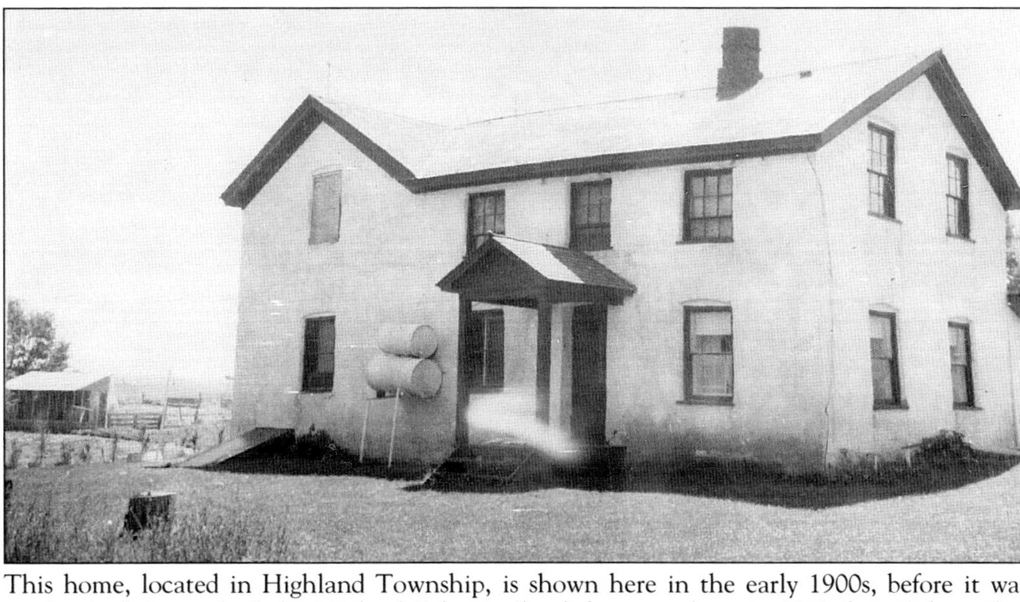

This home, located in Highland Township, is shown here in the early 1900s, before it was modernized. It was built by Michael Schouweiler (who came here in 1856 from Schoweiler, Luxembourg), and was always referred to in the family as "the old stone house" in Conception. It is now owned by John Eversman.

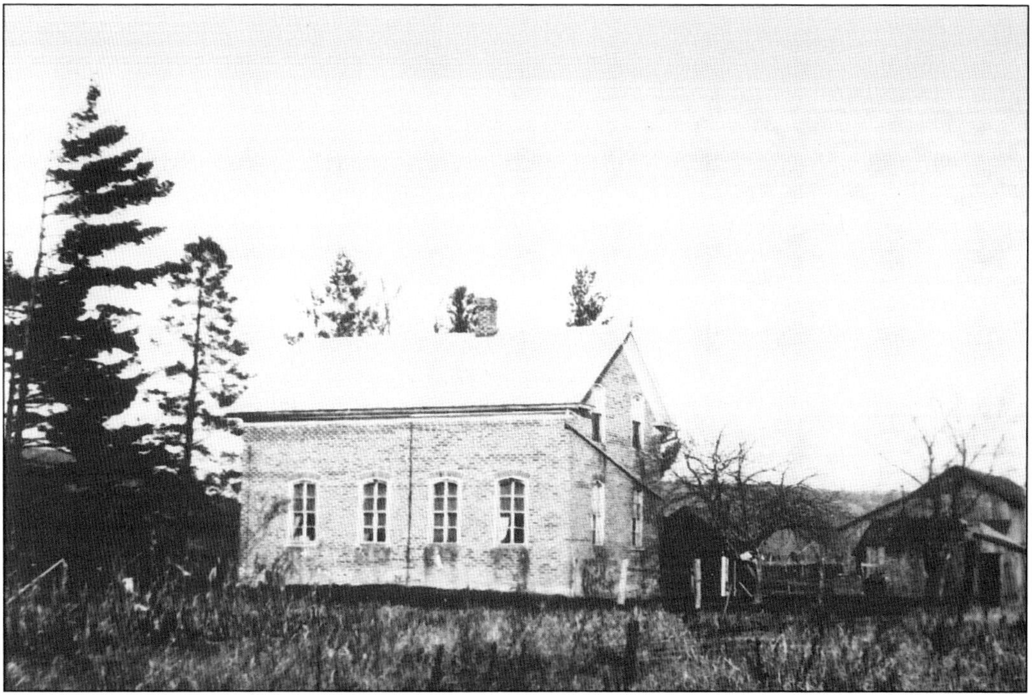

This house was built in the 1860s by Thomas Hellinger in Glasgow Township near Dumfries. Glasgow Township is named in honor of the city of Glasgow, Scotland. The first settlers—Charles Foreman, Hugh McGowan, William McCracken, Hugh and Robert Cochrane, and a few others—arrived here in 1855.

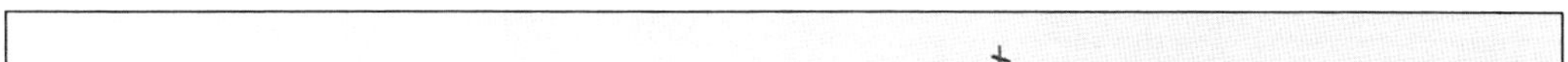

St. Patricks, the wonderful limestone church located in West Albany Township, was erected in 1875 from a quarry across the highway. The rectory was built in 1882. The first marriage took place between J. Ryan and Elizabeth Hayes, and the first funeral was for Patrick McCulligan. The church is famous for six murals painted on its vaulted ceilings by artists Anton Gag, Christian Heller, and Alex Schwendinger.

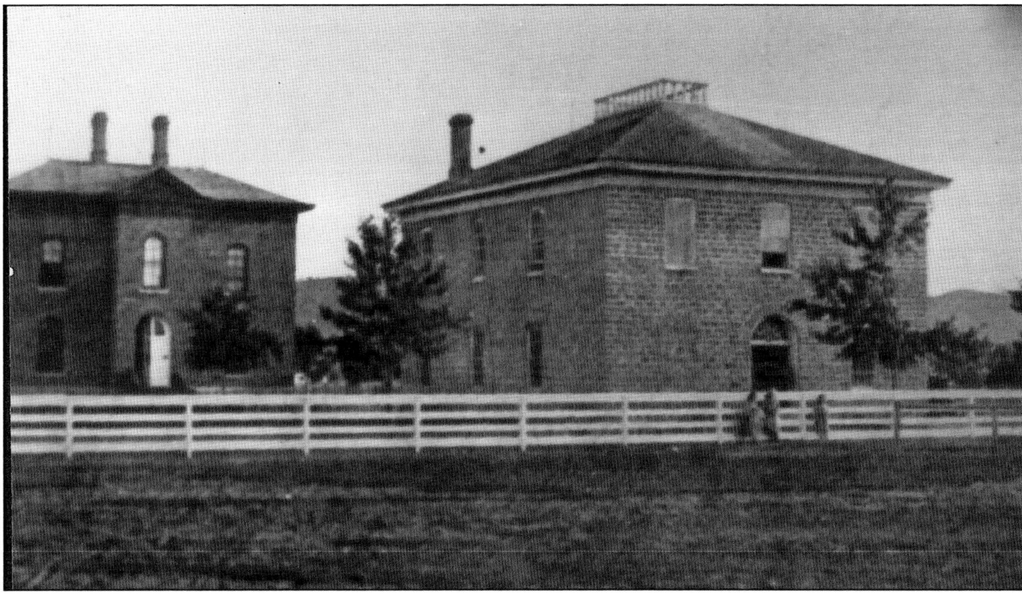

This is the earliest known photo of the Wabasha County Jail (the building on the left), which was erected in 1871 at a cost of $25,000. The building on the right was the old courthouse; the new courthouse was built in 1891. The jail had cells to accommodate 25 inmates, and also sported an attached residence for the sheriff and his family. In 1853, Levi Murphy officially became the first sheriff in Wabasha.

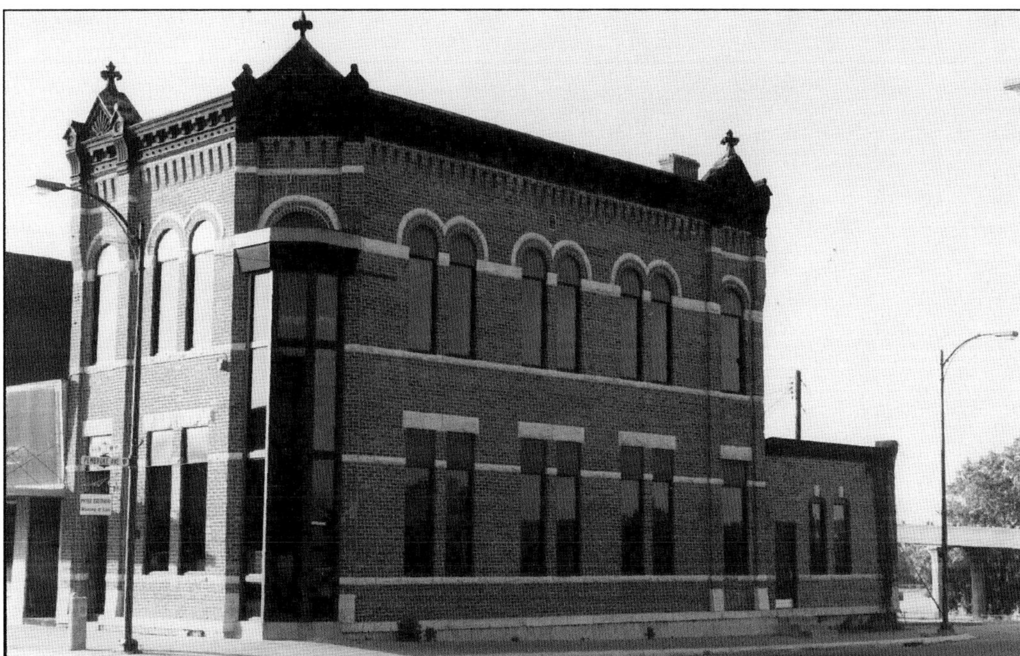

The People's State Bank was erected in 1886 at a cost of $7,500. The business commenced on February 15, 1887, on the corner of Main and Pembrook Streets, and it featured a large Hall's burglar-and-fireproof safe with an automatic time lock attachment. It is now a law office and radio station.

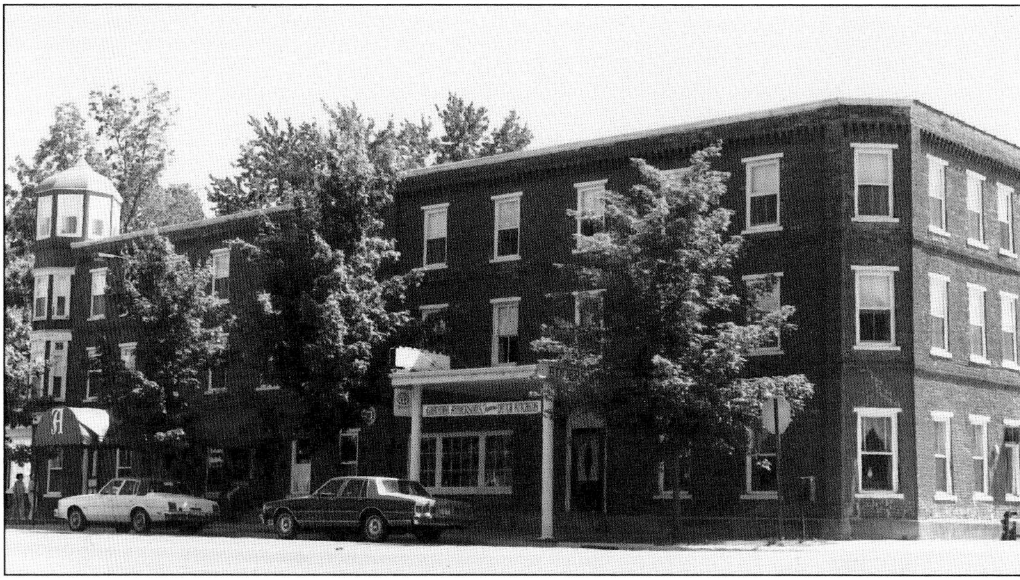

The historical Anderson House (also known as the Hurd House) began in 1856, when Blois S. Hurd erected a small building in Wabasha. A private school was taught here for a few months by Miss E. Hogard. Emma Hurd, the daughter of Elois and Lavira (Isham) Hurd, married Mr. Ziba C. Goss, a carpenter, following the Civil War, and Mr. Goss nearly doubled the building's capacity by erecting a western wing in 1887.

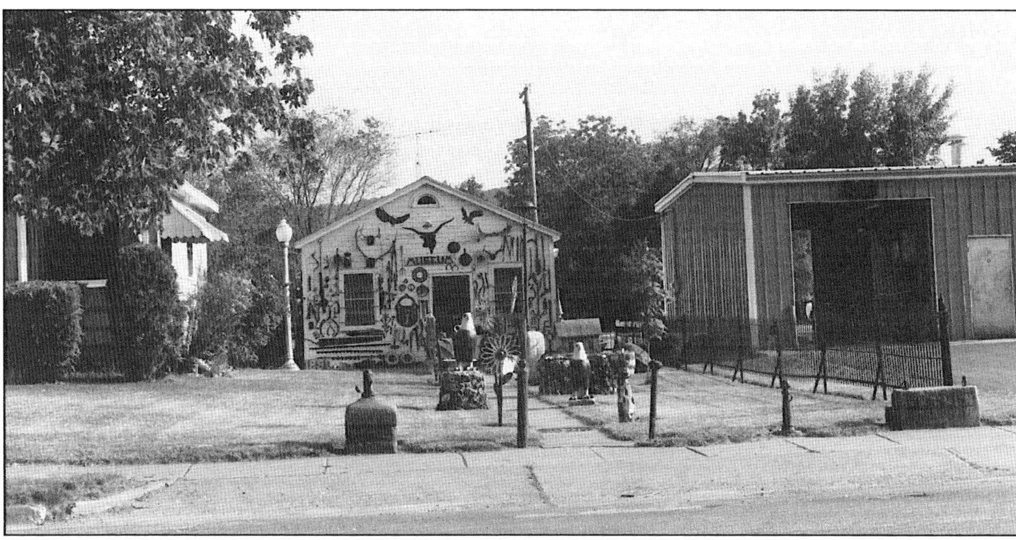

The Joe Suilmann Museum is located by the corner of Pembrook and East Hiawatha Drive in Wabasha. Mr. Suilmann started collecting items when he was 12 years old. In 1951, he built this building to house his collection.

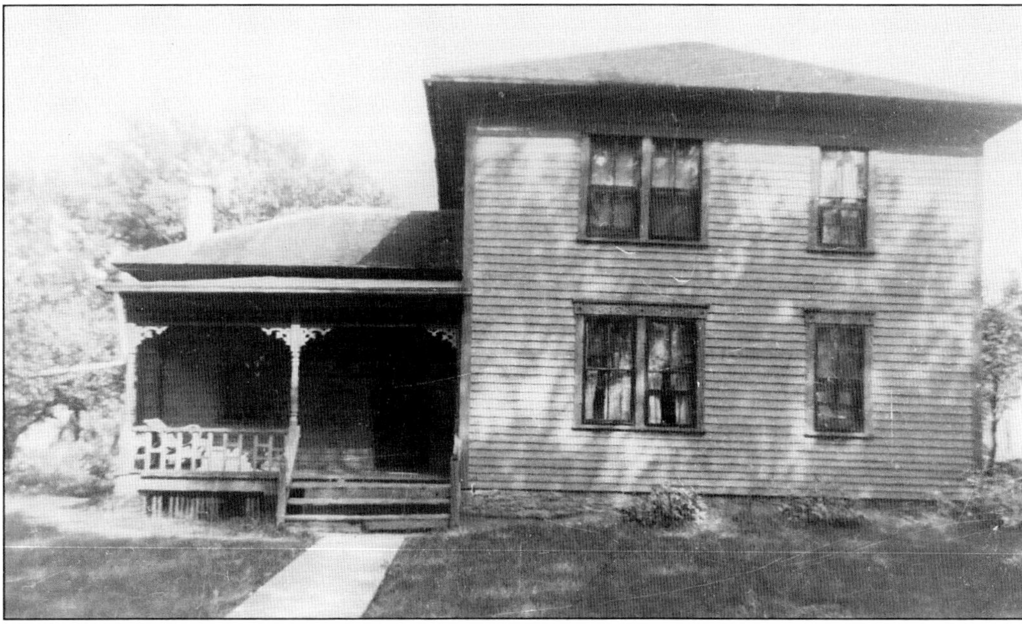

Hosea C. Chadwick and his sons built this home, originally located at 106 East 4th Street, around 1900. It stood in the middle of the block until 1951, when it was demolished (the St. Felix playground is now located on its site). Hosea was a carpenter by trade; with the help of his sons, he built the house now occupied by the Dan Aitkin family at the corner of Washington Avenue and Rustic Lane.

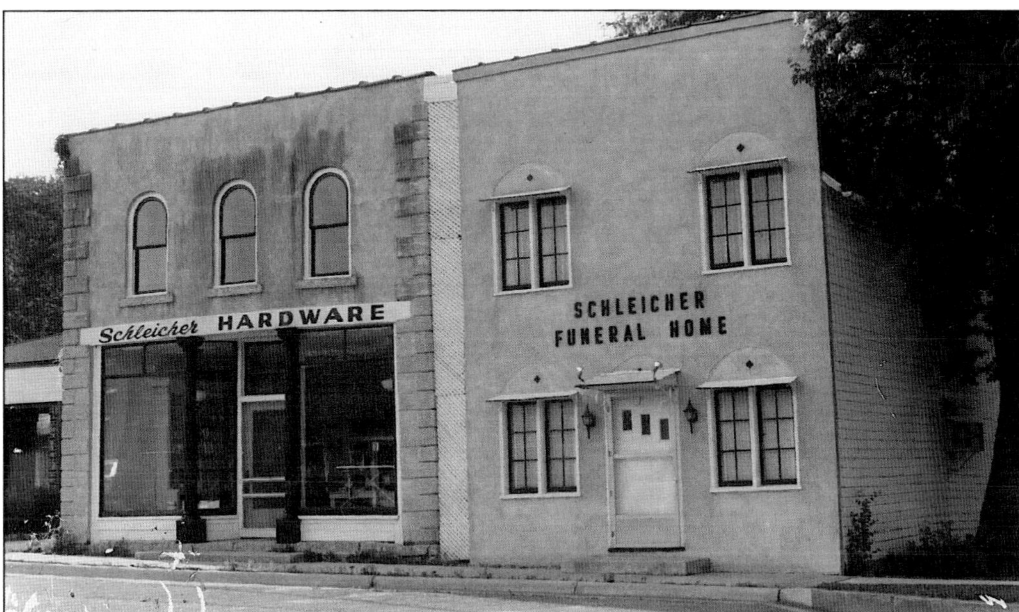

This business was founded by August Carl Schleicher, who came to Millville from Wisconsin, where he had been a Milwaukee Railroad agent. He purchased the Bisbee Hardware Store and later started a furniture store and a funeral home. August attended the University of Minnesota class in embalming; his son, A.R. Schleicher, also attended the School of Mortuary Science at the University of Minnesota.

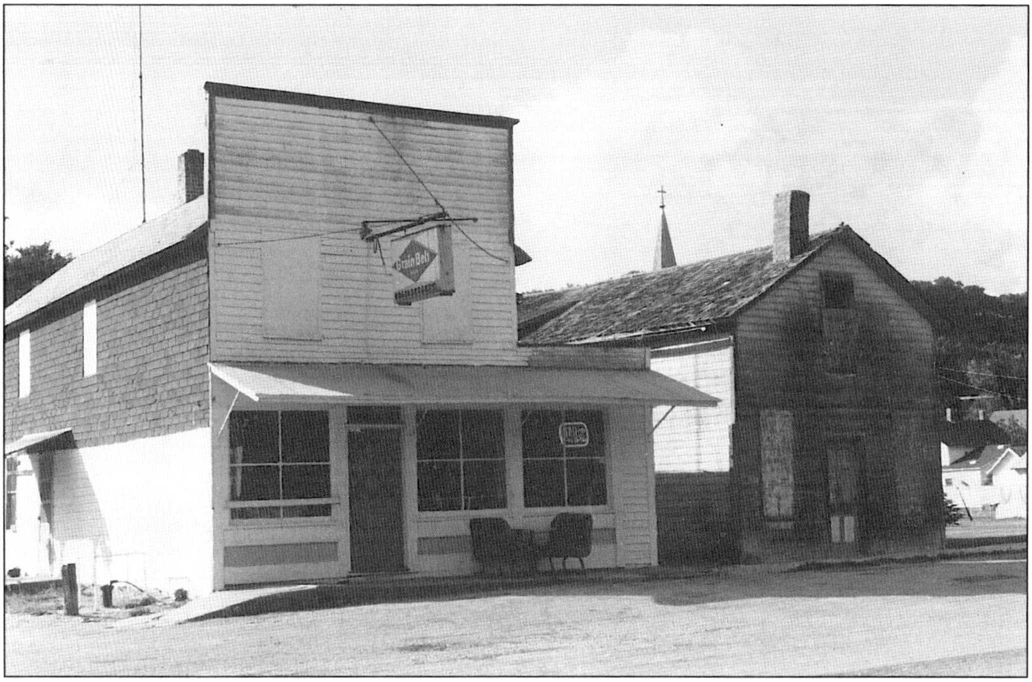

Owned by the Eggenberger family for over a century, this building was the birthplace of Roy Eggenberger and his sisters, Sally Schurhammer and Mary Lou Schuth. Roy took over the structure in 1969, and it became well known as "Roy's Tavern." When it was condemned, the residents of Theilman organized a fund-raising drive to help replace the bar. The building was razed on September 6, 1987, and a new one has been erected in its place.

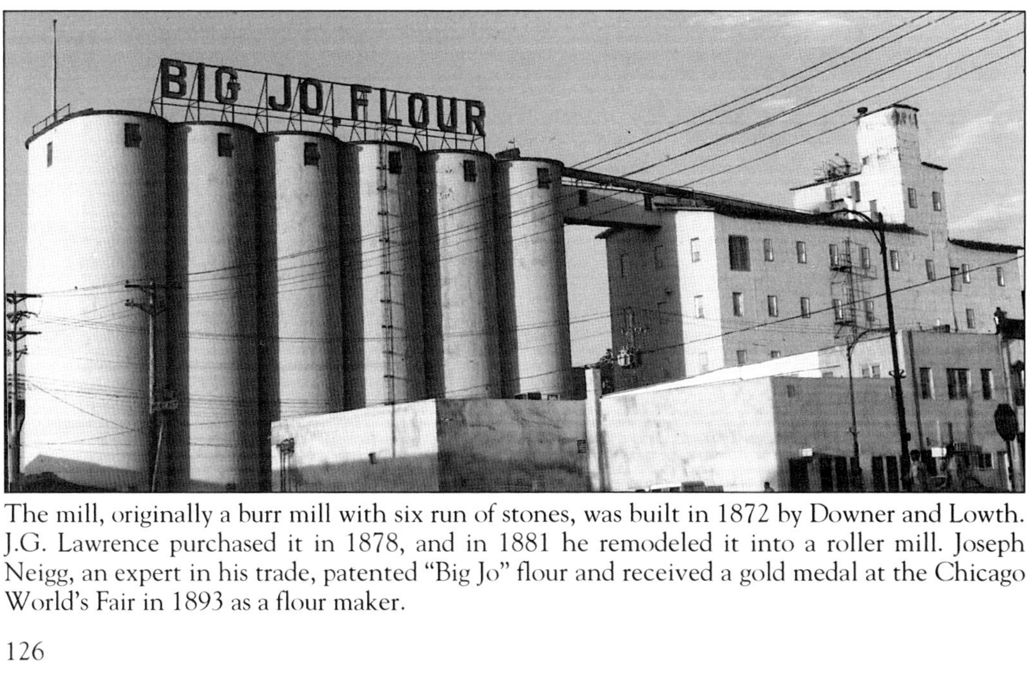

The mill, originally a burr mill with six run of stones, was built in 1872 by Downer and Lowth. J.G. Lawrence purchased it in 1878, and in 1881 he remodeled it into a roller mill. Joseph Neigg, an expert in his trade, patented "Big Jo" flour and received a gold medal at the Chicago World's Fair in 1893 as a flour maker.

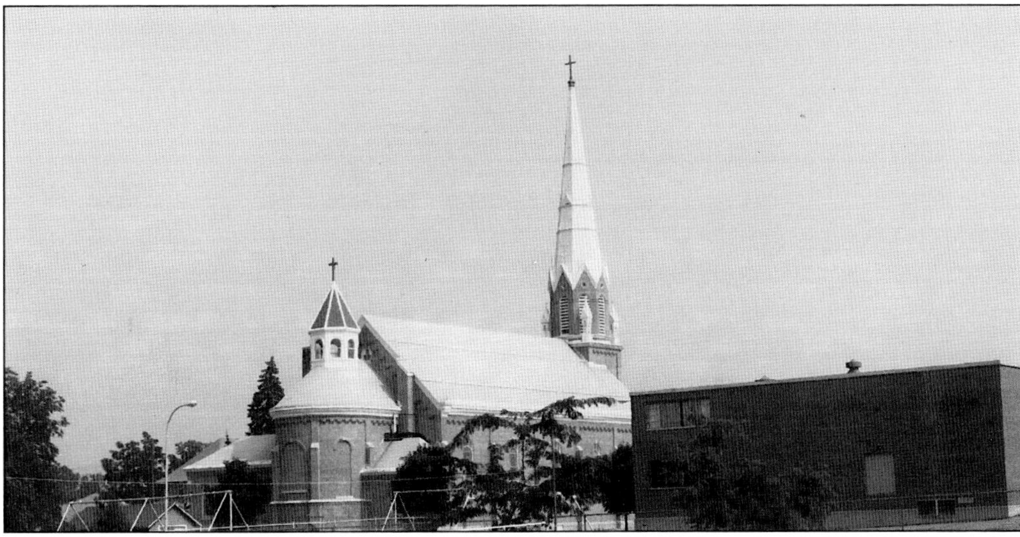

The cornerstone of St. Felix Church, named in honor of Father Tissot's patron saint, was laid on Lot One and half of Lot 2 in Block 26 on July 14, 1874. One year later, on July 18, 1875, the church was dedicated by Reverend Bishop Grace. It was destroyed by fire in 1893 but rebuilt by Reverend Max Wurst, with improvements. Father Wurst built the present rectory.

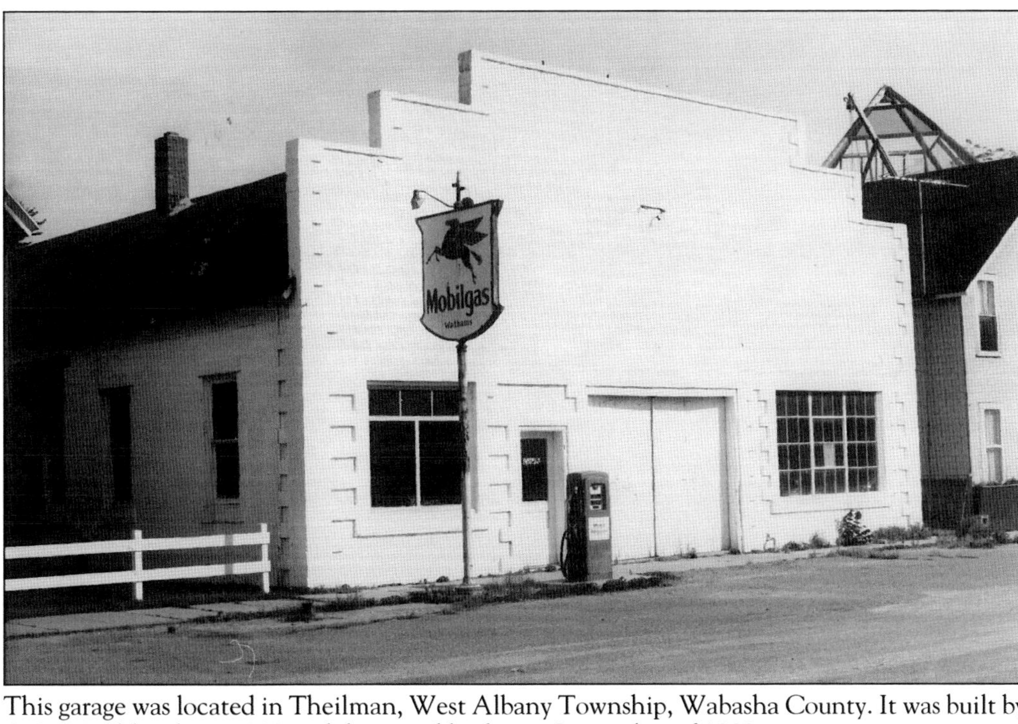

This garage was located in Theilman, West Albany Township, Wabasha County. It was built by A.G. Mischke about 1920 and destroyed by fire in September of 1982.

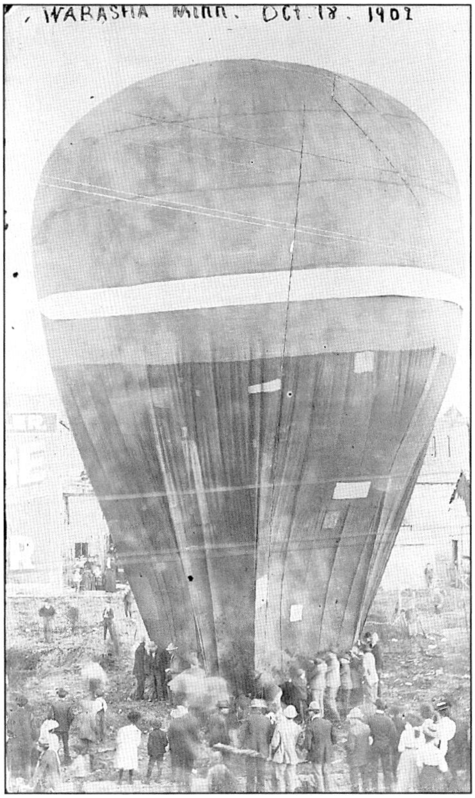

Peter J. Paul is prepared to go aloft in his hot air balloon. After leaving the ground on Saturday, October 18, 1902, from Wabasha, Professor Mais, the youngest aeronaut and undisputed high-diving champion, made a parachute descent from Paul's balloon in addition to a free dive into a life net. The balloon was decorated with political banners. Following this exhibition, there was a football game between Wabasha and Winona and a dance later that evening.

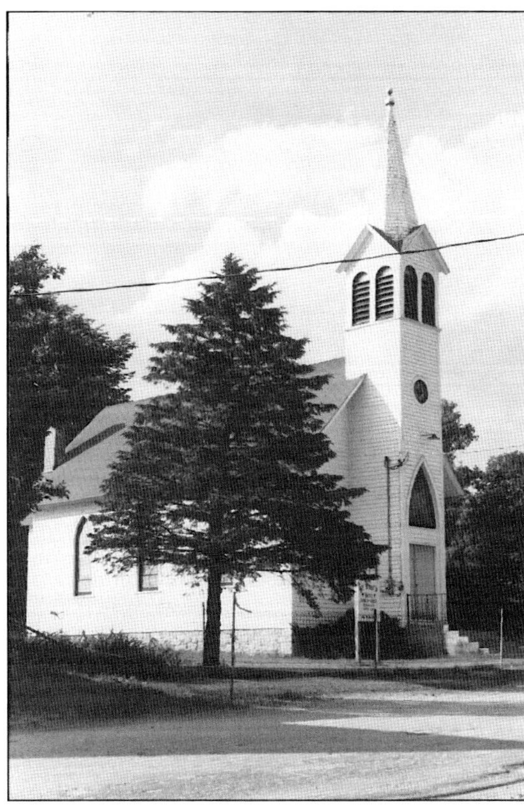

St. Paul's United Church of Christ, 110 years old as of 1998, is located in Theilman. Christian Theilman donated the land for a church and cemetery in 1888. The first church services were held in the late 1860s.